The Ship Hits the Fans

Hereward Kaye

First published in Great Britain in 2022

This first edition published in 2022 by
Lapwing Publishing Services
2 Siren Cottages, Horsgate Lane, Cuckfield RH17 5AZ

http://www.lapwingpublishing.com

Copyright © 2022 Hereward Kaye

Hereward Kaye has asserted his moral right to be identified as the Author of this work in accordance with the Copyright Designs and Patent Act 1988.

Every effort has been made to trace copyright holders and to obtain their permission for the use of copyright material. The author and publisher apologise for any errors or omissions and would be grateful if notified of any corrections that should be incorporated in future reprints or editions of this book. Any perceived slight of any individual or organisation is purely unintentional.

All rights reserved. Apart from any use permitted under UK copyright law, this publication may not be reproduced, distributed, stored or transmitted in any form or by any means, including photocopying, recording, or other electronic or mechanical methods, without the prior written permission of the publisher or in the case of reprographic production in accordance with the terms of licences issued by the Copyright Licensing Agency.

British Library Cataloguing-in-Publication Data
A catalogue record for this book is available from the British Library

ISBN   978-1-9993226-2-5

Printed and bound by TJ Books, UK

Cover design: Tamsin McGee

Only You – Pat

This book is a memoir. It reflects my recollections of experiences over time. Some events have been compressed, whilst dialogue has been recreated from my day-to-day diaries. The entries were written at the time of events and conversations described. I therefore believe them to be representative.

Hereward Kaye

Contents

Overture		vii
Prologue		xi

Part One: You Weren't There

1.	Are You Experienced?	1
2.	Trigger	13
3.	Café Society	21
4.	Golden Mile	31
5.	Flat of the land	41
6.	Midsummer Night's Dick	55
7.	Old Profanity	61
8.	Liverpool	67
9.	Ba da da daa	81
10.	Alf	95
11.	Firebomb	107
12.	Ship ahoy	111
13.	Wham bam wallop	115
14.	Romance	119
15.	Sweet mango	123

Part Two: A Whale of a Tale

16.	The Old Firestation	133
17.	Hope	141
18.	Carve up at l'Escargot	151
19.	Knobsworth	161
20.	Waiving and drowning	167
21.	Ba da da d'aargh!	181
22.	Pinkerton	195
23.	Orchard Road	201
24.	Dystonia	207
25.	Perg	215

Part Three: The Nearly Man

26.	Campo Dog	223
27.	New York	241
28.	The fridge	253
29.	Fin	265
	Acknowledgements	279

Overture

Above the theatre blazed a huge green and yellow school tie, all lit up. Chase lights glamorised the title: 'Moby Dick!' A giant grinning white sperm whale leapt through a sea of blue paint, winking at theatre-goers already building up on the street below. Life-size pictures of the girls of St. Godley's suspended all the way round the theatre. Splashes of water were speech bubbles shouting 'Stuff Art, Let's Dance!' and 'A Whale Of A Tale'. On Shaftesbury Avenue, every other London bus that came along seemed to have our school tie logo on the front and 'Stuff Art Let's Dance!' emblazoned along the side.

I picked up the plethora of post awaiting me at the stage door: good luck cards and gifts from cast and crew, letters from those I had not seen or heard from for decades, some since schooldays. Backstage I changed into a crisp white shirt and a pair of new shoes, then hit the pub. I needed a fucking drink.

My wife Pat and sons Leon and Joe barged bright-eyed through the swing doors, agog with expectancy, dressed in their finest. I caught a brief glimpse of Denman Street, clogged up with tooting limos.

"Dad, come and look at this!" My 16-year old boy Leon prised my fingers away from my drink and led me outside. Television arc lights bathed the front of the theatre and lit the sky. "Michael Winner, getting out of that taxi," gabbled Leon excitedly. "Smith and Jones getting out of that cab dad – and look; that's Peter Cook!"

Inside the bar, old friends continued to materialise. They knew exactly where they'd find me, of course. "Hello Star!" gushed Marsha, striking a pose in the pub doorway, Hollywood sarcastic. I hadn't seen her since Martha's Vineyard days. Hubby Pete followed her in. He's seen me snatch defeat from the jaws of victory so many times in the past, he regarded me as a master of the art. He was grinning through his ears as we inserted ourselves at the counter.

"Chateau Shite?"

"Oh the show's not that bad," I responded. "Here, let me." For once, I was getting the drinks in – it was easier; he would never have believed I couldn't afford it.

"What are you on?" he asked, and he didn't mean drugs and alcohol.

"Three and a half per cent of box office."

"Tonight?"

"U-huh."

"Full?"

"U-huh."

"Sixteen hundred."

"Fourteen hundred and sixty pounds," I corrected. "I have an agent.'"

For once, I didn't see the layer of withering cynicism in his eyes I had come to expect. In fact, there was almost grudging respect.

"I've seen all the publicity," he said.

I bet he had; we were everywhere. Moby Dick was Cameron Mackintosh's latest musical extravaganza back in that year of 1992 and eagerly anticipated, having become a minor cult on its way to The Piccadilly, and having been written by two complete unknowns. British! Would Robert Longden be the new Tim Rice? Would Hereward Kaye be the new Andrew Lloyd Webber? Or, would it fail and give the Press the first chance they'd had to plunge knives into Cameron? The Guardian had flown executioner Michael Billington back from Australia especially for the occasion - an occasion that was now terrifyingly at hand.

"You know what mate?" Pete said, looking me squarely in the eye. "Even you would be pushing it to cock this up now."

I drained my glass and held it up to the bar staff to signal another.

"Just watch me."

Pop star Tom Robinson appeared - another old friend who knew exactly where to find me. My sister Rosamund arrived minus fur coat mercifully, or my Animal Rights activist wife Pat would have had to kill her.

This was it then. I took a deep breath and with friends and family at my squared shoulders, shuffled in with the general public.

In the foyer Chris Biggins and Ed 'Stewpot' Stewart were sharing a laugh. Biggins had already seen the show at the preview stage and told me he loved it. Melvyn Bragg

Moby Dick at the Piccadilly Theatre, London, March 1992.

– who had last seen the show when we'd performed it at the little Firestation Theatre in Oxford the previous year – came sweeping towards me flanked by personal assistants. He broke off from dictating notes to hold his thumb aloft, grin hugely and say "terrific," just like he does on the telly. Up above in the mezzanine bar, people were shouting their orders over the heads of others and booking drinks for the interval. Through all the clamour, the three minute bell could be heard ringing. A disembodied voice was announcing: "please take your seats ladies and gentlemen. This evening's performance is about to begin."

Wearing my family around me, I presented my ticket to be torn by an usherette dressed as a schoolgirl, and through we went, to take our seats. Settling back, I was quite horrified to see Clive Anderson settle into the seat in front of me. Biggins was one thing - this cynical presenter of 'Who's Line Is It Anyway' was entirely another. His wit was cruel, his comedy cutting edge. Ours was old school. He was intelligent too, which didn't help. He would hate it.

I cast my eye around. Shirley Bassey was taking a seat, amidst much attention. Two rows away, Sheridan Morley was greeting Jack Tinker. I was playing 'spot the critic' and they were easy to spot, even the unrecognisable ones. They were the ones who weren't smiling.

Soon, every seat was taken. Then the lights were dimming and the din of a steam train sliding to a halt rent the air, followed by a prolonged and flatulent hiss. We heard the station master's announcement boom. It was my co-author Robert Longden:

"Knobsworth, all stations to Knobsworth!"

Clive Anderson's back bristled immediately and he wriggled impatiently in his seat. As for me, despite the fact I held Pat's hand in a death grip, I was tense to the point of eerie calm. A protective shell had formed that nothing could penetrate.

And then lights came up on the cast, the band struck up the School Hymn, and Judgement Day was upon us.

Moby Dick the Musical set sail in London's West End.

Prologue

I was 10 years old when I saw The Beatles play live. It was a night I would never forget and, as it happens, neither would the rest of the world. November 22nd, 1963. In America, the man in the motorcade they called The President was in his last minute. Five thousand miles away in the North of England, Jimmy Tarbuck, popular compere, prowled the stage of the Stockton Globe before my eyes.

"Four young lads from Liverpool, where else?" he crowed, only for his words to drown in a sea of screams as one of the four stuck his Chelsea boot through the crack in the curtain. Fidgeting on the lip of my tip up seat flanked by my sisters, I felt I was about to explode.

"John!"... Tarby kicked into countdown. In Dallas, a hired assassin settled to stillness, only the barrel moving, Kennedy in a quadrant of his sights.

"George!"

...the President's magnificent brain was primed to implode.

"Paul!"

...the killer's forefinger tightened on the trigger.

"Ringo!"

...the trigger started to move. Fate's swollen waters swayed in awesome pause.

"The BEATLES!"

A crack of a marksman's shot and the opening chugga-chugga of 'Twist and Shout'.

Blasted back into my bucket seat, riddled with rock and roll, my life had just begun.

John was smack in front of me, wrenching out words like tortured metal and pulling stupid faces. Paul was on the left, his violin bass pointing up at his eyebrow, which he

Hereward aged 10, 1964. Tab collar shirt, Beatles moptop, first guitar.

arched in mock innocence, stirring the soup of screams. George commuted between the two, his shiny Gretch black as a Cadillac. A big guitar, big hair, a slow grin. Ringo was on a drum riser behind his grey Ludwig kit, Beatles logo on the bass drum, fringe flopping every time he hit the snare.

Matching hair, matching suits, matching amps – though Paul's was bigger – Wizard of Oz lighting, electric guitars and the world at their feet.

I checked the sisters. Ros was sobbing, Corky wailing "George!" hand outstretched.

The Beatles did the 'ooo' thing they nicked from Little Richard, sending a tidal wave through the soup of screams and another batch of fainted girls into the arms of the St John's Ambulance Brigade in the aisles.

"Shurrup!" yelled John, the hard knock.

"Could you just perhaps, you know," asked Paul, reasonably, "just scream a little quieter, so we can hear what we're doing?" The eyebrow arched fatally.

"We've written another… SHURRUP!… we've written another song. For Ringo! But he hasn't learnt it yet, 'ave yer, Ringo?"

"Can I just say," said Paul, "would you mind not throwing any more Jelly Babies? We've had lots and lots and lots of Jelly Babies and we don't like them anymore."

"This is the last one!"

"Last one!"

"Cos we can't hear ourselves!"

"SHUURRUUUP!"

"It's our new single."

"We hope you like it as much as the larst one." John the sarcastic, John the hardcase, John the clown.

"It's called 'I Wanna Hold Your Hand'."

Prologue

Starry-eyed I crawled from the wreckage, an avalanche of screams ringing in my ears. From Dallas, Texas, emanated a cavalcade of sirens to freeze time itself to the spot.

Dad picked us up, grave-faced with the news, but who cared? His old world was as dead as a Kennedy.

My baby heart was beating in four/four and the future had a soundtrack.

Part One

You Weren't There

Chapter 1
Are You Experienced?

I had no idea how I was going to harness the musical euphoria I carried with me from the night in 1963 when I saw The Beatles – until I met Tom Robinson, four years later.

Someone who knew us both as two aspiring musicians sent him along to my house in Orchard Road, Middlesbrough. There filling the door was a big lad in a donkey jacket with a bass guitar. He had deep eyes, acne, and a tumble of curls. He looked like Paul Jones from Manfred Mann.

His right hand was already out: "Tom Robinson."

The grin was sheepish, the handshake warm, the eye contact magnetic. When Tom plugged in, he took care to turn down the volume on the amp first. He gently bent his ear and fine-tuned to the harmonics, tenderly adjusting the giant keys at the top of the neck.

He played the bass properly and had the ragged voice of a seasoned bluesman. Whatever twelve bar jag we set out on, he managed to steer it towards a proper song. Then Tom padded to the piano and sang a song I didn't know.

"Who wrote that one?"

"Me actually."

"You write your own songs!" Now I was impressed. "I wish I wrote songs. I write poems instead."

"Perhaps you should put tunes to them and then your poems would become songs" he said wryly, and casually changed my life.

Tom went to a school called Finchden. It sounded well weird. Everybody just did what they wanted. They didn't have lessons and they didn't have holidays.

The Ship Hits the Fans

Finchden Manor, 1969. Back left: Raphael Doyle, Foreground: Tom Robinson. Right: Hereward.

"But next time I come up I'll bring Ray," he said. "He writes songs too. He's a singer."

It was a few months later that we met. Ray Doyle had long hair, a smelly green jacket and flip-flops in the middle of winter. His Irish eyes were gentle but fucked-up. His real name was Raphael.

Raphael sang with his eyes shut, by candlelight usually. His eyes fluttered behind his eyelids and his words were delivered with almost holy care. When the loud bits came he squirmed agitatedly behind his guitar, clubbing the strings crudely, hamfisted and fat fingered, spittle, hair and words flying. Jesus! The lyrics were all his own and smelt of trouble. How I longed to be deeply troubled like him! Although I too was setting my poems to music now, my words were waggy-tailed Scotties, jumping up to lick your face and over eager to please.

Tom sat by Ray, the two of them cradling acoustic guitars. Their voices rose and fell in cadence, Tom's harmonies taking a rasp to the rich mahogany furniture of Raphael's voice. But what Tom took away from the vocal purity of Ray, he repaid instrumentally, smoothing over Ray's acoustic guitar playing with pearly strings of chords, most of which neither Ray nor I had seen or heard before.

I felt privileged to belong to their secret club. It was a joy to make music with them, but always so short lived, as we were at different boarding schools. I use the term loosely; as the boarding school they attended wasn't like any school I'd ever been to. Finchden Manor was a sprawling rural retreat in Kent. The place was a tip. Hippies crawled all over it, cross-eyed with introspection. They had names like Nose and Pash. Tom, I discovered, was Head Girl – they didn't have a head boy.

The musical bond between the three of us grew stronger, and as our school days fell away, continued to strengthen without interruption. Tom and Ray poured such respect into my songs, that my songwriting couldn't help but flower under their encouragement. As time went on, the two of them became the three of us.

We only had one contact in the music business, but it was a good one. Alexis Korner. He was Finchden Manor's most famous son. As well as touring the country as a musician and presenting his own weekly jazz and blues show on BBC Radio 2, Alexis was also a great mover and shaker in the music business. He introduced Mick, Keith and Brian to one another, thereby bequeathing the world with The Rolling Stones. He was instrumental in the creation of other groups besides, such as the mighty Free, who I loved. So when I first dared to dream of moving down South when I got a bit older and trying to make it in music on my own, it was Alexis I turned to first.

I sent him a demo of my naïve and earnest early songs, on the first of many dusty cassette tapes I was to bandy around the capital over the coming years. My letter asked him plaintively: is it worth me giving it a go? Alexis's answer was crucial to me. Though I was only 16 years old and had to write songs that were a hell of a lot better than these ones, maybe he sensed my urgency, because he sent me a very nice letter in reply. Get in touch, he said when you move to London.

I couldn't wait to be old enough; I cherished that letter for the next two years. It was the ticket to my dreams.

I first set eyes on Pat when our drama teacher led her up onto the stage at Billingham Tech, to introduce her to the rest of the group. We were rehearsing for the 'Wizard of Oz', but we didn't have our leading lady.

"This is Pat," said Ken Parkin, "Pat Lord. She's going to play Dorothy. And she's going to sing for you."

Which she did. Like a nightingale! As I was already cast to play Scarecrow, I scrutinised her closely. I remember thinking she looked old, about 30, even though she was just a few months older than me. And Pat remembers thinking I looked really baby-faced, she didn't see me as boyfriend material at all. But she did say, in that final scene, turning to me after pinning a heart to the Tin Man: "Goodbye Scarecrow, I think I loved you best of all." Whatever resonance that phrase came to take on, at the time it was a just a line in a play. She was going out with the Cowardly Lion and I, so recently released from captivity in a boys boarding school, was joyfully having it off with the Witch of the West.

With my long hair and red sandals in winter, I was far more flamboyant than other guys at college. I put it down to my mother, an exotic mixture of Dutch and Indonesian, who once had the family car resprayed to match her nail varnish. I ignored the sniggers on the campus corridors as I passed, or the calls from across the Middlesbrough street: "Are you a boy or a girl?" I spent all my time on the Billingham Tech stage in a world of my own, hammering out my newly-minted songs to the other drama students.

I was a waggy-tailed 16-year-old who threw my arms around everyone and thought you could talk to anyone about anything. My mother's influence again. But Pat be-

Pat Lord in 1969 aged 17, riding her pony Peridot.

came tense the moment I got on to anything personal about her. She was fresh out of a broken marriage – her mother and father's. Dad was a Methodist minister (The Reverend Lord!) and both parents were marriage guidance councillors, ironically. But you couldn't discuss her broken family; the subject was private, closed off.

Pat and I seemed to be in the local papers on an almost weekly basis. All my articles were about me, I noticed. All of hers were about saving endangered animals: 'Horseback Pat Saves Billy the Kid!' Out riding, Pat had found an emaciated goat wandering by the A19, slung it over her saddle and taken it home. 'Pat Saves Rag 'n Bone Pony' – she came across a pony sprawled in its shafts beside an overthrown cart, led him home and back to health and into the pages of the *Northern Echo*.

Meanwhile I was telling *Middlesbrough Evening Gazette* how I'd replaced my opening monologue in Our Town with a self-composed song of which I felt sure playwright Thornton Wilder would approve, or how I'd had my long hair cut for a drama course production of Antigone and my mother had turned it into a hairpiece for her own hair.

In time I came to regard Pat as my best friend, as we cried on one another's shoulder, as each of our individual romances went wrong. The Cowardly Lion was badly beaten up. The Wicked Witch of the West flew away across the skies, cackling back at the red trail of smoke she was leaving behind – my burning heart.

Then we were into the second year of our course. The Wicked Witch of the West and Cowardly Lion had followed the yellow brick road down to London and both of us were left bereft. Months of consolation passed – in the Astronaut mainly.

"Mick came back" she told me, "talking of how he'd met this amazing lady, they smeared each other in chip fat and had the most unbelievable sex."

This was a little beyond our innocence. We hadn't yet moved to London, we were that crucial year behind with lives parochial, to their lives metropolitan. 'Are You Experienced?' wondered Jimi Hendrix on the cover of my favourite album. No, we weren't. But they were, those we had loved and lost and who were now apparently fucking in chip fat. It made you feel sad. It made you feel like another beer and rolling back late for class. Then, when you did:

"Do come in!" Johnny Moore gushed, all expansive gestures, cutting a swathe through the class to the door, where I'm in the act of insinuating myself into the room. His every muscle bristles with aggression. After Art, Johnny Moore teaches weightlifting.

"Kaye everybody" he proclaims, arms aloft. "Now Kaye doesn't come here very often, do you Kaye? Cos 'e doesn't need to, do you Kaye? Maybe you know something we don't know. Maybe you think Art is ten percent perspiration and ninety percent inspiration like the rest of your – 'Derama Geroup'!" You can actually see the spray of derision as it leaves his nose. "Whereas we all think it's the other way round!"

But he was right. I did think I could make it on inspiration alone.

Then came the day when our theatre course was over. Pat was accepted into a drama college down South. I hadn't bothered to audition – the straight choice between a life in theatre or a life in music was never in doubt. I couldn't be a Beatle, that job was already taken, but I could be a musician. This was the moment I'd been waiting for and I had to get myself out there.

I drove Pat down to London in my battered Ford Transit van. She was in the passenger seat, weeping over the gear stick, overwhelmed with guilt for leaving her mother behind – she was all her mother had left for company, at home. Pat's Irish Setter was on her lap, being sick out of the window. Someone with the power of clairvoyance could have saved me a lot of time at that moment, by saying: "get used to it mate, welcome to the rest of your life". But they didn't and the rest of my life remained unrevealed, as I dropped her off for her connecting train down to Guildford and turned to face the city of my dreams.

I arrived in London at the age of 18 with two things in my pocket: a letter from Alexis Korner and a cheque for £200 courtesy of my Dad. My father was beyond disappointed that I'd dropped out of boarding school, been uninterested in the idea of university and turned down the gift of a family business, to which I had been born.

"He wants to be a musician for God's sake! He's going to… (here he waved his fingers up by his ears) 'make it'."

Dad blamed the Beatles, and though a little worse for wear, he was right.

I was one of the lucky inhabitants of Middlesbrough to have been born with a silver spoon, but I really didn't have a clue about money. That £200 in the black soon became £200 in the red and the bank manager – who had called me in – was addressing me soberly as 'Mr Kaye' and referring to my 'embarrassing situation'. I had my metaphorical feet up on his desk, sitting back blowing smoke rings from an imaginary cigar as I assured him it was absolutely no problem at all and I would 'make arrangements'. You have no idea how ambitious I am, I wanted to tell him. I'm a musician, I'm gonna make it.

The bank was a NatWest, directly opposite Finchley Road Tube station, connected by an underpass. Unwilling to go cap in hand to my father, who was waiting to see me turn his £200 into an empire, I made the underpass my workplace and became a busker. With a flourish of theatre, I borrowed my mate Jessalinda Franks who'd just had a baby. There she sat on the cold concrete beside me, nursing her babe-in-arms as I crooned Simon & Garfunkel:

I am just a poor boy, though my story's seldom told...

The very first person to come along was the bank manager.

Such was the start of my musical odyssey. That was the money gone, but I still had my letter from Alexis in my pocket. I straightened out the battered sheet of paper and looked him up.

By a quirk of fate, Alexis Korner had a hit in the charts at the time I rocked up on his doorstep. Though he was a venerable and celebrated musician, such commercial success had never happened to him before or since. 'Tap Turns on the Water' was in the Top Ten and he had an upcoming gig at the Albert Hall. He promptly put me on the guest list.

"This way Sir," said an attendant as I arrived in the foyer, unclipping a golden-plaited rope that separated the hoi polloi from wherever next I was to follow him. He opened a door in the curved wooden wall and I found myself in a box – and not just any old box; the Albert Hall's Royal Box! A buffet was laid out and I was at the centre of what looked like three generations of family celebration.

The family were most welcoming, showing me a peg where I could hang my coat, inviting me to help myself to food, pulling up a chair to the brass rail where I could enjoy a birds eye view of the magnificent Victorian arena laid out before me.

The lights dimmed. A gentleman took his place in the vacant seat alongside and offered a polite hello. I hope I didn't do a double-take, but I suspect I did.

Muddy Waters. Only bloody Muddy Waters!

Back at boarding school, the Blues was my Bible. Whilst everyone else had a trunk and tuckbox, I had a Vox A.C.30 amplifier, liveried in colours of the night. The hot dust burning off the valves is a perfume I shall never forget. My blues band was called 'Screw' (the teachers were dead against the name but as the logo on the posters was an actual screw, they couldn't do much about it). 'Hoochie Coochie Man', 'I Just Wanna Make Love To You' – the songs we played were by Muddy and the words that fell from his lips were the word of God. Now I was sitting next to this man in the Royal Box of the Albert Hall. Muddy Waters, King of the Chicago Blues, on a night out with his family.

Tom was still at Finchden Manor when I first arrived in London, but Raphael had left and so he came and joined me there. Alexis put us together with a couple of other musicians and my first London band was formed: 'Bodie'. We only managed one gig: a private party in the middle of a wood. I don't remember how good or bad we were, but the American guy who bounced up at the end I won't forget in a hurry.

'Great set man!'

It was the American singer Harry Nilsson, flanked by two young ladies – 'chicks' was the term we all used back then and they looked like baby chicks, with almost identical gamine features and the same peroxide white hair, cropped tight. They were beautiful and desirable, and one of them was waving a joint.

Harry said: "Wanna come and join us? We're over here." He motioned towards a rug beneath a tree. "Bring a guitar!"

"Do you smoke?" purred the chick with the joint. She put the lighted end in her mouth and her face to mine, leaving me very little choice but to suck on the other end. Tough job, but someone had to do it.

We must have smoked a hundred joints and sung a hundred songs that night, there on the rug, me, Raphael, Nilsson. I hadn't noticed the chauffeur waiting discreetly beside a distant white Rolls Royce, till he came over at around four in the morning. But Lennon's 'lost weekend' buddy wasn't ready to leave yet; he waved his chauffeur away. The evening ended unforgettably with Raphael power-vomiting between the two of us, as Harry and I marched him vigorously about the woods this way and that, in an attempt to straighten him up.

That was Bodie's first gig and as it happened, our last. As John Lennon sang a decade later, life is what happens to you when you're busy making other plans. So when my father collapsed in the street in Middlesbrough and my tearful mother came on the phone, it was time to go home, for a short while at least, to take over the reins of the family business I didn't want, till Dad recovered.

I had lasted in London for less than a year. Pat had lasted even less than that at Drama College, before she too came home. Her mother Dorothy was living on her own and it was more than Pat's guilty heart could bear. As the only two friends of our old circle still in the North-East, we immediately sought one another out. We were ridiculously relieved to see each other; we felt like old friends.

It was a little confusing that her mother was called Dorothy, because the fact was, my own mother called *her* Dorothy! Had done, ever since she'd seen her in the Wizard of Oz. "Oh Dorothy," she would sigh, opening the door to Pat as if it was Judy Garland herself on the doorstep, in sparkly red shoes. Though my mum's grip on the English language was good, she did have a fabulous talent for getting hold of the wrong end of the stick.

The long evenings Pat and I spent in my attic bedroom grew longer, as, for the first time, I managed to get her to confide in me. Pat was the Minister's daughter whose family had exploded. Being a man of Faith, her father's unfaithfulness had sent shockwaves through the church and scandalised his parishioners, who regarded the family as the very model of decency. Pat had been an eleven-year-old girl on an upstairs landing, hugging her rocking horse as she heard the awful words floating up to her from the hallway downstairs. Her father was leaving. Her mother was sobbing. "I drove my finger into the rocking horse's mouth until it bled," she whispered, as we lay side by side.

Sometimes we lay like that talking till the early hours and I felt Pat's mistrust melting away in the dark. And when she finally gave herself to me, I was the only guy she'd ever allowed to get that far. A line was irrevocably crossed. With any other girl I knew, I could still have described us as just good friends – but not this one.

Our relationship gained in intensity. Deep feelings were freely flowing between us, now I had melted Pat's wary mistrust into giving. I didn't know if I could handle the weight of that responsibility. I'd spent four years away at boarding school and was emotionally cauterised. If I'm honest, I started to feel trapped.

I was back in my hometown in a committed relationship I simply wasn't ready for. I was filling in for my absent father at the helm of a family tool business I never wanted.

I was spectacularly unsuited to the mantle I had inherited at Kayes (Middlesbrough) Ltd. I was utterly clueless going into work. I watched the staff beavering away on the shop floor below and knowing I too should be bustling about, all I could think to do was go down and empty the till, bring the bundle of notes back up to Dad's office and count the money. Senior members of staff gave me a satisfied smile as I passed. Chief Buyer Jim Carling proudly told me I was the third Mr Kaye he had served under.

When others passed, they addressed me respectfully as 'Mr Hereward'. I wanted to bolt straight out the shop door and run screaming down Newport Road.

There was one person working at Kayes Tools who didn't call me 'Mr Hereward' – Phil Vickers, in the Workshop Dept. He referred to me as 'H' and his eyes twinkled in tacit acknowledgement of my unsuitability to be boss. One long afternoon when the minutes seemed like hours, he rapped knuckles on my office door and walked straight in. He found me gazing out of the window. Over the road, rooks cawed in bare trees under leaden skies. It had been summer when I arrived. Seasons had changed and I was still there.

"What's up H?"

"I'm being buried alive here Phil, that's what. I've got to escape."

"Yeah," he agreed, taking me in. "I think you do. Where are you gonna go mate?"

"Not London again, not yet." I was in no shape to pick up the reins of my ambition.

"The South of France is very nice apparently…"

"South of France…"

I turned it over in my mind. On that mournful day in Middlesbrough, the more I considered the idea, the better it sounded.

"And there's a smile on his face for once," said Phil.

"That's because I'm going to go for it."

"Just like that?"

"Yeah, I actually think I am…"

My impulsive nature always did get the better of me. "Hey," I found myself saying, "wanna come with?"

His eyes clouded. His face cleared. "Sure H!"

Pat and I were at our regular haunt of The Kirkleavington Country Club, sunken back into a sofa in the soft fireside glow, when I broached the tricky subject. She sat bolt upright, immediately adrenalised.

"You're leaving me?"

She dashed the Southern Comfort from my hand into the flames, which sputtered sparks of indignation. With a sigh, I unpeeled myself from the brown leather upholstery, queued at the bar and returned with another expensive one. It went the same way as the first; dashed from my hand into the logs. Gasping for a drink by now, I watched

Rehearsing with first band Bodie, London, 1971.

in anguish as another day's wages went up in flames.

We had a terrible argument in the car park. It seemed to be coming over her in waves. On the drive home, Pat slapped me so violently around the head that I careered off the road onto the pavement and, still under physical attack, veered in and out of a stranger's front garden.

Instead of dropping her home, I foolishly coaxed her back to Orchard Road to talk it through. We ended up nodding off over a half-drunk bottle of wine, up in my attic bedroom. At 4 am I was awoken by Pat raising all hell again, as another wave of anger overcame her. She made so much noise my mother shot up to the loft to see what was going on. She walked in on me trying to protect head and privates simultaneously, as a snarling Pat came at me, brandishing the bottle.

"Oh Dorothy!" she sighed.

In the South of France, Phil and I went from boat to boat in Cannes harbour, seeking employment. Fabulous yachts bobbed and gleamed on their creaking ropes, pools of sunlight playing across their bows. The further we walked along the pontoon, the bigger and flashier the boats became. Emperor of them all was the Northwind at the far end, a magnificent charter yacht with two decks, a crew of eleven and luxury quarters for a further eleven paying guests. As luck would have it, the crew were down to nine that day and they were recruiting. At a stroke, I went from stand-in Manager, Kayes (Middlesbrough) Ltd, to crew cook on a pornography millionaire's yacht.

Our captain on board the Northwind was a disgraced former Admiral of the British Fleet. His world fell apart when he had an affair with an innocent male rating he could not resist. His relationship to actress Dorothy Squires collapsed (she went on to marry Roger Moore) and disgraced, he was stripped of his rank and expelled from the Royal Navy. Still wore the uniform though, every day and night up there on the bridge, admiral now of a porno-king's charter yacht for the rich and famous.

Our first sea voyage was a short trip down the coast from Cannes to Monte Carlo, where we had been chartered by racing team Yardley McClaren for the Monaco Grand Prix. Their drivers were Peter Revson and Jody Scheckter. Security was paramount and we were drilled with protocol. They stationed Phil on the gangplank. 'Don't move!' he was instructed. 'Stay alert! Don't let anyone on without a security pass' – Phil stood riveted to the spot all day, eyes peeled, like one of those coppers facing the crowd at football matches who miss the whole game.

At the end of the race Jody Scheckter, helmet under arm and reeking like an exhaust, staggered towards the gangplank after 55 gruelling laps of the 1972 Monaco Grand Prix. But Phil had learnt his lesson well. He wouldn't let him on. No ID you see. Could have been anyone, couldn't he?

There was an after-race party on board the Northwind that night and I ran the bar. Surreally, the first pint I pulled was for Stirling Moss. As I went around gathering empty glasses I was overhearing clipped English tones declaring: "so there I was rounding the tenth at Monza and the bloody brakes failed!"

Parties became a regular feature over the next few weeks and once they realised I could play guitar, I of course was the minstrel. For some reason, I particularly remember one eye-watering party moment off the coast of Sardinia, where I strummed my instrument with one foot up on a stool, wearing only Donovan's kaftan (I swear this is all true). As I sang, a former Miss Sweden stuck her hand up the garment and strummed my instrument too!

Pat was having a less interesting time. Letters arrived bearing the Stockton-on-Tees postmark. 'Bored, bored, BORED!' went one. 'I'm thinking of taking up Scottish country dancing' went another. Then the letters dried up and danger bells began to clang. Why had I not heard from her in a while? I wrote. A letter came back: 'I've found a boyfriend who looks just like you, he has long hair and big spaniel eyes and he does it five times a night.'

This was my 'Dorothy' moment – I had to get back to Kansas! Before I lost her forever, I had to get back to Pat and unpick every stitch of my betrayal.

The answer was there all the time: this was my girl. And though I would always come a poor second to every endangered animal on the planet (particularly spaniels), I would embrace it as my penance.

Another truth was staring me in the face too: Tom and Raphael – how good were those guys? We had to form a band! Together the three of us could surely take on the world. We would need a manager, but I knew one: John McCoy, owner of the Kirk, where Pat had dashed successive Southern Comforts from my hand. McCoy wasn't just a club owner, he also took artists under his wing and developed them. He was a manager, and if there was one thing I'd learnt this far, I needed a manager.

Next time we docked in Cannes, I slammed the van into gear and raced out of the harbour. I didn't stop driving until I hit Middlesbrough. I was running on at least 90% inspiration. All the way, I thought of the people who little knew the whirlwind that was about to hit them: Pat, Tom, Raphael, McCoy. I wouldn't stay in the North East long; I had to get back to London, but first I had to hit my home town, to lay claim to the things in my life I truly needed.

One was my band. The other was my girl.

Chapter 2
Trigger
- 1975 -

Welcome to Christmas – come in, grab a bar stool or a seat in an alcove, if you can find one. Here in Martha's Vineyard, a wine bar in Hampstead, they're doing a roaring trade. Owners Jackie and Des are dispensing wine and bonhomie behind the counter. 'Leather freak guy' straddles his usual stool, a man who looks like Tom Waits sounds. His fringed arm's slung low around the waist of a blond girl young enough to be his daughter. From behind dark shades he gazes into her eyes. She has a bottom like a Golden Delicious and his wrinkly, ring-festooned hand moves around it continuously, as they talk.

"Who is that pervert?" Pat mouths at Jackie.

"He's my Dad," Jackie tells her above the din, far too loudly.

And here comes local legend Larry Viner, sporting a handsome kilt and – bending to present it to the roaring crowd - a plastic arse. Last week he flitted around the wine bar dressed as a butterfly. The week before, dressed as a nun. Larry organizes a fancy dress outing from Martha's to the seaside once a year, with a weekend in Paris for two as first prize. People go to great lengths. Little Frank looked odds on to win the year he hired an astronaut's costume from the BBC, though boarding the coach was a problem – he was too wide for the aisle. We had to pass him over our heads to the back row, where he was forced by the strictures of his costume to lay horizontally for the whole of the journey. He didn't win, after all that. First prize was snaffled by a pair of nonagenarians. They clinched the deal on Brighton pier, when the old girl took a lusty glug of Lucozade from her bewildered husband's catheter.

Bronco the Tramp – in defiance of his nickname 'The Barred of Hampstead' – is passing from table to table and through all the din, faint tinkling tones from a piano man belting out Billy Joel for all he's worth can just about be heard. He is completely ignored, it's a thankless task.

Has he no ambition? I mean, what self-respecting musician would want to do such a thing?

Well, me. I am that piano man.

Four years down the line from busking Simon & Garfunkel in an underpass, the furthest my ambition had taken me was belting out Billy Joel's 'Piano Man', to a pissed-up crowd at Christmas in a Hampstead wine bar. The job fell a long way short of my delusions of fame and grandeur, but it was a hell of a lot warmer than that underpass. I was even more ignored now than I was back then, but my beautiful wife Pat, I couldn't help sourly noticing from behind my upright, was being positively embraced by everybody. A quite fabulous flirt, especially in the half an hour or so before she had to go round with the hat – it always paid dividends.

Sing us a song, you're the piano man, sing us a song tonight

Cos we're all in a mood for a melody, and you got us feeling alright…

Can't say I was listening to my own song either. I must have sung it a hundred times. I was amusing myself gazing around trying to spot a character I'd been told to look out for. Our mutual pal Charlie Hanson had the idea to put us together.

"A friend of mine wants to say hello. He's coming down to Martha's tonight."

"Who?"

"Robert Longden" replied Charlie. "An actor who writes."

"Writes what?"

"Musicals; off-the-wall ones. He's looking for a musical collaborator."

"What does he look like?"

"I'm sure you'll spot him."

Sing us a song, you're…

There, in the corner alcove; that had to be him. Hair dyed red, slopey-looking, he had the aura of a performer. Red glasses matched the hair. He looked hip, but a bit Clark Kent too, frowning over something he was writing. The Robert I had been told to look out for was playing Riff Raff in 'The Rocky Horror Show' apparently and this guy seemed to fit the bill.

I finished the Billy Joel number, closed the piano lid, lit a fag and crossed the floor.

"Robert."

He jumped to his feet.

"Oh hi!"

It was a beatific smile, almost childlike. He had a sheath of lyrics in his hand, which he shoved towards me now. I squinted at the top one: 'Knucklehead Meadow'. Good grief.

"I've written it for us," he said brightly, "just now."

I was startled; people were meant to ignore me. But Robert had been absorbing me all evening, in-between intense bouts of scribbling.

He appeared on my doorstep the very next day, shoving a gift at me this time, a great glossy book about Vaudeville. It was a generous present and it was almost as if he wanted to educate me. Then he was hands and knees on the kitchen floor, crawling about with our baby boy Leon. Over the next hour or so Robert proved to be hilarious company, a breathless succession of funnies and slapstick. I don't think we actually got round to discussing his search for a songwriting partner and I certainly hadn't agreed to anything by the time I saw him out, but as I turned back indoors, I noticed his sheath of lyrics, there on my piano.

I went to see Robert in the 'Rocky Horror Show', playing in a theatre down the King's Road. It was the original production of this landmark musical and Robert was the first change to the cast. He'd taken over the role from actor, musician and creator of the whole show, Richard O'Brien.

As spooky manservant Riff Raff, he was first called upon to open a door to Brad and Janet. Wow, did he open the door! Boris Karloff had nothing on this boy. The script then called on him to utter just the one word: 'Yes?'. The script presumably did not prevail upon him to bend over backwards before he delivered the word and touch the stage behind with the tip of his forefinger, before reassuming vertical status and arching his back like a black cat. But that's what he did.

"Yes?"

The audience was riveted. So it went with every scene he was involved in, Robert inventing a piece of 'business' to ensure the audience's attention never strayed for one second from him to one of his fellow performers.

When it came to the walk-down, the company necklaced the front of stage in time-honoured fashion and, taking their cue from the one in the centre, bowed deeply in unison. Robert was on the far end. Each time he bowed, the tip of his forefinger met the boards in front of him. I looked around. Every eye in the place was glued on Robert's finger to see if he'd do it again.

As well as comping me in to 'Rocky Horror', he invited me round to his house. Robert lived in the basement of a huge place in Holland Park and the first time I went there, I rang the wrong bell. I was mortified when John Cleese stuck his head out of the attic window.

"Sorry to bother you", I called. "I came round to s…"

"Just a minute" he said with infinite weariness and closed the window. I waited nervously. The front door opened. John Cleese was in his striped pyjamas and immensely tall, glowering down from the top step. I was face to navel with Basil Fawlty on a bad day.

"I'm really sorry, Mr Cleese. I didn't realise you were asleep…"

"I wasn't asleep. I was ill".

"Ah. Er…. I'm here to meet Robert Longden. I must have the wrong address."

"Robert lives in my basement. He's got his own door round the side. And his own doorbell."

Crawling with embarrassment I shot round the corner and rang the right bell. A beaming Robert answered. Arriving in his living room I wished I'd bought a gift, as he had done. I gushed about his book on Vaudeville and admired the bookcase behind him, similarly crammed with books on the history of theatre and the cinema. He seemed to belong to a time where Max Miller told risqué jokes on the Music Hall stage and Myrna Loy batted sleepy bedroom eyes across the big screen.

My genre was pop music and had been since the Beatles. Actually, even earlier, ever since The Shadows came to my hometown. Four men in red hunting jackets, moving in perfect sync. Forward on the right and across with the left and a step back and change, all to the jingly jangly thrill of 'Apache'. My favourite was Jet Harris on bass, with his dyed white-blond hair and a provocative smirk amongst smiles. He was a loose clone, something that went wrong in the lab. The Shadows live on stage in Stockton kickstarted my musical world and, apart from my big sister's Elvis collection, I knew very little of what came before. All these books at Robert's apartment however, spoke of someone steeped in a theatrical history of a world where pop music had never happened. It was all a bit beyond my comfort zone and I was far from sure I could commit to being his collaborator. Robert seemed more than sure though, and I sensed he saw me as some kind of protégé.

"What got you started on all this?" I wondered, waving my hand vaguely to take in the wall of books behind him.

"Well," he replied emphatically. "When I was about eight or nine, I used to go to Cinema Club on a Saturday morning."

"Where was that?"

"Our address was Shangri-La, Nab Lane, Bollington." As he giggled, his face went as red as his hair and his glasses slid down the bridge of his nose. The coffee in his hand slopped onto the table. It was messy, but he regained his decorum and narrative.

"There was always a bit of fun from a grown-up on the stage," he told me, "then a film. Well, the film this Saturday was 'Son Of Paleface'. Do you remember it?"

"Yes," I lied.

"It starred the singing cowboy Roy Rogers and his horse, do you remember him, Trigger? We all absolutely loved Trigger. Anyway, the cinema manager came on and he said: 'I've got a very special guest for you this morning children!' – and on to the stage wandered Roy Rogers."

"The real Roy Rogers?"

"Absolutely! Wearing fabulous leather chaps, giant Stetson, the lot. He was so glamorous. We weren't used to real Hollywood stars in Macclesfield. He sang us all a song" – at this Robert broke into 'A Four-legged Friend' with the well-modulated tones of a trained singer – "and then Roy Rogers asked us: 'do you want to meet my friend? He's come a long long way to say hello to you all. Can you guess who it is boys and girls?' And on to the stage came Trigger."

"No!"

"Yes. It was absolutely magical."

"And you've been chasing that feeling ever since."

"Well sort of."

We were smiling and nodding at one another.

Now it seemed every time I played at Martha's Vineyard, there was Robert at some point in the evening, slipping into an alcove. Like myself, he was both part of the crowd and not part of it; a loner in his candle-flickered world, dreaming, writing, waiting for me to finish, for me to come over. I watched him, pen in one hand, fingers of the other grinding away at the palm; there was a sense of suppressed tension, evident even from a distance. And he was still there at the end, watching me close the piano lid, return my guitar to the case and lay the strap carefully along the strings, willing me to come over, share in his vision. And it must have worked, for soon I was painting seaside scenes upon the walls of a room above a pub in Islington, The Old Red Lion. Robert was creating a new theatre venue for 'our' shows apparently and I was now a founder member of the 'Primeslot Frontcloth Gang'. Musicals weren't really part of my plan but I was carried along by Robert's persuasive personality. I found myself donning a pair of white gloves to play Mr Interlocutor in Robert's revue: The Primeslot Frontcloth Show.

As master of ceremonies I was in an umpire's chair, with the cast ranged in a semi-circle to either side of me. Upon my invitation they would spring from their seats singly or in pairs, to perform little monologues or comedy scenes from Robert's imagination, or one of his memorable and charmingly old-school songs. It was a minstrel show, essentially, with Music Hall at its roots, though it had an experimental modern twist to it all and potty-mouthed jokes. An uneven piece; at times it was hilarious, at other times awful.

The Primeslot Frontcloth Show played in the run-up to Christmas and was good enough at least to transfer to The Institute of Contemporary Arts (ICA) on The Mall, early in the following year. By the time we began rehearsals Robert had changed almost everything about the show. This was something I was seeing for the first time but was to become very used to in following years, where musical theatre was concerned. My role of Mr Interlocutor for instance, was now to be played not by me – but by Robert! I was recast as The Headmaster. What Headmaster? There was no Headmaster! There was now, apparently. And sharing a scene with me was new cast member Connie Booth – John Cleese's ex-wife who had co-written Fawlty Towers and starred in it too, as Polly. I was apprehensive about having to deliver dialogue opposite a proper actress off the telly.

"You won't have to say anything dear," Robert reassured me.

"What do you mean?" I said sharply. I'd already lost the central role since our last production and now it looked like I was losing all my lines as well. And yet, there they were, in the script, in my hand.

"You have to sing them." Robert giggled and pushed his red glasses further up his nose. Robert was a great giggler. He'd almost lose it – drop whatever he was holding on the floor or catch his specs as they slid off his nose. His face would turn the same colour as his hair, there was a little spittle. He was enormous fun, but there was tension below the surface, evidenced by the crater of hard skin that scarred the ball of his right thumb. The fingers of the same hand would continuously gouge at it, even as his face was beaming beatifically in your direction.

Kooney Wacka Hoy, 1980. Left to right: Anita Dobson, Linda Dobell, Ian Bartholomew, Caroline Quentin, Stag Theodopolis.

"But, what about the music, have you written something of your own?"

I was more rattled and defensive now; I had been led to believe I was writing the music.

"No, you just have to make up a tune on the spot. Something highly operatic."

So there I was on opening night sitting in my Headmaster's office on stage, gown around shoulders, gazing out on the first night audience, with John Cleese unmistakable even in shadow – his head was higher than everybody else's. On breezed Connie and flung open the curtains behind me. The stage became flooded with light.

"Good morning Headmaster, tra la laa! It's a beautiful mo-o-or-NING!"

Her eyes locked into mine, which widened in alarm. We stared at one another helplessly. When I eventually managed to summon the inner Pavarotti, my eyes were brimful with tears. "Good morning He-he-he-he, He-he-he, He-he-he- Head Girl!"

After that, I could only manage to summon enough masochism to appear in one more of Robert's masterpieces: 'KooneyWackaHoy' back at the Old Red Lion. I don't know how he got them all along to that cold and miserable room but, night after night, you'd come out from behind your little curtain and there they were gazing impassively at you – Hayley Mills, Anthony Andrews, Ian McKellen… there may well have been only twenty people in every evening, but half of them were household names and the other half were agents.

Our cast included Anita Dobson who wore four different engagement rings on her finger, and a baby Caroline Quentin. They were as yet unknown, but the audience made up for it. The one time someone from the general public did appear, he heckled us so loudly that Robert beat him up in the toilets after the show. It came as quite a shock – Robert's level of commitment; his lack of democracy, the blood on the wall.

And so, for the time being, that was that as far as he and I were concerned. When Robert's 'KooneyWackaHoy' at the Old Red Lion closed, I didn't hear from him again until 1983, when he rang and uttered the two words that would propel us on a whole new joyride.

"Moby Dick".

Chapter 3
Café Society

I was 22 with a young family to support and a mortgage. Money was tight: by day I busked, Thursday and Friday nights I had my residency at Martha's Vineyard (Saturdays were taken already by a singer called Annie, much to my annoyance). I had been on some sort of strange theatrical journey with Robert that didn't earn a penny, and I had my band with Tom and Raphael – likewise. The band, I was sure, was where glory lay. Our manager John McCoy came up with the name 'Café Society' and assured us that the whole Café concept was the next big thing. McCoy was king of the next big thing so we believed him.

Ray Davies of the Kinks came to check us out at the Troubadour in Earl's Court, where we had a weekly residency. He'd formed one of England's early independent record labels and he was shopping for talent. It was the night Alexis Korner appeared as our 'Special Guest' for the princely sum of a bottle of Scotch. A special guest of the highest esteem and the great Ray Davies reportedly coming along to check us out. We were getting somewhere!

Alexis arrived late, sneaking through the crowd to our cubbyhole behind the arch, where we were tuning up our acoustic guitars. He produced a huge spliff.

"Red Leb," he rasped. "It's extremely strong!"

It had a devastating effect. Our tiny cell became a cocoon and started to revolve. Now it was a pulsing womb. Outside, the final Leadbelly track of side two crackled and died away. Coughs and shuffles settled to silence. Our audience was waiting. We three stared at one another in open panic. We were totally incapable of performing, we couldn't move.

"Take off your shoes and socks," Alexis croaked benevolently, "Get your bare feet on the cold floor. Always works!"

Café Society cartoon by Dominic Poelsma.

Alexis stepped out into the spotlight, while we cooled our heels. The bluesman played until we'd straightened up enough to follow him on.

Café were mid-song, underneath the arch, just suitably stoned when a fashionable stir occurred at the back. Raymond Douglas Davies was amongst us, old melon grin. He was pop royalty, a man we had grown up watching on 'Ready Steady Go' and 'Top of the Pops'. Tom, Raphael and I would have had all the Kinks singles I'm quite sure, and to recognise his familiar face there at the back had a galvanising effect on us; on the whole room actually. Many of our audience were friends and supporters and there can't have been many who didn't have a copy of 'Days', 'Waterloo Sunset' or 'You Really Got Me' somewhere at home. Inspired, we sang our hearts out, and when the interval came, word came back to us in our cubby hole that "Ray would like to perform a few songs."

Next thing, we're onstage with him, providing backing vocals.

Us: "La la laa!"

Him: "Chilly chilly in the evening sun, Waterloo sunset's mine…"

After that he was 'Uncle' Ray. The record deal was as good as signed.

I dashed up north to my hometown of Middlesbrough to share the good news with my mates at the Kirklevington Country Club. Apart from sofas and an open log fire into which angry girlfriends could smash Southern Comforts, 'the Kirk' was quite a venue. I saw Lindisfarne there, belting out 'Fog On The Tyne' before it was a hit. I missed Jimi Hendrix, but the barmaid told me he was so loud that half the glasses broke. It was where I had held my 18th birthday party and Dave Coverdale, who worked in a clothes shop in Redcar, came across to say hello.

"Happy Birthday man!"

"Hey, how you doing? Haven't seen your group The Government around for a while…"

"Yeah well, something extraordinary happened!"

"Oh yeah?"

"Yeah! You know Mick, Mick Moody? He insisted on driving me down to Sheffield to audition for this important band. Anyway, I got the gig."

"Oh yeah, which band?"

"Deep Purple."

"Fuckin' hell man."

"Yeah, I know. First thing they did was stick eighty grand in my bank account."

"Eighty?"

"Said I had to get used to money…"

"Eighty thousand pounds?"

"I know!" (Next time I saw him, I was bald and 53 and he was on MTV driving a convertible across the Mojave desert, lip-syncing his latest Whitesnake megahit, one arm around a girl, another beautiful female draping the bonnet, and the long hair of all three of them streaming behind).

Anyway, here I was now, in a band being produced by Ray Davies and awaiting success of my own. The burger chef at the Kirk was a songwriter like myself and another member of club owner John McCoy's stable of artists: Chris Rea. We sat there on his fag break, betting which one of us would make it first. I can't remember what the stake was, but we were both confident. My band Café was signed to Konk, the record label owned by Ray Davies, whilst Chris had just signed with Magnet Records. And though he was still flipping burgers and I was a member of Robert's ludicrous Primeslot Frontcloth Gang, both Chris and I were convinced it was all about to happen; why wouldn't it be? We had the conviction of youth, we had the record deals and both had singles scheduled for release. I wasn't massively convinced by the quirky song Ray Davies had chosen (even though it was one of mine) but this was the moment for both of us – next stop, the world!

We travelled back to London together in our manager's car. McCoy sat in the back, Chris drove. Like a maniac. The man who would go on to write 'Drivin' Home For Christmas' was high-tailing it in the opposite direction as fast as horsepower could carry him. Even though he was much more 'Middlesbrough' than me, it seemed he just couldn't get away from the place quick enough. We were doing a 120mph when the bonnet catch popped and the bonnet slapped up against the windscreen, completely obscuring our view of the A1. Chris was very calm; gradually dropped his speed, indicating from fast to middle lane, edging it back some more, insinuating the vertically-bonneted vehicle into the slow lane, then coasting onto the hard shoulder, killing the engine.

He got out. Put the bonnet down, checked the catch. When we set off again, nobody said a word about the incident and the needle on the speedometer resumed its former position. Way off the dial. At Golders Green, I was spat out upon jelly-legs.

Smash Hits declared 'Café Society' their album of the month, but it didn't do much for the sales figures, which finally settled on the 600 mark after my mother went out and bought eight copies. To promote it, we supported Barclay James Harvest on over thirty British dates for no money at all, in fact I think we paid – quite difficult when you're on a lousy record company retainer of £25 a week. At sound-check, we shoe-horned into the postage stamp of a stage they'd left us, and had to make do with the few moments still available till doors open.

We were terribly green. At Malvern Winter Gardens the local promoter asked us if we would like any girls after the show. We all stared at our feet. Nobody said anything. The promoter was startled. He'd never had this reaction before. Usually, bands crowed like cocks and played air guitar.

"I'm married," Raphael mumbled.

I was reluctantly forced to mumble "me too" having recently tied the knot with Pat.

Tom brightened and looked up. He'd just thought of something.

"Have you got any boys?"

At the Victoria Hall, Hanley, Tom developed an eye-catching manoeuvre where he banged his right foot up and down like a maniac during the groovier numbers. As we left by the stage door a bunch of kids waiting for Barclay James Harvest crowed: "There's that mad bastard with the leg!" It was in every night after that.

At Glasgow Apollo – with a large stage so elevated you were staring the balcony in the face – the promoter came to us in our dressing room immediately before we went on and warned us starkly: "They dinnae fuck around wi' support acts here. If they dinnae like you, they'll let you know." I won't say we went down well – we delivered our whole set to a quite deadly silence – but they didn't throw anything, and they all had bottles.

With our acoustic guitars and three vocal mikes, we were an easy act to get on and off. Barclay James Harvest, in comparison, seemed ludicrously overblown. Guitars came double-necked. Drums came with great gongs. One particular song culminated in a giant butterfly arising over the stage and opening its wings. Except, they never opened, something always went wrong. I think it came off maybe once or twice in 30 dates. With utter delight we took to the side of the stage to witness the moment. We sang along lustily to the next number, too. All their songs had the same ponderous rhythm to which we bellowed, in rhythm: "Shittybumweewee, fuck wank SNOT!"

We sang safe in the knowledge they couldn't hear a thing. In fact, Barclay James Harvest would look across, approvingly. 'Support band are diggin' us!' you could see them thinking.

We were offered more support slots: three dates with Leo Sayer (his wife watching from the side as he sang 'The Show Must Go On' in the clown's outfit she'd made him) and a mini-tour with Lindisfarne's Alan Hull. Impressively, every night without fail by the time he went on, he'd drunk at least six pints of Guinness and he was still sober, and he was still thin!

We did a few UK dates supporting the Kinks. In fact, they offered us the support for an entire US tour but my visa application didn't happen in time and we were left behind. I wasn't the most popular member of Café Society…

I loved watching the Kinks perform. Ray was a great showman. A rattling skeleton was brought on and he, mortarboard on head, ruler in hand, pointed out the salient parts of the cadaver. "The hip bone's connected to the thigh bone" he sang, "the thigh bone's connected to the knee bone". 'Dem Bones' was an unusual choice of song for a band, but that was the Kinks. Another tour-de-force was Demon Alcohol, where he balanced a wobbly bottle of beer on his head. During one show, he soaked a woman in the front row who complained bitterly and Claire in the office moaned to us later about having to pay the dry cleaning bill.

Ray wasn't very kind to Debbie and Shirley, his backing singers. "Have you farted?" he murmured one night into his microphone, as he passed them. He wasn't much kinder to members of the band either. Laurie the trumpet-player – a bit of a short guy – was made to stand on a box for his trumpet solo one night, "because it's his birthday," Ray told the audience. When it came to the solo, the whole band went up a semitone – the whole band apart from Laurie that is, who hadn't been informed of this arrangement.

Baptist, the keyboard player, had a particularly hard time. Despite having been in the group for 10 years, he still had to fly economy, with original members Ray, Dave and Mick in first-class. Baptist's tour-de-force was his 'Phantom of the Opera' intro. Back in the days I am describing, Andrew Lloyd Webber had not yet purloined the title as his own. This mighty organ intro by the Kinks keyboard player was a Gothic throwback to the old movies, from Lon Chaney's silent deformed creature, through to Claude Rains and Herbert Lom. He delivered it with camp, Hammer-horror intensity. Phantom was his signature and he pulled it off brilliantly. But once the curtain

Café Society, 1975.

came down, Baptist hit the bottle. When the Kinks returned from the US tour, of which the less said the better, Mick Avory told me (in between demonstrations of the golf stroke he had pulled off at the fourth hole in Augusta) that the organist had passed out so senselessly in bed, members of the band were able to move his bed out into the corridor, with him in it. They set him up outside the lifts, bedside table, standard lamp, Gideon's Bible and all. When Baptist awoke, he believed he was still in his room. He couldn't understand why there was this pinging sound every two minutes and people emerging to gawp at him.

Café did a few dates supporting jazz singer George Melly. He wore flamboyant jackets that appeared to have been made out of deckchair material and, though he seemed old to me at my tender age, there were echoes of decadent youth about his face. Conversationally, his intellect, wit, appreciation of art and philosophy (he was President of the British Humanist Society) put him quite out of our league.

George would drink half a bottle of scotch before the first set and polish it off before the second. His party-piece was to turn his back to the crowd and, as the band vamped, stroke his portly sides with his arms wrapped around himself, as if being caressed by a woman. To a roar from the crowd, he flipped a pair of red high heels upside down on his shoulders and gyrated his hips. Pat was with me in the audience one night as I watched this little pièce de résistance. George's eyes lit upon her and he came across at the end of the performance to be introduced. He'd sunk a bottle of whisky, his eyes were gleaming and he was licking his lascivious lips.

"Oh no," I muttered.

"What a beautiful pair of breasts" he growled, arriving. "May I?"

"Sure!" Pat laughed without a moment's hesitation and pushed her bosoms towards him. He kissed one and then the other, bowed in worship before my young wife's décolletage. I'll be honest, I was a little put out.

Our British dates were drawing to a close. We wound up in London at the 'Hammy Odeon' with Barclay James Harvest. I donned a top hat and cane to give our debut single 'Whitby Two Step' that extra push. As it turned out, it didn't bother the charts.

Meanwhile, Chris Rea's first single, 'Fool If You Think It's Over' went to number one in the States. Er… cancel that bet.

3. Café Society

We took on a new manager, Colin Bell. He was a milkman when we first met him, but he was going places faster than Ernie. We acquired drummer Nick Travisick, and Nick South, bass player with Vinegar Joe. We got out there and pub-rocked London: Hope and Anchor Islington, The Brecknock, The Nashville Rooms – we were becoming a proper rock band. *Sounds* thought so, anyway. They dubbed us 'Most Promising Band of '76' – though with hindsight, perhaps that title should have gone to the Sex Pistols.

Tom saw the Pistols at the 100 Club. He saw the future. One week later he played a solo gig at the ICA and turned up at our rehearsal the next day with a wrecked guitar.

"I had this moment, this joyful moment, when I just threw it at the floor!" he exclaimed, eyes ashine.

That was our guitar, Café's guitar. Tom knew that! Had an alien replaced him? I realised we were in trouble.

Trouble doubled. Having a peaceful pint with friends in his local gay pub, The Coleherne in Earl's Court, police moved in for the bust. Tom found himself herded into a group and pushed up against a wall. It politicised him, instantly. He went home and wrote a song, then steamed straight round our house on his motorbike to sing it to me, trembling with excitement.

"The British Police are the best in the world" it began. I was startled. We didn't write songs with first lines like that. Then he got to the chorus: "Sing if you're glad to be gay, sing if you're happy that way, hey…"

It was a greater song than anything he'd written by far and we both knew it. In fact, it was so powerful it filled me with tears. Once introduced into our set, it blew away every other song we had written, as far as audience reaction was concerned. I still sang original songs about me, and Raphael still sang original songs about himself, but it was no contest. Tom's songs about himself were just more interesting.

Soon, every review seemed to begin: 'Darlings of Earl's Court' or 'Gay band Café Society…'

Ray and I were trapped. Sympathetic to Tom's cause was one thing, tarred by the same brush was another. After a while, when we got to the chorus, Tom sang: "sing if you're glad to be gay," Ray sang: "sing if you're glad to be Ray," and I sang: "sing if you're glad to be Kaye". But Tom's world had changed. He was a political animal now. Life divided neatly into Them and Us. He started writing angry, sloganistic songs: 'You'd Better Decide Which Side You're On', 'Up Against The Wall', 'Ain't Gonna Take It'. Raphael and I were still listening to Cat Stevens' 'Tea For The Tillerman'. Tom's new songs didn't square with ours and he was dancing with frustration on the spot where loyalty tethered him to us.

Against this backdrop we went into the Konk studio to record our second album, not with Ray Davies this time, but a team of producers of which he had approved, led by Jon Miller and calling themselves Triumvirate. Day one was edgy. On day two, Jon Miller sacked our keyboard player and drummer.

Colin Bell convened a hostile meeting between Ray Davies and us. Colin was good. He put Uncle Ray under enormous pressure, to the point where, halfway through the meeting, he excused himself for a moment and disappeared.

We sat and we waited. Eventually, secretary Claire appeared.

"What have you done to Ray?" she said accusingly.

"He's just gone to the toilet," I informed her – naïve to the last.

"About 20 minutes ago," Colin added grimly.

"The toilet?" She was quite incredulous. "No he hasn't," she assured us. "He's just left in an ambulance."

Tom departed in disgust to form his own band, leaving the two of us on the kindergarten floor, trying to fit together the pieces that were left. Raphael and I carried on recording but suddenly it was as if we had a Beatles album with only Paul and George's songs left on it. It made even 'Tea For The Tillerman' sound like the work of some rabid fundamentalist…

The first time I saw Tom's new band, the 'Tom Robinson Band' (TRB), was at The Stapleton, a pub round the corner from Konk, where Raphael and I slaved over a not-so-hot record. You could hear them down the road. When I walked in, Tom was playing bass lying down on stage, his head inside the drummer's bass drum – a startling transformation from his sedate presence in the Café Society line-up. A desultory few watched over the top of their pints with amusement, but six or seven young lads went mad at the end of the number, pulling each other about by the fronts of their T-shirts and pouring beer over their heads.

When Tom came over to hug me, the same six or seven followed and stood around him, beaming, wearing him like a badge. He introduced me to them one by one; he knew all their names.

There were more disciples the next time, and they knew all the words. Third time I saw him, the pub was The Brecknock and it was heaving. Illegally full. Don Arden, legendary Jet Records boss and manager of ELO was on the prowl. Steve O'Rourke, manager of Pink Floyd was similarly competing for Tom's signature, along with eager teams of A&R men. Imminent success was so tangible it smelt of hot metal. Tom was surfing his own power-surge, grinning, winning.

But first, he had to get out of his contract with Konk. He had good contacts at *NME*, *Melody Maker* and *Sounds*. Music journalists had been charmed by Tom's courteous habit of sending a bunch of flowers to anyone who gave Café a decent review. Now Tom took every opportunity to rail at the injustice of his recording and publishing contracts with Ray Davies. Punk was billowing up all around us and music journalists were only too eager to document any challenge to pop music's established autocracy.

After the umpteenth slagging off in the *NME*, Uncle Ray finally picked up the phone. Tom was free from his contract. With one bound we all were unbound. Like two caged birds whose door has been accidentally left ajar, Raphael and I waddled to the edge and waddled back. We were in the middle of Café's second album. It was all our own material. We didn't want to be free.

Tom signed to EMI and '2-4-6-8 Motorway' went to number five in the UK charts.

His first British tour (via 'Top Of The Pops') wound up at the Lyceum. Raphael and I entered the arena together. A clenched fist stood 30 foot high, a towering backdrop to a vast stage. A jostling circus thronged, ready to cavort at the first powerchord. It reeked like an arena of Christians and lions. And we were the only two Christians there…

A phalanx of press photographers amassed at the front, separated by a barrier from the rabble. When the house lights died for the mighty advent of TRB the air seemed to fry. The mosh pit contracted, sucking in a hundred more, and to the screaming of seagulls, in a battery of flashlight, the band appeared. They were wearing school uniform. So was the audience. Tom's jacket was covered in the same badges as theirs. His guitar had the Ford logo on it. Except it exclaimed 'Fraud'.

Danny Kustow hit the opening chords of 'Motorway'.

Chank Chank Chank Chaggang!

It was the death knell of Café. Days I'll remember all my life.

Chapter 4
Golden Mile
- 1977 -

After Café Society fell apart, I wrote a dubious collection of rather aggressive songs. They weren't really me at all, but in '77 for musicians like me it was adapt or die. The Sex Pistols and clans of following bands like The Clash, Sham '69, The Damned, had not only stormed the music establishment's castle walls, they were inside. Up in their ivory towers cowered rock's royalty, the likes of Pink Floyd, Genesis – even the Rolling Stones! They hardly dared peep through the crenelations at the marauding army swarming below, brandishing guitars for axes and spittle flying, all got up in studded bondage gear held together by safety pins, screaming: "No Future!"

Punk was the filter through which all music was judged. Overnight, all my musical heroes were zeros. And as for me, the composer of a previous song of which I was proud that the *NME* had described as 'enough to make a body cringe'. I was a goner; 24 years old and a rock dinosaur already, one of the unknown types, an elaphrosaur perhaps or a liopleurodon. As I desired something more than a dinosaur in Hell's chance, it was time to change my tune.

That singer/songwriter tag was the first thing that would have to go. What I needed was a band, and not one like Café that could knock out a killer version of 'Morning Has Broken'. I needed a proper rock band (was it still okay to use that word, for I could never pretend to be a punk? I could, however, be a little more cross). Fallen Angels, I decided I would call them, after a line in a Leonard Cohen song – though maybe I should keep quiet about the connection for now; he was another of my great heroes to have fallen out of fashion.

I advertised for musicians in the back of *Melody Maker*, somehow convincing successful applicants that big things were just around the corner and promising to pay them as soon as I had some money. I organised a couple of out-of-town warm-up gigs, then lined up The Golden Lion in Fulham for our all-important London Showcase.

The Kinks office helpfully lent me their van and I felt excited as I piloted Fallen Angels to our first gig. Driving them home a few hours later I felt less of the excitement and more of the apprehension.

"When can you pay us man?" they asked good-naturedly, as I dropped them off at a central point in Town. It was the question I had dreaded them asking. God knows where the money was going to come from. Pat and I had barely the thickness of a Rizla paper to rub between ourselves and poverty. I was pretty mean about that Rizla paper too – I needed it to skin up.

"After the showcase," I assured them, "I'll pay you then, I promise."

"Oh… okay."

"It'll be worth it when we're signed to a major label!"

Guitars on backs that arched slightly against the skinflint cold, I watch them disappear into the downward throng of the Tube. I had sold them a dream and they'd bought it for now, but when you don't pay your musicians, patience has a short shelf-life.

Another week's rehearsals and another gig. Goodwill was now becoming stretched. But the big one was coming up, our London showcase. The Kinks office helped me organise the guest list for Fallen Angels' gig in Fulham. They got on the blower and three or four different record labels agreed to come and check me out. Ray Davies magnificently offered to lend me his white stage suit and looked on from the bar in wry amusement as I twisted up my face and spat out the lyrics to my sneery new songs to the curious drinkers, dotted with industry insiders.

At the end of the show, three labels weren't there anymore. One table however, remained. The Beatles label: EMI. They beckoned me over.

I felt the bands' eyes burrowing into my back as I crossed the empty dance floor. I felt their eyes glimmering over pints as I talked to the record company executives, monitoring my body language from afar. Maybe they stifled the impulse to cheer as I stifled the impulse to punch the air, as the words I had waited my whole life to hear dripped from the lips of Brian Shepherd, Head of A&R.

"We'd like to sign you."

"Ah great!"

EMI wanted me. I was leading my band, Moses-like, to the Promised Land.

"Just you."

4. Golden Mile

Keenly the band watched me all the way back to their table, no doubt observing waves of elation being wrestled from my face by competing convulsions of panic.

"Well!" I said emphatically, arriving. "There's good news, and there's bad news."

The multinational music empire cuddled me to its corporate body with a 5 year, worldwide deal, insulating me from the icy bitch of existence with a ReadyBrek glow. I was where I always wanted to be, signed to a major label. Suddenly I had an annual retainer to clear all my debts and £500 from Artist Development to blow on clothes. A suit was being fashioned for me from yellow shot silk. Vidal Sassoons' dyed my hair blond. Pat's face fell when she opened the door to me.

"I know, I know!" I called over my shoulder, hurrying up to the bathroom mirror where a blond alien stared back at me with an expression of horror. I was outside Vidal Sassoon's at the crack of dawn the next day, to get it dyed dark again.

A&R started talking Producers. Big names were bandied about and demos of my songs went out to them. Then John Darnley, in his A&R office where unlistened-to tapes were cascading from the cupboards, said: David Hentschel's interested."

"David who?"

"Producer of Genesis." I could only guess Genesis were laying low in the current climate and through a miracle of timing, I was the lucky recipient of a top notch producer twiddling his thumbs.

"Fucking hell!" I began to stammer, then, feeling his eyes weighing up my suitability for stardom, adjusted. "Yeah sure, why not, give him a go…"

David had a sensitive tax situation so – poor me – I was forced to record in Paris. Worse still, I was given a suite at the Hilton and a 24-hour stretch limo. It felt a bit big, I must say, after our Ford Escort.

"Qui avez vous au derriere last semaine?" I asked chauffeur Jean Claude, playing with the electronic partition, sending it up and down.

"Rod Stewart, Sir."

I felt a bit nervous. I'd never had a chauffeur before, I didn't know how to treat the guy. When we got to the hotel I gave him the night off. Er… wrong.

"I shall be 'ere," he said disappointedly, "waiting in ze foyer for when you need me."

I bulleted up to my penthouse suite to change then sneaked down in the service lift, out the back entrance and down onto the Metro. But you know, you soon adjust to luxury. By the end of the week I was phoning Jean Claude at three in the morning to come and open bottles of beer with his teeth.

The Ship Hits the Fans

What an imposter I felt, feet up on the mixing desk in Studio One of EMI Paris, with Thin Lizzy in Studio Two. I had Howie Casey in the booth, slaving over a hot saxophone. Howie Casey – only the Beatles' bloody horn player! On the sofa behind me waiting their turn were drummer Dave Mattacks from Fairport Convention and the awesome Pete Wingfield, who'd already had a hit record of his own, '18 With a Bullet.' Here they were, and more, flown across the channel to bring to glorious life my dog-eared collection of scribbles and chord symbols in notebooks, my snatches of piano and singing on back pocket cassettes full of bumfluff. The experience was thrilling. It ran the former Miss Sweden a very close second.

Somehow, it fell to me to take back to London the master tape of the four songs recorded in Paris.

"Whatever you do" cautioned David, "don't put it through the X-ray machine."

At the airport, after tipping John Claude every last franc I had in the world, I watched, traumatised, as the giant spool of multitrack sailed towards the scanner. Airport security had insisted on me putting it through, even though I caused such a fuss it almost became an international incident. Throughout the whole flight home I was horror struck at the thought of returning to the record company with a blank reel of tape.

Pat was dutifully waiting for me at Gatwick. In the chill wind of the multi-storey, when we eventually found where she'd parked the car, I automatically climbed in the back.

"Get out of it," she snorted. "You can drive."

"Sorry darling, I'm used to a chauffeur," I apologised, climbing behind the wheel.

"You've only been there a bloody week!"

"I know," I agreed, brushing away dog hairs already settling on my jacket. "How quickly we change."

Back in the foyer at EMI the roster of artists stared down intimidatingly from the wall. Sixty names, mainly household. It was a rock 'n roll call of the great and good. Top, Paul McCartney. Somebody had graffiti'd 'God' next to his name. Underneath, Cliff Richards. Some wag had put 'God' next to his name too. Beneath that, the almighty Queen. It was rock royalty. But the company was shrinking fast. They had invested all their Beatles profits in a state-of-the-art brain scanner. Then the Japanese developed the same thing but better, for half the price. EMI had taken a massive financial hit, been forced to merge with Thorn Electronics and in its aftermath, belt-tighten. The roster of artists shortened by the week and it was the lower orders getting the chop, not the golden Gods at the top. Mercifully, my mastertape had turned out to still have music on it and my place on the roll of honour was preserved. Where? At the very bottom.

Recording continued at Maison Rouge in Fulham, a studio owned by the band Jethro Tull. Chas & Dave came in for a couple of numbers, reminiscing about the jellied eels you used to be able to get off a stall in Edmonton. It was just the kind of conversation Chas & Dave should be having. We'd borrowed drummer Preston Hayman from Kate Bush – another label-mate – and Tom Robinson was on bass. He was a rockstar these days, our Tom, and it's true I could have found a greater exponent of the instrument, but I was hiring more than a bassist. Here, sharing the studio floor with me once more was my old Café bandmate, my musical mentor and big brother.

After 6 weeks of sheer happiness, my debut album 'Golden Mile' was finished. To my ears it sounded quite beautiful. But what would the label think? Brian Shepherd, Head of A&R turned up at the studio, gangsters in tow. He took the leather-upholstered producer's chair and bade me pull up the tape op's slightly less salubrious one – the one with gaffa tape in all the places where stuffing erupted. He chopped out two lines of coke and motioned with his hand. I dutifully, if rather guiltily, sat down beside him and hoovered up the nearest line, under the accusatory glare of my wife, who had never seen me do such a thing. Producer David Hentschel pressed play, Pat reluctantly subsided against the back wall and as the opening riff kicked in I felt a surge of confidence. A simple thumbs up from this music industry Nero beside me would unlock the low door in the wall of humdrum existence, beyond which lay Nirvana.

Yep, the drugs were definitely working!

Not a soul stirred during playback, not a word was spoken between tracks. The only movement was the chopping out of another two lines at the end of Side One and the beginning of Side Two.

As the final powerchord ebbed and faded away, the back wall gangsters who held my career in their hands, wordlessly unpeeled from shadow and followed Brian out of the door. Not one of them had a word to say. Pat had though – she propelled herself off the back wall and gave me holy hell.

Taking the stairs two at a time like a mighty rock giant I came face-to-face once more with the roster of artists on the first landing. Gazing upon it, I felt the deathless breeze of the Grim Reaper's scythe across the back of my neck. In the 6 weeks I had been in the studio, 60 acts had become 31.

I was the one.

The Ship Hits the Fans

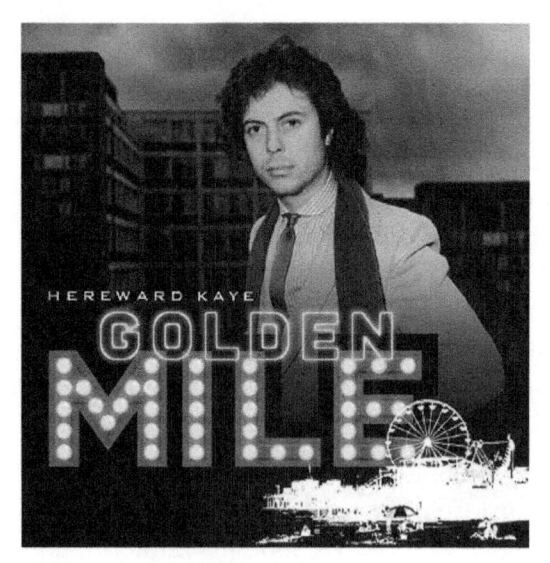

Publicity shot of Hereward, taken on the roof of EMI Manchester Square, London, 1979. © EMI

I reached A&R. Where was everyone? Torch-bearing enthusiasts of mine had been mysteriously supplanted by lawyers.

Nero appeared in his doorway and beckoned me in.

"Great album," he gushed, "I can honestly say it's one of the best four albums ever delivered to me."

He beamed. I beamed, I'll say I did! The ReadyBrek overcoat was back on.

"Great album…" then he frowned "… with one fatal flaw. It doesn't have a single. And until it does, we can't market it. I was thinking, would you be willing to co-write with someone else? I've spoken to B.A. Robertson about this one. He loves what he's heard. He'd be delighted to help."

"No, it's okay," I said lightly.

"He's got one hell of a track record as you…"

"I can do this myself."

"Are you sure?"

"Yeah."

The breeze turned chill. "Okay, I want you in the basement studio here every Monday morning, with a new song. We'll keep going until you come up with a single."

The more I had to write a single, the less I could. Boy, I came up with some turkeys! 'Boom Sha La Boom' was the title of the first miserable effort. There was a third-rate Elvis Costello pastiche called 'Infatuation'. After a month of Mondays and 'Julie Joined The Police' – what was I thinking? – I thought I'd never write a decent song again. The only tune I could hear in my head was the toll of doom. The option for EMI to renew my contract for another year (and ramp up my income by another grand) was coming up in 3 weeks time. Being dropped was not an option. I had more mouths to feed now; our two young sons, Leon and Jody, and Pat's mum Dorothy, who'd moved in with us. Not to mention Pat's ever-expanding menagerie of animals.

4. Golden Mile

But of course it was about more than money. I was within touching distance of chart success, of fame. Making that final leap depended on EMI believing in me and investing in me as an unbroken artist, in the way they had just done with Kate Bush. They needed to put their hand in their pocket and push, push push me as a breakthrough act. They had record pluggers going into radio stations every month with a pile of new EMI releases. My record needed to be top of that pile. The decision was down to Head of A&R. Nero's mighty thumb would swing up… or down.

Instead of going home, I walked out of EMI's Manchester Square headquarters and hitched around the country. I needed time to think; I could see which way the thumb was swinging. One week later back at Manchester Square, I knew what I had to say.

I looked Brian Shepherd straight in the eye. "I want you to commit the same budget to promoting my album as you did to recording it."

"Sixty grand?"

"I'm a new artist. I need to know you're really committed to putting my album across, otherwise I'm afraid I'll have to look elsewhere."

Like the vacancies board at the Job Centre maybe? What was I saying! Bad move.

One A&R meeting later and I had my answer. Sadly, in the current climate, they could not commit to a marketing budget of such enormity on an unknown artist. In a daze, we shook hands and I walked out, head just about held high, for at least I had not been dropped. But as an example of snatching defeat from the jaws of victory, it was up there with the best of them.

I had seriously blown it.

Now I had to go home and tell Pat.

At Martha's Vineyard, all the usual suspects were assembled. Behind the counter, West Indian Desmond was slick with endeavour, opening two bottles at once. Beside him was Jackie, just back from the Middle East fighting the Six-Day War. Little Frank was being eaten alive by Big Alison. Randy Roger, 70 years old and bent double, was telling anyone who'd listen he'd cured himself of multiple sclerosis by cutting out wheat. Leather freak guy straddled his usual stool, Larry was a First World War General, with bars across his chest.

And me? Stuck behind the piano, clanking my way mechanically through someone else's song, delivered in tones changed somehow, grown darker. But then, your voice does change when you've received a kick in the balls. Pete and Marsha came over and plonked a bottle of house white on top of the piano for me. "Ah, my favourite, Chateau Shite." It was an old routine.

"I'll have you know, this is what the Pope drinks," countered Pete, on cue.

"No wonder they have to carry him round in that little chair."

"When's your wife going to sing instead of you? She's better."

And so it went on – and on. Every Thursday and Friday the wine bar party beckoned and I was the one-man band leading the parade. It could make you forget what you were meant to be doing, or who you planned to be. I'd been playing this wine bar far longer than intended, there should have been a plaque on the wall. Annie, the other live performer at Martha's who commandeered the prized Saturday night slot, had long since moved on to better things. Now we all knew her surname too – Lennox.

Looking across at Pat, she was no longer going from table to table as I used to see, head thrown back in laughter, receiving a hug. Her face was more serious now, buried in her new book: 'The Fat of the Land' by John and Sally Seymour. This title worried me. We had two horses we couldn't afford in a stable yard out at Stanmore, beyond the end of the Bakerloo line. We had an enclosure of rabbits at the end of our narrow garden. Pat threw them fresh broccoli from the greengrocer's. Fresh! We couldn't even afford any for the fridge. The garage was full of rabbits too, to the exclusion of our car, gaining winter rust out on the curb. And somehow – somehow – I had agreed to an African pygmy goat. George, we called him. Pat took him with us everywhere. Tied up outside the Co-op, the sight of the creature pulled old ladies up in their tracks. "'Ere, what kind of dog's that?" They weren't used to goats on North Harrow High Street.

We were just in the wrong place to fulfil her needs. I hadn't realised until we moved to London, how much Pat would hate the great metropolis. She couldn't even get on the tube without a panic attack. She wanted the natural world, not this one. She didn't belong to Bond Street, her clothes were always shedding bits of hay or straw. I'd borrowed her jacket to pop outside recently and there was a dead dormouse in the pocket! And how had I ever thought she would grow out of horses? Whenever we went on a night out, back in the 'Boro, we'd have to swing by Cherry Prince to put him to bed. I'd watch her from afar, feeding him a carrot from her own lips before she climbed back in the van and gave me a great snog, as I protested. Giving up horses would be like me giving up music.

There were other books fanned out around Pat's dripping candle: 'The Farming Ladder', 'The Cottage Economy', 'The Smallholders Guide'.

Worrying. Every comment she made these days came from the pages of these books and started with a: "did you know": "Did you know twenty per cent of gammon in a supermarket is injected water? Did you know veal calves are crated and kept in the dark so their meat turns white when you cook it? Did you know pigs are bunged in farrowing crates to suckle their litter?"

Her voice was shot through with urgency as she said: "Listen, just listen how factory farmers kill chickens and turkeys. They're hung by one leg on a conveyor belt that takes them through to the stunner. But they're swinging and every tenth or twelfth one gets missed. They're alive when they go through to the throat slitter. Some miss the stunner and the slitter and go through to being dipped in boiling water and plucked in mechanical plucking machines!"

"That's terrible."

"If you only ever read one book read this one."

Pat had discovered her next big thing. It wasn't remotely compatible with our life in London, but Pat hated London and in that summer of '79 no one could blame her, with the National Front at one end of the street, the Anti-Nazi League at the other, and batons across constabulary chests, the Special Patrol Group in between. Pat dreamed of the country, where she could scatter corn from an apron or lick the warm milk running down her fingers from the juicy udders of goats. As I sang beside her, Pat found shelter in imaginary fields where ponies in their multitudes nuzzled her palm. Her imagination floated like the sleepy dustmotes above a candle as she dreamed of another future, a better life elsewhere.

It was winter now and a quiet one tonight. Trickles of dripping wax drew patterns around old wine bottles like hoarfrost, as lovers gazed at one another over the candle-light. Couples huddled over their tiny wrought-iron tables in cosy nests of light, deep in conversation, tongues loosened by the wine. In this soft glowing oasis everyone looked like a character in a Renoir painting and no one wanted to know about the world outside, which, on this night, was a pity. For beyond the window assembled the National Front.

Ugly chanting could faintly be picked out in the far distance. Violent thugs with skills honed every Saturday as they spilled from the terraces, were spoiling for a fight. I abandoned my song as vile slogans permeated the walls and derailed the melody. All conversation stood suspended in mid-sentence. Even eye-locked lovers looked up.

The English were coming!

Skinheads appeared at the window. Then they spotted Des, mine gentle host - from Jamaica. The shouting grew louder, more violent. A Union Jack was brandished above hate-twisted faces. The plate-glass went through like a time-bomb. Fear detonated in us all, jumping to our feet, indignant with no time to react to invaders swarming for the bar. Jackie's Star of David was wrenched from her throat and rising pathetically to defend her, leather freak Dad got a bottle in his face. Through all the shouting and chaos, came a cavalcade of sirens. The cavalry I thought, thank God! Blue light tracked spattered walls above the piano where Pat and I cowered, faces buried in one another's clothing. One of us was whimpering – I think it might have been me.

The boys in blue made straight for Desmond, cornered and fighting for his life. They lobbed him in the back of the van with a few skinheads for good measure and, having got their man, were off. Siren tones merged and melted into the sound of city traffic, a snowflake falling on snow.

Silence settled. The fascists – and the National Front – were gone, leaving behind the desecrated landscape, the framed Renoir with a boot through it.

Pat and I faced one another across the debris. She didn't have to say a thing. We both knew.

I'd married a girl who had stuck it out for 8 long years and denied herself because she didn't want to hold me back. But I'd had my go. It was her turn now.

London would have to turn without me.

Chapter 5
Flat of the land
- 1982 -

Welcome to Stickford, Lincolnshire. You can find us by driving 10 miles north from Boston upon a road as unwaveringly straight and unforgiving as a Quaker. There are no corners in this part of the world and even if there were, it's unlikely that you would find success around any of them. Our road heads humourlessly for the far horizon, a horizontal demarcation between sprouts and sky, uninterrupted by trees or hedgerows or copses or dells or nooks or dips or hills.

Just the sprouts; and the smell of them.

Companion by its side and lying in wait, runs an endless 'Drain', a Venus Flytrap for the booze befuddled farmhand, swatting at the windscreen of his Morris Minor as fog and dark descend.

Splish!

You see it a mile off, The Crown. The casual traveller, bowling like a tumbleweed up the road towards it will find me in here. Everyone round here knows me – I'm the one who doesn't fit in.

Slightly further up the road there's a petrol station and on the right, a great dilapidated house. These three buildings, so startlingly grouped together, comprise Stickford, as comparatively exciting to the surrounding sea of sprouts as is Las Vegas to the Nevada desert.

The house is ours. So remote is its location that the RAF target it, screaming out of Coningsby 18 miles away and dive-bombing us moments later. To be out in the yard when the fighters come in low and hurtle across, too fast to see and too loud to hear, is to momentarily experience insanity. The world cracks open like an egg.

All colour fades like hope from the face of the day. Light wanes into waxing darkness. Snow fields slide away, wan listless ghosts, yesterday's already. My two North London sons shiver up a tree, trapped by geese. Turkeys, ducks and hens mill about crapping, waiting for me to get home from the pub and strangle one of them. They don't know which yet and neither do I, but one of them.

We'd been away from London and penniless for two years now, out in the wilds of Lincolnshire, living on whatever we could grow ourselves. And all because of a book: 'Self-Sufficiency: The Science and Art of Producing and Preserving Your Own Food', by John and Sally Seymour. The book was our bible. We wouldn't need shops or money or products, we told them; we'd grow our own, raise our own, eat our own. As responsible meat-eaters we would feed our animals and they in turn would feed us. All we'd ever need to go to a shop for, in fact, was toilet paper! We shone in the face of scepticism from our friends. We felt we had stumbled upon the secret of life.

It didn't get off to a great start. After seeing a sign by the roadside, 'GOTES', I'd brought home two nannies of quite ferocious strength – brutes that would wrench me across the courtyard, down the steps and onto the lawn every morning as I attempted to tether them. I soon grew to hate them. Goats and I were clearly never meant to get along. As for milking the bastards, it didn't come naturally at all. Teat in hand for the first time, it felt like a very small, very old man's todger. My first tug on it made the goat jump and I soaked my inside leg. I angled the teat towards myself to see if I could spot the hole in the end, and a milky jet blinded me. My next effort whacked the outside of the pan, though it almost felt like a triumph, coming that close. Beside me, Pat had the teat laid comfortably along the palm and her knuckles worked rhythmically inwards, one hand waxing as the other waned. Milk rose steadily in her vessel, as mine shot cobwebs off the wall.

Nothing seemed to come naturally. I was wary of the geese; we'd just glare at one another. I was uncomfortable around the horses after one of them stood on my foot. The pig we bought bit me on the knee. I brooded about my inadequacy over a pint that evening, as the locals nudged each other and with some justification muttered "Townie" under their breath — though maybe they just thought I was called Tony, it was hard to tell with the accent round here.

With each pull of the landlady's arm on the pump, up crept my overdraft. It was only a matter of time before the bank manager over in Boston called me in. If I had to keep drinking (and I did), I would have to start making my own. Now I was smiling over my pint for once, as the locals threw me funny glances. Here would be a demonstration of commitment to the cause. I'd prove myself to the lot of them with this one: wife, mother-in-law, John and Sally Seymour. I'd show them all just how self-sufficient I could be.

Sadly, wine-making wasn't a huge success either, though God knows desperation dedicated me to the task. I gathered up all the windfalls in the orchard and created two huge binfuls of wine. Too impatient to wait for it to ferment naturally, I stuck the wine in a neighbouring manure heap where it percolated viciously for a month. At which point I twitchingly declared it ready. It wasn't, but we were prepared to think the unthinkable and drink the undrinkable.

We popped the cork, glugged it into the glass and chinked.

"Cheers darling!"

Windfall wine made Chateau Shite taste like Chateau Neuf du Pape. It was utterly hideous, almost impossible to imbibe without an expletive and a startlingly loud, involuntary retch.

"I think you should have taken the worms out of the apples first," croaked Pat, attempting to be kind. Then a violent shudder shook her whole body. I don't think she drank another drop after that.

I endured the psychotic episodes it induced, but for the sake of my art alone; Windfall wine simply had to replace nightly visits to The Crown. I needed my bankcard to work – please God – to get to London to demo up my new creations. As my creative life was that of an impoverished artist starving in his garret, I'd poured my all into these songs. They were honest and heartfelt; they were me.

Jon Miller, producer of Café Society's ill-fated second album and owner of Redan Recording in Bayswater, had generously donated me an afternoon's free studio time. But three hours wasn't long; this would need to be a highly focussed session. I was just happy to be getting on a train, back on track, on a mission. And when I got there, what a joy it was to sit behind a grand piano, lid raised, microphones trained upon the strings as the velvet hammers danced, with spools of tape turning as I sang:

No more sweeping up the fingers on the factory floor

Run and hiding from the strong arm of the law

No more looking for a job that no-one else can stand

I'm leaving the city for the fat of the land

'Fat of the Land' had been the first song off the press arriving in Lincolnshire, when I was still burning with evangelical zeal for the life self-sufficient. There was another recorded that day, 'Flat of the Land', which as the title would suggest reflected my suffering soul as the dream of a better life faded and the sense of bridges forever burnt took hold:

Let's find a house, just a little house on a street

Doesn't have to be surrounded by miles of sugar beet

Just a room with a view of the neighbour's windy sheet…

At the end of my three hours, the recording engineer gave me the thumbs up through the control room window. His voice appeared in my headphones.

"Come in and have a listen."

Jon Miller entered and stood beside me nodding his head listening to the playback through the giant speakers.

"They're good Herry," he said, throwing me an appreciative look.

"Thank you."

"Pint?"

"Only if you're buying."

"Haven't you got any money at all?"

"None whatsoever."

He rolled his eyes. "Come on."

And in the pub next door, later that evening, just as I was about to leave…

"Rick," beamed the tall chap striding towards me, blond hair swinging. "I couldn't help overhearing your name – are you really called Hereward?"

"Yes, after Hereward the Wake!"

"It's only that I'm actually descended from Hereward the Wake," beamed Rick. "My surname's Wakeman – man of Wake."

He extended a friendly hand. I popped a cassette in it.

"Fascinating Rick, have a listen to this. Just recorded it next door."

And with that, I ran for it. Having no money to overnight in London, I couldn't miss the last train.

The bank manager called me in, as I knew he would. My trip to London had pushed finances over the edge. "Six thousand pounds overdrawn Mr Kaye. A huge amount. What plans have you made for repayment?"

"Oh, it's not a problem at all," I assured him. "I'm making arrangements."

5. Flat of the land

It was exactly a decade since I'd spouted this crap to another bank manager, who then came across me busking in a London underpass with a borrowed baby at my side, singing "I am just a poor boy..." How far I'd come. Anyway, he wasn't buying.

"Can I have your bank card please?"

Ceremoniously he cut the card in three before my eyes. Humiliated, I went home and gagging at the mere sight of my windfall wine, sought solace in the piano, carving out a bitter song, which I called 'IOU':

It's made of paper and it's green, it bears a picture of the Queen

It pays the bearer on demand, it passes from your hand...

A couple of days later, the telephone rang.

"Hello?"

It's Rick Wakeman? "Hi! I liked your voice Hereward, it's... different, very distinctive. Do you fancy being lead singer on my next album? Yeah? I'll get The General to give you a call."

The General turned out to be his manager, Tony McArthur.

"Rick kinda likes your voice so lucky you, how much money do you want?"

Taking an outrageous leap, I asked for three hundred pounds a day.

"Alright," he immediately agreed. "But if it's a day you don't record, a hundred quid, alright?"

I was quite stunned when I came off the phone and told Pat. This was the early 1980s and three hundred pounds was actually worth a lot of money back then. The relief was incredible.

"How many days do they want you for?" gasped Pat.

"He wants me for an album, a whole album's worth of days!"

"What's it called?"

"What's it matter! 'The Cost of Living' – ironically."

She threw her arms around me. "Spin it out darling."

"I will, I will baby!"

Windfall wine played no part in our celebrations that night, thank God, but down the road we beat all-comers at pool, demolished pickled eggs and pork scratchings

Front cover of Rick Wakeman's Cost of Living album, 1982. Sleeve design: The Artful Dodgers. © Charisma Records Ltd

and, after several flexes of the landlady's quivering bingo wing, left The Crown even happier than we went in, if that were possible.

Recording on Rick Wakeman's album took place at Jacobs Studios in the stockbroker belt of genteel Surrey, so-named because of the Jacob sheep they raised on their land. I slipped into a routine of working and sleeping in Surrey during the week and driving home for weekends. What I hoped would be at least a couple of week's work slipped into six. This was a godsend, particularly as I was the singer and half the tracks on the album were instrumentals! But Rick was so bloody sociable and he did love a jar back then.

His house in Godalming was on my flightpath to the studio. "Just pull in here old boy" he said, as a salubrious country pub came up on the left. There we stayed half the day as he regaled me. I heard all about Yes in their pomp; how the band were so at war with one another they travelled to gigs separately, each with their own team going on ahead with their own section of stage. Yes didn't deign to use the stage on offer at these huge venues, they brought their own segments which fitted together, each with its own distinctive carpet. "And woe betide you if you stepped on anyone else's carpet!"

"Why, what would happen?"

"Well, we'd have to talk to one another for a start!"

He and bassist Chris Squire were particularly conflicted. Rick was violently anti-drugs. Chris I gathered… wasn't. I felt more sheepish than a Jacob sheep as I nodded in agreement with every word of his anti-pot, anti-coke tirades. Booze however, in his world, was clearly fine. But then, he'd never tried my Windfall wine.

We would rock up at the studio four hours and four pints later, band all waiting. A TV crew awaited in the studio next door too, impatient for Rick's return. Channel 4 had just recently launched and Rick was to be presenter of its flagship rock show, 'Gas Tank'.

I was at the TV studios when they shot the first episode. As Rick interviewed Status Quo, I took a stroll down the corridor in pursuit of a faintly-detected whiff of dope. A door was slightly ajar with someone on the lookout. One conspiratorial grin was enough to gain entry. Within I discovered 10cc, sneaky little schoolboys as the joint went round.

5. Flat of the land

"Quick! He's coming!" hissed the look-out. Roaches were stubbed and 10cc dived for cover. Obviously the 'Man of Wake's' abhorrence of pot went before him.

One night, Rick invited me over for dinner. He lived in a surprisingly small terraced house on a street. His girlfriend Penny, aka Nina Carter, one of *The Sun's* top page three models, answered the door.

"Hi! Rick's out the back, watering the vegetables."

I wandered down the little garden path and there was the caped maestro, very much sans cape, playing his hose this time, instead of the keyboard.

"I used to have four gardeners doing this job for me, back in Switzerland" said Rick, eyes on the hose as I arrived. The story began to unfold; in divorce proceedings the judge had settled everything in favour of his third wife. "He saw me as a jumped-up pop star and her as the injured party. Cow got everything, even my cellar full of classic vintage wines. When I got back into Heathrow, I had nothing – only enough for a phone call."

"Who did you ring?"

"Toby, my roadie. I'd paid him to keep all my stuff in storage when I moved out to Switzerland, plus a retainer of three hundred quid a week to keep an eye on it, which was pretty generous, I thought. I rang and said 'Tobes, I'm back, I'll have to come and stay round your house while I sort myself out'. He said when will that be Rick? I said tonight mate. He said I don't think that'll be possible. I said Toby y'cunt, what am I paying you for? You haven't had anything to do for three years, I'm coming round now. When I got there, can you believe it, his missus didn't even invite me in, I had to crash my way past her. First thing I saw was my beloved smoked-glass chess table. And when I looked round the room, there was all the rest of my stuff, hand-carved antique furniture, the lot!"

Rick had clocked up three wives and three heart attacks, loads of living for a guy of 34 – not that it seemed to have done him any harm. He could play the arse off all of us, critiquing one piece of music coming out of the speakers as he absent-mindedly composed another, scribbling musical notation on sheets of manuscript paper. As our bandleader he was dominant – but playful also. He did love a practical joke.

As I set off for home in Lincolnshire at the end of week one, I detected a hideous rattle. I found a sweeping brush sticking out of the exhaust. The following week, setting off from Jacobs Studios I discovered – too late – the steering wheel was plastered in honey. I was sticky-handed all the way home. The week after that it was a spray-can windscreen penis. There were buckets of water balanced precariously on top of doors and once, feeling a gathering in my buttocks (I can put it in no more genteel a fashion), I discovered Rick had stretched clingfilm across the toilet bowl, under the loo seat. All of this brought him unalloyed joy. Rick was a child – no other word for it.

Three weeks in, mysterious lyricist 'Tim' appeared. Tim turned out to be Tim Rice, who tied in his visit with an after-dinner speech he was booked to deliver at a cricket club up the road. He dropped into the studio on the way back, well-oiled. Tim stepped into the vocal booth, asked the engineer for lashings of reverb and went into his Elvis repertoire, curling a lip, dipping a hip, giving it the full 'uh-uh-uh'.

And somewhere along the line, all my lead vocals got recorded. It had taken six weeks to get down five songs. Then the fairground ride was over and how different our diverging lives became in that moment. Rick went off as guest of honour to the World Cup Final in Spain and I went back to the middle of nowhere. But the cheque that followed from The General's office a few days later came to six thousand pounds – exactly the sum I owed. As if pulling a rabbit from a hat, I produced it at the bank, in return for a bankcard.

We were solvent.

To celebrate, we sat down to a meal of fresh, home reared roast pork. Obviously I had lacked both the guts and the expertise to do it myself, but we were proud to have raised this 'wreckling' ourselves (so called because the mother had rolled upon her as a piglet). We had given her a good life. Then, when the time came…

Halfway through a mouthful, Jody became suspicious.

"Is this Petal?" Jody's bottom lip began to quiver. "My little pig?" It was almost heartbreaking, but I was so happy to have brought home the bacon I had to bite my lip to cover up a perpetual smile; there was Petal, in his mouth, which had fallen open.

"Is it Daddy, is it, is it?"

"I'm afraid it is darling, yes."

"Eurgh!" He spat out Petal and pushed the plate away. His sullied lip began to wobble.

"Don't think I want any more."

"I didn't kill it Joe!' I protested. 'I got someone else to do it!"

Jody's eyes burnt into me with pure and utter hatred. All our compassionate farming had managed to do was produce the first rabid vegan in the family.

5. Flat of the land

Another year sailed by in a sea of sprouts. Argentina invaded the Falklands whilst I invaded nowhere whatsoever. I was too far from everyone and everything to do anything. And try as I might, I was rubbish at self-sufficiency. What killed me more than the sense of failure this engendered was the sense of road networks out there with people going from somewhere to somewhere. Where did I have to go?

Nowhere. Through my own pig-headedness I'd turned a worldwide deal with EMI into a pub window view of endless vegetables, disappearing into the mist, just like vegetating me. If I ever found my way back into the game, I would settle for less, far less, than before.

What the hell am I doing? I asked myself, casting a baleful eye around an almost empty Crown. The only other bloke in the bar caught my gaze.

"You're from London then?"

"Sort of."

"Never been to London. Ain't never ever been to Boston."

"Ten miles away?"

"Me father went there once. Said folks was stuck up."

"You're joking!"

"Me father," he said, rhyming it with 'bather' and fixing me a look, "he should know."

I supped up and under bruised skies walked the road less travelled home. It was so less travelled I walked down the middle of it, even stopping to take a piss. Entering our scruffy yard, I crossed to the chicken run, setting off a kerfuffle of activity.

I'd been leading up to this for weeks, months, years.

My first murder.

Pat emerged from the stables seeing what I was about to do and hurried for the kitchen door.

"Don't start till I'm out of hearing range!"

"Okay."

"Why do we have to kill one of them?"

"Because it's in your fucking self-sufficiency book!"

"'Don't do it wrong, I don't want it to feel anything!"

I lunged about wildly, setting off a squabble of hen gossip as they evaded my clutches. "Grab one by the foot!" yelled Pat from an upstairs window now, before ducking down beneath the parapet.

Playing God, I feinted left and grabbed right.

"That's Sophia LeHen, we only eat males!"

"Says who?" I yelled. "St John fucking Seymour?"

I hunted another instead, pouncing upon its scaly ankle just above the three-nailed foot with the lethal fourth at the back, hauling it upside down high into the air, above feather and din.

"Not that one!" shrieked Pat, "that's Moby Duck!"

I bestowed the gift of life and Moby scorched off scandalised, to gabble with the rabble. Grabbing a third, Gregory Peck, I strode from the arena like the winner of the Victor Ludorum, my inverted victim now curiously becalmed, as if coming to terms with the dreadful card that fate had dealt: the Grim Reaper.

I stalked across the gravel toward a sweeping brush leaning like a layabout against the wall. Holding Gregory Peck high in the left hand, I snatched the sweeping brush with my right and smashed it against the wall. Wood splintered and the head came away; perfect practice for the murder I was about to commit.

"What was that?"

"Don't worry, just decapitating the sweeping brush."

"It's the only one we've got and we can't afford another!"

Our children came charging around the corner and pulled up dead. Guilty as charged under the judgement of innocents. Jody broke ranks, hammering into the house, not stopping till he hit the attic where he hid under the bed.

"I don't know how you can Dad," said his elder brother Leon with quiet dignity, passing indoors.

Neither did I, to be honest. All this effort for a mouthful of chicken – killing, plucking, gutting and cooking; all the months leading up to this brutal act, putting it off, trying to wriggle out of it. But it was in the gospel according to St John. There was no escape, for me or the chicken.

I have the long sweeping brush handle in my right hand and a philosophical bird in my left. Keeping the bird well up I gingerly drop the pole down to the ground and stand on one end, poking the toe of my left foot underneath the other. I lower the bird till its gullet scrapes the ground. I introduce the head into the small gap beneath the pole and continue lowering until neck follows through and head is out the other side.

I still have the ankles. The chicken is in situ. Poor old Gregory arches his neck obligingly, looking up to see the world for one last time. I find myself involuntarily looking around, sharing the moment as if it were my last moment too. Patchy gravel, puddles floating soiled straw, gunmetal March sky.

Removing my foot from under the raised end I stamp down hard on the pole. Both hands wrench skywards. Greg's neck elongates, stretches and stretches. Choked of air, strong wings beat a frantic tattoo against my legs, never-ending, though I pull and pull.

From nowhere, a monstrous noise rips open the skies. For one dislocated moment I think it is I who is dying. Then the two fighter planes are gone, twisting away towards Mablethorpe and the sea.

In my hands, a headless, twitching torso. Gregory Peck's unblinking face lays beside me on the ground. His neck drips like a loose hose, turning my trousers crimson.

"Herry!" screams Pat, from the window.

For heaven's sake, she thinks I've killed the wrong one.

"It's not Moby Duck!"

"No!" she yells, "it's Moby Dick!"

"What?"

"Robert on the phone!"

"What does he want?"

"He's got a Musical for you in London, Moby Dick!"

I hammered indoors and snatched up the phone, which squirted from my slick fist.

"Hello? Hello?" I heard Robert saying, from somewhere near the floor.

"Hey" I said, snatching it up. "Sorry, just wiping down the receiver."

"Oh!"

"You caught me red-handed Robert, don't go there. What's up?"

"We've been asked to do something for the Capital Jazz Festival."

"Where?"

"Camden Lock, in the open air. Eric Reynolds the administrator wants something watery. I thought we might do Moby Dick."

"Whereabouts in Camden Lock?"

"We'll do it on the Lock itself, shall we? Might as well," he giggled.

"Have they got a Lock in Camden Lock?"

"Well. You know as you go through the archway into the cobbled bit? There's an oblong of water. We'll do it on there."

"Underwater?"

"I thought we might find a boat. Tow it in. Paint 'Pequod' on the side. Don't worry about that, I'll sort all that out."

"How much?"

"Nothing. About a hundred pounds."

"I'll do it. When?"

"Three nights in June, around Midsummer Night's Eve. They want an hour, eleven till midnight. I'll need half a dozen songs. Think nautical, but with a rock edge. Think 'ye' instead of 'you'; quohogs, clams, grog, Quakers, Heathens... you know what to do."

"Yeah. Read Moby Dick."

"No need for that, I'll send you a copy of the film. Have you seen it? Gregory Peck?"

"Funny you should say that."

* * *

With a slight pause, I emerged from Kings Cross station and out onto Euston Road, which was a pageant of pandemonium. Traffic kept coming, a jockeying cacophony bearing down upon the lights. An armada of red buses sailed a sea of diesel, pluming skirts of poison. To my right, a semi circular loop of black cabs fed voraciously off an impatient cue of commuters. To my left, down-and-outs lay on the pavement, backs to WH Smiths, a Hogarthian tableau of low lifes feuding over the Tennents. I drank it all in; it had been a lifetime.

5. Flat of the land

I bought an *Evening Standard*, *Time Out*, *City Limits*, *Event*. Beyond the kiosk, a smell of warm dust and rubber wafted up the steps from the underground. A rising surge of humanity struggled elbows-out through an equally determined downward tide.

With joyful heart I joined humanity's throng.

Chapter 6
A Midsummer Night's Dick
- 1983 -

And so, the first ever performance of Moby Dick took place at London's Camden Lock, in the open air. Whilst I had sat at home carving out tunes, Robert had been in search of a boat to tow into the lock, as a stage for our presentation.

Rehearsals took place in Dingwalls, a live music venue located within the Camden Lock complex. On that first morning, performers just kept arriving: out of work actors, comics, punks, show offs, friends of friends. By the time I sat down to play my new compositions, there must have been forty of them around the piano.

Faces shone up at me as they heard the music and I saw excitement. Mostly. Some were far too good looking to be excited, some were far too cool, being professional thespian types, there to keep the class act muscle-toned, sleek for the agent's offer one phone call away. These included Caroline Quentin, Kate Robbins – female impersonator and cousin of Paul McCartney who went on to find her niche as the Queen in Spitting Image – and Kate's twin brother Ted, who went on to find his niche as a game show host. Then there were the two punk-pretty Eurasion boys, Fritz and Dee, who simply despised all twelve musical notes of the octave, whatever order they were in. They had a band called Flex. With their multicoloured cockscombs, they would dress the ship in contemporary colours. They didn't have to do anything more. Creator and director of the show Robert simply cast them as cabin boys, left them to play and got on with it.

Referring at all times to his drawings of all the major moments, Robert staged his set pieces frame by frame, almost like a movie director. There was no doubt in his mind, watching him, that we were on the path to glory, that we were the new kids on the theatrical block. Having marked out the floor himself, he bestrode its boundaries like a colossus, berating and cajoling, chatting up, teasing out, tensing up or freaking out, inspiring love and fear and above all, big performances.

Between rehearsals I killed time walking around outside, just happy to be in the north London sun. Camden Lock looked beautiful to me. The market was a patchwork quilt of hippy merchandise. Hard-faced mothers and beatific fathers minded the beaten silver and unbeaten bongos as their children dodged beneath hanging folds of heavy fabric. Overhead, metal body parts performed a jerky dance of death along a network of wires. Tiller girl legs gangled towards flailing arms, Londoners pointing in laughter at the mechanised ballet.

I went in search of the boat. I'd been sceptical about this part of the arrangement, but Robert had found one, as said he would. A couple of friends slung from the side in the sunshine, painting on the name: 'PEQUOD'.

Rehearsals moved out to the boat. With much palaver, our company tottered aboard whilst Robert and I observed their wobbly progress from dry land, alongside our choreographer Linda Dobell, decked out in purple and black, as ever. She delighted in belittling Saul, our leading man, a dead ringer for Ahab, if a little on the short side.

"Saul darling, do try and do better, there's a love. You're standing on people's feet, people with a left foot and a right foot. You wouldn't know about right feet would you darling? Let's go again from the beginning."

Groans on board, as they darted paranoid glances from their feet to the murky deep. Back on dry land they crossed the cobbles to underneath the arches, taking up their starting positions behind the wall to an accompaniment of giggling, shushing and farting.

"Quiet behind there!" snapped Robert, voice pinging off the walls. Onlookers sniggered. "Try and imagine the music, ladies and gentlemen" he asked the concealed company a little more softly, as if 'ladies and gentleman' would soothe away the indignity of being forced to walk the gangplank – in the pitch dark come showtime – when they were doing this crap for nothing. "And sing properly!" he added, for my benefit, I think.

"And go!" screamed Linda.

I didn't know anything about musicals in those days, and I'd started our show with the most miserable sodding dirge known to man. Robert had simply told me to write something for Quakers boarding a boat. Now here they came, under the archway, a Mogadon army, shuffling in procession towards the dreaded gangplank.

"Punish us Oh God, we are so weak" they droned. "Shipwrecked are our souls until you speak."

Onlookers noticed the yellow duty free bags Robert had given every Quaker, to try and lighten the awful effect of my song. Cartons of Marlboro protruded from the tops of carrier bags. I felt we were on to something.

"No No No!" Linda clapped her hands in the air with each scornful repetition. "Per-lease! You're meant to be halfway up the gangplank by now."

Stifling mirth, Robert was boggle-eyed behind his glasses, bright red in the sun. "You'll have to get there a bit quicker" he managed.

"Can we take the tempo up a bit?" asked Linda, touching my arm and, seeing my eyes dither: "No? That's okay." She touched my arm again and raised her voice. "You'll have to take bigger steps. Try and look brave going up the gangplank."

She turned her attention upon our leading man.

"Saul. How are we managing in the rigging?"

"Fine," came a weak voice.

"Jolly good. Don't fall in darling." To me: "yet."

Robert cleared his throat: "positions please, ladies and gentlemen" – and off we went again.

The actors adjusted to the Pequod. Before long they could have been up and down that gangplank on skateboards, asleep and in the nude. Knowing Robert, I'm surprised they weren't. I adjusted to being part of the management, looking on from the shore, a dog-eared paperback of Moby Dick in my pocket, much dipped into but never finished – the book was a tough read. Hermann Melville would surely have been turning in his grave if he could see the way we were mangling his story, though we did have utmost respect for his characters.

Melville's tale in a nutshell (or at least, our version of it) is this: It's 1838. Ishmael, a young innocent starting out on the adventure of life, arrives in Nantucket, whaling capital to the world. Having almost no money, he is forced to share a bed in The Spouter Inn with Queequeg, an exotic South Sea cannibal. Meanwhile, Captain Ahab, with his tender-hearted Cabin Boy Pip in tow, returns from three years at sea to his sex-starved wife Esta. The reunion doesn't go well! Ahab reveals his missing leg, lost to a gigantic, rogue white whale. Esta becomes hysterical. Enraged, Ahab puts a curse on her, driving her backwards over a sea wall to a watery grave fathoms below. Horrified and remorseful, Ahab's descent into madness and obsession begins.

Back in Nantucket Harbour, Ishmael and Queequeg survey the ships. The Pequod catches their eye. Seeking to sign up as whalers, they are welcomed aboard by Mr Star-

Cast of A Midsummer Night's Dick, 1983.

buck – devout Quaker and First Mate of the Pequod, and his Second Mate, Mr Stubb. Just as they are about to sign, Elijah – Nantucket's resident loony and prophet of doom – warns them against it. He has a vision that all but one of the sailors on the voyage will die – a prophecy they choose to ignore.

The Pequod is to be captained by Ahab, who is roused from prolonged wallowing in drunkenness and despair by the vision of his dead wife Esta, imploring him to go back to sea and seek out the white whale that has destroyed their lives. And so, on Christmas Day, they set sail, the start of an epic three-year whaling mission. Ishmael, the bright-eyed rookie whaler, heathen harpooner Queequeg, upright and responsible Mr Starbuck – determined to reap great profit for the ship's owners by harvesting as many whales as possible – and obsessed sea captain Ahab, plagued by visions of his dead wife Esta and interested in only one whale in the whole watery world; that white freak waiting in the blue: Moby Dick!

Time and again, in the three long years they sail the seven seas, Ahab orders them to abandon their latest catch, as none of the whales are the one he's looking for. Starbuck's attempt to lead a mutiny against the Captain fails, as Ahab rules by fear and bribes the men with promises of ever more gold. And now he causes a second death of a loved one. Cabin Boy Pip, banished by Ahab from his cabin and forced to sleep on deck, is washed overboard and, when rescued, dies in the arms of his crewmates.

Distressed English Sea Lord Captain Gardiner hoves to in his ship The Rachel, comes aboard and implores Ahab to turn about and help search for his son, lost overboard when their boat was attacked. Ahab refuses, for he has heard in Gardiner's tale a description of the beast that did the damage – a gigantic white whale, and just a day away. The hunt is on; finally Ahab meets his great nemesis – and Elijah's prophecy comes to pass.

This was the multi-layered story we had to get across in one hour flat, out in the open air at pub chucking-out time!

Further tricky set pieces were negotiated. Meanwhile, Robert had to find yet another boat to double as The Rachel. The one he found was 'come in number six, your time is up' size. We trained our Captain Gardiner to heave to at the same time as appealing to Ahab to help search for his missing son. It was with some apprehension we watched

Gardiner round the corner for the first time. It's not easy standing up in a wobbly rowing boat and throwing your arms out in supplication, but she did it.

Choreographing the fight scene, Linda had her first man overboard, not that she gave a fuck. Luckily, the Royal Free Hospital had just opened over the road and they were able to stitch him up. As if he hadn't been already…

Posters went up – 'The Primeslot Frontcloth Gang Present: A MIDSUMMER NIGHT'S DICK'. Programmes were printed. The band arrived for the final two days and set up on the poop deck. Robert discovered one of the cast was a member of the London Ravens American Football team, so they had to be worked in somehow. By now the ship was groaning with humanity and though we weren't ready, the day had arrived, and it was better to get on with it, while we were still above the Plimsoll Line.

Outside, a large crowd were gathered clutching drinks, loquacious and happy. I wouldn't say they were there to see us exactly, or even at all, they were just there. They'd cruised the side shows, trawled the stalls, pubcrawled and Dingwalled. It was a hot night. Bars were jammed. As the bell rang for last orders drinkers spilled out on to the cobblestones where they continued to hold court over flat lagers, as pot-men ducked and dived for plastic glasses, to alleviate the crisis at the bar. And then the clock struck 11pm and the faint sound of singing could be heard from afar – not that anyone was listening.

"Punish us oh God, we are so weak. Shipwrecked are our souls until you speak…"

The drinkers hardly seemed to notice the procession of Quakers nudging a path through their midst. When the cast were on the gangplank I think somebody noticed the duty free bags and it caught on a bit. There were a few laughs as conversation dipped then picked up again. The Rachel came and went more or less unseen. The singing was inaudible, the company had to bellow their lines across the water at a seething mass caught in the dilemma of a closing bar.

The London Ravens rode to our rescue. When they rushed the gangplank in their shoulder pads and helmets we were four goals down. The Ravens hit the deck and performed forty fast press-ups to huge cheers (1-4) then took up battle formation to more cheers (2-4) and launched into some sort of all-American chant (3-4). As they joined forces with the forty strong cast of punkish singers and out of work actors, swaying and singing along to 'Save The Whale' it was four all, the crowd was drawn back in and I was a shipwreck.

The fireworks got the winner in extra time.

Chapter 7
Old Profanity
- 1984 -

It was New Year's Day, hung-over and dull. London was picking up the pieces as I headed for the Cornet in Clapham, a former gay roller disco. It was 'Carry On Up The Gangplank' time – we had been offered an exciting opportunity to stage a second production of Moby Dick. I waited at lights to turn the corner where the venue would hove into view, half expecting to see 'MOBY DICK' in spangled neon against the sky. There was nothing, of course, just a pub. But could this be the year? You never know!

I took the stairs two at a time into a stratosphere abloom with trills and vocal pirouettes. In the rehearsal room ankles were full stretch on icy radiators, at right angles to sinewy Lycra torsos. Other performers hovered around the Musical Director's piano. Our MD was Martin Elmer Cotton, possessor of a fine old-fashioned cricketer's beard. Outside this spot of moonlighting, Martin had a perfectly respectable job in charge of the BBC sound library, which gave him a certain amount of freedom of movement. But now he was beginning to wonder what he'd got himself into and when he'd catch up with his department. It was a position of some responsibility – and it paid.

Robert, when I found him, was one floor further up. "Look," he said, instead of hello, "we've got an office."

It was true. There was a typewriter or two and a phone, fresh paint and fresh people. Best of all, there was a photocopier.

"This is home now," declared Robert following my gaze, "our home."

The phone was ringing and he snatched it up. I watched as delight suffused his features. "Someone's donated a backdrop," he explained, when he came off.

"Great!" I said. "Does it fit our storyline? Is it a seascape?"

There was a pause in which it seemed the whole room stopped what they were doing.

"Venice."

Whether Venice fitted our subject matter or not was irrelevant; the fact is, this was penniless fringe and the backdrop was free. With an instant leap of Robert's imagination, Moby Dick changed direction like a goldfish. Word was passed downstairs for all actors to adopt Scottish accents. The costume department (a grumbling girl ironing inside a cupboard) was on red alert: all costumes, male and female, were to be creatively adapted into girl's school uniform. The lost property department at the local girls' school was mysteriously denuded of every badge, garter, tie and hockey stick. I meanwhile, was programmed to produce a school hymn to replace the disastrous Quaker dirge I had come up with last time around.

At the end of a long day in the recently abandoned rehearsal room still hanging with the day's endeavour, I worked upon the song. From downstairs came the clamour of our cast bonding round the bar. My fingers fumbled across the black and white teeth like those of someone new to Braille. I was orienteering in the dark. My compass was Robert's few words: "Think Jean Brodie. Her girls are happy, singing the school hymn as the train pulls into its destination."

"Let me guess…"

"The Piazza San Marco, Venezia!"

"Where they are presenting…?"

As if I needed to ask. Next morning when I took the stairs two at a time, I came face to face with the poster: 'MOBY DICK IN VENICE'.

Our Captain Ahab, Stephen Beard, was given the rather mystifying instruction that he would now be playing Muriel Spark's famous literary heroine, Scottish school teacher Miss Jean Brodie.

"Not Captain Ahab?"

"Both dear." Robert succumbed to a trademark fit of suppressed giggles, his face growing redder and his glasses slipping down his nose.

"How does that work then?" asked a confused Stephen.

"You're Jean Brodie playing Captain Ahab."

"Ah…"

David Auker was informed he would now be playing Mr Starbuck, the Pequod's First Mate, in a dress. This was meat and drink to a performer like David, a man who was the spit of Tony Hancock and performed in a similarly hangdog manner, redolent

7. Old Profanity

Cast of Moby Dick In Venice, Cornet Theatre, Battersea, 1984.

of the roar of greasepaint and smell of the crowd, from a bygone age of comedy. David's roots were in Vaudeville, as were Robert's. Each reaffirmed the other's old-fashioned view of comedy, harking back to a golden era; they were almost a double act, the two of them, like Flanagan and Allen.

It turned out David was also a trained carpenter and, together, the two of them built the stage upstairs at the Cornet, for our production. For two nights a week, their lovingly-crafted stage played host to waves of alternative comedians plying their trade. The venue became 'Jongleurs' as BBC executives rattled up the stairs pursued by gales of general public blowing in off the street. Whilst Moby Dick played to half-empty houses and nobody got paid, the same room on the two nights of alternative comedy was fuller than a Tokyo train and the take on the door was a whopping great wad of banknotes. It forced one to measure the marketability of our brand of humour against theirs.

Comedy was the new rock 'n roll. A revolution was redefining what was funny; long established TV comics and game show hosts, feeding off a plankton diet of racist jokes and mother-in-law gags, were challenged as never before. Taxi for Freddie Starr, Jim Davidson and Bernard Manning. But they weren't all bad guys, those old-school comedians using those go-to gags; Les Dawson's mother-in-law humour was an elevated art-form, Bob Monkhouse had written a million good gags (and had them all stolen) and every night of the year Ken Dodd seemed to be somewhere or other delivering four hours of funny for the price of two. But where were female stand-ups? Where were the black comics who weren't prepared to lampoon their colour to gain an appreciative audience? Pacing the boards of our hand-made stage on Jongleurs nights, that's where.

I knew the train was a-comin'. Four years earlier I'd headed for the Nell Gwynne Strip Club in Soho one Saturday night and taken the rickety lift up to the Comedy Store on the top floor. Word was, something amazing was happening. I walked in on a bear-pit and a crowd baying "The Gong! The Gong!" There stood Master of Ceremonies Alexei Sayle, bonger in one hand, his other cupped to his ear, a hapless entertainer by his side. Alexei's arm hovered, then swung. BONG! Raucous cheers, exit of defeated contender.

On came a twitchy specimen, wearing a long student scarf and branding a little red book, as the crowd mocked. "I'm going to read you my poetry!" he heckled back at them. "Vanessa, oh Vanessa," he began, to an avalanche of jeers. "Shut up!" he excoriated, "just SHUT UP!" His eyes stared intensely. The scarf was re-flung around his throat and his book held higher, as if to ward off evil. The audience lapped it up. They even shushed one another; everyone wanted to hear the next line.

"Vanessa oh Vanessa" – another disruptive pause – "I shall take your memory to the grave." Then, triumphantly: "but at least it will be a Redgrave!"

This was newcomer Rick Mayall. I saw him with Ade Edmondson one night too, calling themselves 20th Century Coyote, knocking one another about. It sounds standard stuff, but in those pre-Bottom, pre-Young Ones days, it was electrifyingly anarchic.

So an audience was washed into the Cornet on comedy's new wave on the two nights of the week we weren't performing Moby Dick, and stayed away on the four nights we were. Missed a bloody good show though! The belching, spittoon-rattling sea dogs of America's greatest book, portrayed by a pack of straining luvvies with highly dubious Edinburgh accents, doubling as Miss Jean Brodie's 'crème de la crème' and half of them in drag, what more do you want for your three quid? It was certainly an improvement on our last effort – and 'Moby Dick the Musical' was about to take yet another turn for the better.

Immediately following the production at the Cornet, we were offered another opportunity to develop Moby Dick. Our 'theatre' this time would be the Old Profanity Showboat, a converted grain carrier moored up in Bristol harbour.

The news didn't go down well at all with Pat. An absent husband she could accept, but one who wasn't earning money? She said you've never had a penny from Moby Dick. I said well, a hundred pounds from Camden Lock but fair enough.

"Where are you doing it this time?"

"On a boat!"

"It's meant to be about a boat not on one," she scathed. "Who's going?"

"Almost everyone from the Cornet, though we've had to cut down a bit."

Neither of us were happy with the way the conversation was going. She said what about so-and-so and so-and-so (the good looking leading ladies) and I said well, yeah. After a quiet moment, Pat asked who was going to play Ahab.

"Robert."

"Robert?"

"Robert. He was born to play the Headmistress."

"Hmm." Another silence. Then: "I thought you were just the guy who wrote the music?"

"And some of the lyrics!"

"Okay, but do you have to be there?"

"Yes."

"Why?"

"Because I'm playing the piano."

"Piano? Can't they get someone else to play the piano?"

"No, they can't!"

"Why not?"

"Because there's no fucking money for anyone else!"

"Great."

Now I was curled up in my bunk on the Old Profanity, staring out the porthole. It was a shit feeling, parting on an argument.

The Venetian backdrop wouldn't fit onto the boat, so Venice had to go. It was too late, however, to jettison the girl's boarding school setting. Stockings and wigs, lacrosse and hockey sticks spilled from trunks and littered the deck. These costumes and props were our currency. In the absence of money, they were all we had, so school was in. But while we were throwing things overboard… after you Miss Brodie! She was too mannered, too soft and earnest for our needs. The little 'gels' followed her over the side like lemmings, and their irritating accents drowned with them. Sixty dernier stockings morphed into fishnets and grew suspenders – even mine, behind the piano. 'La crème de la crème' turned from needlepoint to hooch and hornification. The gentle school hymn became a battle cry as we rang out old heads on young shoulders and rang in the Belles of St Trinians.

Most alarming of all – with a horrible rightness all the same – was Robert at the centre of it all, playing the Headmistress playing Ahab (in a frock, with a cricket pad for a wooden leg). Within Ahab's twisted soul there now lurked a smirking Alastair Sim – and with David Auker still playing Starbuck – Robert had his straight man (in a dress).

We needed more numbers. The two of us went back and raided another of our creative masterpieces and adapted the lyrics. Thus, the rise of a new Paris from the ashes of destruction in 'Hunchback': We're building Paris, Paree / Working for Notre Dame, we're working for Our Lady... became an anthem for hard-bitten whalers with hope in their hearts, as the Pequod finally set sail: We're building A-me-rica! Accruing oil to light the lamps of a darkened world...

We had a Show, and whatever else it wasn't, it **was** original.

At the end of the run, just when I was meant to be returning home, I was offered a role in a show called 'Return To The Forbidden Planet', at the Liverpool Everyman. The offer included something I'd heard about but never actually seen in musical theatre, having only ever worked with Robert: a wage packet! It was a proper paid job in a proper theatre and in Liverpool – a city I had wanted to know all my life, the city that gave birth to the band that changed my life.

Now, after the last performance of Moby Dick, on a night where I should have been hugging myself at the thought of going home, instead I was gazing out of the porthole at the slopping waterline and wondering how to tell my girl I was back, but I was off again, for three long months.

Chapter 8
Liverpool

The house was a mausoleum, glimpsed through veils of overgrowth. I checked the address on my slip of paper and rang the bell.

Echoey footsteps from within. I was unsurprised when my new landlady resembled Morticia Addams.

"Mrs Williams?"

"Beryl. You're in the new show at the Everyman."

"Yes, Return To The Forbidden Planet."

"I've heard it's going to be very good. Come in, let me show you to your room."

It was a dark corridor, lined with black and white photographs, all of similar composition. They featured Beryl and, one presumed, her husband in front of a black Commer van. My eye was moving along the corridor, spying identically framed photographs, more populated now. They pictured Beryl surrounded by young rocker types in black leather, lounging against the van with guitars. I tried not to boggle.

"You knew the Beatles?"

"My husband Allan was their manager at the time."

"Where were these pictures taken?"

"Hamburg."

I'd only been in Liverpool five minutes and I'd run into The Fab Four. Did every home have pictures like this on the wall? Maybe the boys had been managed by every householder on Merseyside at some point or other?

"This door here's Bob, been here for years, won't bother you. This is you. Kitchen's opposite, help yourself to crockery. Here's your front door key."

The Ship Hits the Fans

The following evening, I came back from the first day's rehearsal, let myself in and went through to the kitchen, which was occupied. I felt a bit awkward at first, clonking my shopping on a surface, making room in the fridge. Though the kitchen was big, I felt I was invading the privacy of the two 50 year-olds at the large refectory table, bottle of red on the go and old friends, clearly. Allan and Bob. They were there the next night, and the one after that. Their positions didn't change, or the words that passed between them. Only the bottle of wine was different. They were indifferent to my presence as I went about meal preparation, pretending not to listen. But I couldn't help it, I was far too interested in what they had to say. I gleaned that not only was Allan Williams the Beatles first manager, he had sold them to Brian Epstein for a mere three thousand pounds. As for Bob Wooller, he was the original Cavern DJ back in its heyday. At Paul McCartney's 21st birthday party, a drunken John Lennon had thrown Bob downstairs and broken his rib.

"I can't believe I sold the Beatles," moaned one.

"I hate that bastard John Lennon," spat the other.

I always seemed to come in to the same litany of despair. Whilst Allan and Bob were bemoaning their luck, I couldn't quite believe mine. I'd turned a key in exactly the right front door in Liverpool to walk in on the Beatles Story.

One night I found myself in the kitchen with just Allan Williams, stuck for company. He motioned for me to join and I set my plate down on the refectory table, hungrier for his hard-luck story than the food I had prepared.

"I went to see the boys once, years later," he confided, "down at Apple. Fair play to the lads, they all agreed to meet me."

"How did that go?"

"Awkward. We all sat round in a circle. Come on I said, gimme some money. I got you going for fuck's sake and I got nothing, three thousand pounds. You've got loads of money, come on give me some you bastards, you know I deserve it."

"Blimey! what did they say?"

"They all looked at their feet," said Allan, "One of 'em said we haven't got any Al, we don't carry cash around. I said I don't believe you. One by one they turned out their pockets. See said George, told you it was true. And then I swear to God, when it came to Harrison, he turned out his pockets and out fell seven uncut diamonds!"

* * *

The show in which I was performing, Return To The Forbidden Planet, was The Tempest in disguise, with space suits and electric guitars. We were all actor/musicians, moving from one instrument to another whilst declaiming our lines in iambic pentameter, though not in Shakespearian cadences. We had to ham it up in the style of a sci-fi B movie. 'Planet' caught on hugely. When it came back later that year by public demand, I too made the intergalactic journey and my role was upgraded from Bosun to Navigation Officer.

By this time the writer, Bob Carlton, was flavour of the month in Liverpool and another of his actor/musician 'Shakespeare meets rock'n'roll' shows was commissioned by the Everyman. From A Jack To A King, it was called – Macbeth in disguise. I was brought in as Musical Director and they kept me on to direct the Christmas show up there too. A further four long months were spent at the Everyman acting in football-dreary You'll Never Walk Alone (dubbed amongst the cast You'll Never Work Again), starring Scottish music hall legend Chic Murray as Bill Shankly. All in all my three months in Liverpool had stretched into two years, off and on, and the city had become almost a second home.

I interacted with my actual home after an all-night train ride from Lime Street after the curtain came down every Saturday. I was at my house for a day and a half, till I had to wave my family goodbye and make the return journey, in time for Monday evening's show. Needless to say, every time I arrived home there was another animal to greet me. And the longer I was away, the bigger the animal I came home to.

Our Lincolnshire pile had long been sold and home was now a tiny terraced cottage, the back garden a long narrow strip sandwiched between two neighbouring houses. It was not much more than the width of a train carriage, though a narrowboat version of Noah's Ark might be a better analogy, and the grass groaned under the weight of animals. There were horses heads poking from stables, ducks and hens milling about behind endless yards of chicken wire, rabbits in multiple hutches – the lawn was crawling, clucking and whinnying with all creatures great and small. In fact, when Leon's teacher asked the class to write a poem about their garden, this was his: 'My garden is a tip, my garden is a turfed-up mess / Dirt made by chickens and ducks / the stink of old eggs / you could break your leg walking up my garden.'

There was a neighbouring field tucked away between houses and, thanks to my visiting father who had taken pity on us all, it was now ours. We could spread out a little. The field was where I would invariably find Pat, on my arrival back home from Liverpool on a Sunday morning. "Oh!" I said one time, discovering a new creature standing there chewing grass. "That's not a horse."

"No," Pat explained, "she's a Dexter Jersey cross."

"You bought a COW?"

"You always said you wanted one, don't you remember darling?" And she turned on me her brilliant smile, though there was a touch of fait accompli about it.

"Yeah I did," I remembered slowly. "I said I wanted a cow – to eat. Back in Lincolnshire. Are we still compassionate meat-eaters then?"

She changed the subject by throwing me a bone: "you can name her. You know how much you love to name things."

"Sunblest."

"Oh that's beautiful." Pat looked at me with a little love at last. "Oh I like that darling. Blessed by the sun."

"Sunblest, like the bread," I said. "We're going to cut her up into slices and stick her in the freezer."

With a sigh of irritation, Pat disappeared into the dark of the stable. When she emerged: "How was it?" she asked, going about the stable yard with her barrow.

"Knackering! Eighth show of the week last night in Liverpool, then straight off stage and on the train, which took all night by the way. It got as far as Crewe then started to go backwards." I threw myself on my back in the middle of the field and gazed up at the summer sky. "I'm exhausted. So glad to see you baby, so glad to be home."

Pat offered a tight little smile, which wasn't exactly a welcome in the valleys. Sunblest on the other hand, came loping across the field towards me. She sunk to her knees, then flopped onto her side. She stretched her hoof across my chest, then licked the whole side of my face in long slurping rasps of her flapping tongue, from the nape of my neck to the top of my head.

"Yeurgh!" I staggered to my feet, swiping away cow spit yet feeling somehow blessed, shouting at the sun: "No WAY are we eating Sunblest, no way!"

* * *

Killing time one afternoon, I went to the Liverpool Empire to attend a matinée of the musical Blood Brothers. The show affected me profoundly – so much so, I left a note at the stage door for writer/composer Willy Russell, saying it was the first time in my life I had written a fan letter. On an impulse, I rummaged in the bottom of my bag for one of my cassette tapes of home demos. 'Your songs remind me of mine,' I wrote.

He was a great deal further up the food chain than I was – he'd written the masterpiece Educating Rita and would go on to write Shirley Valentine – but I sensed a kindred spirit. He was a writer who composed, and I was a composer who tried to write.

Before the week was out, there in my pigeon hole at the Everyman was a note from the great man himself, asking if I would like to meet him downstairs in the Everyman Bistro. I was there like a shot.

Over a bottle of red, Willy Russell told me he had an upcoming charity concert at the Liverpool Playhouse. He was sharing the bill with Alan Bleasdale, the city's other esteemed playwright de jour, having written the hugely successful TV drama 'Boys from the Blackstuff'. The concert was to be called 'An Evening with Alan Russell and Willy Bleasdale' – "cos everyone keeps mixing us up." Willy wondered if I could put a band around him for the event and musically direct – he wanted to perform some of his own numbers. He'd never actually performed his own material in public before and was a little nervous. I assured him I would be glad to help.

"I was wondering…" Willy looked down at his fingernails. "Would you like to sing a duet with me from Blood Brothers…?"

"My Best Friend?"

"Absolutely."

"It would be an honour."

I came up with three musicians willing to give up their day off to rehearse at his house. By chance, they were all called Dave. "You'll have to be Dave too," said Willy. So, there was our name right there: Four Daves and a Willy. We rehearsed for a month of Sundays – the only day I ever got the chance to go home. It gutted me that I was missing out on so much family time, but having gone from a worldwide deal with EMI to decapitating chickens in the back of beyond, I was fixatedly clawing my way back from disaster. Lincolnshire had deprived me of everything and I never wanted to be in that position again. I would not let any opportunity pass.

On the night of the charity gala, the Playhouse was packed. We performed our set, then the band went off and Willy and I dueted alone together on stage. I could hardly believe that, in the same month I had watched Blood Brothers spellbound from the audience, I was now singing a song with the show's creator, in front of 900 people. How on earth did that happen, and so easily? It was strange; working in the theatre was not a career path I had deliberately chosen – I had simply taken anything and everything that came along – but I now had an Equity card, was working as an actor and one show continued to lead to another, in a trajectory that was inching ever-upwards. And with the next offer to come my way, working life and home life for once came gloriously together.

Return to the Forbidden Planet was going places – London's Tricycle Theatre to be specific – taking me with it. I was booked to play the Navigation Officer and be the MD this time. Eleven weeks work, two pay packets, and I could commute to the theatre in Kilburn from my home.

During the run of Planet at the Tricycle theatre, one of my responsibilities was the pre-show performance. This entailed striding into the foyer or bar in costume and interacting with the theatre-going public. Occasionally, one was confronted with a familiar face from the past. Stan Webb for instance. He was lead guitarist with Chicken Shack, a bluesy band from my teens. I'd seen them whenever they played the Redcar Jazz Club. I'd helped them in with their gear. Once, I swapped my top hat with him for a five quid deal of pot. So next time I see him, he's having a quiet drink at the bar and I'm striding in as an intergalactic explorer, hairdryer in belt (my ray gun). Maintaining my cheesy US space hero persona, I reminded him of our acquaintance and demanded cheerily:

"Whatever happened to that top hat, Sir?"

"Still got it – I put a plant in it mate, it's in me conservatory."

And more than once, there was Anita Dobson. I introduced her to the rest of the cast with pride. Nobody knew her yet, but soon they would. She was filming as Angie in Eastenders, a soap as yet un-aired but about to give Corrie the fright of its TV life.

"This is the new Elsie Tanner everybody," I announced exuberantly.

Anita cringed. "Joan Collins please darling."

I saw her to the bus stop after the show. She still had far too many engagement rings on her finger, but ding ding! Next stop Brian May.

Another time when I – intrepid astral mariner – strode forth into the bar area to hand out safety procedure instructions, there was my old school friend Mike Turnbull. You will have noticed by now my propensity for encountering legendary bluesmen (Alexis Korner, Muddy Waters) – and it had all begun with Mike, back when we were 14, at boarding school.

We'd hitched up to Newcastle in the holidays to see B.B. King, one of the three great blues guitarists whose name ended in 'King'. The other two were Albert and Freddy. Arguments raged about which 'King' was King. Freddy was my man, Albert was Mike's, but B.B. would do for now.

With unbelievable cheek, I'd insinuated myself into his dressing room at the end of the show as B.B. was in the process of taking a fag from a packet. He looked up in surprise. I sparked his Marlboro and that seemed to settle that. And there was 'Lucille' his red Gibson 335 gleaming on a stand, a celebrity in her own right to a blues fan like myself. I took a step in her direction, hand no doubt twitching towards her like a divining rod.

"Don't touch my guitar, man," growled the great bluesman.

There was an even better guitarist than B.B. on the bill that night – Peter Green, lead guitarist with Fleetwood Mac, who were supporting. I'd followed almost every note he'd played since he replaced 'God' (Clapton) in John Mayall's Bluesbreakers. I'd despised Albatross for not being a twelve bar but 'Man of the World' simply broke my heart. So it was a good moment hitching back the next day when a battered car pulled up ahead and waited, as Mike and I legged it, wrenched open the back door and gasped "Middlesbrough please."

A very long stick insect in a battered hat, torn denim kneecaps impeding the steering, turned to face us. Mick Fleetwood.

"Can't take you to Middlesbrough, but we can drop you off at the Middlesbrough turn off, okay?"

"Great!"

From the hair, I thought it was a woman in the front passenger seat beside him, but when she turned round, it was Peter Green.

"Where've you both been?"

"Newcastle City Hall!"

"To see you actually!"

"You were great!"

"How did you enjoy B.B.?"

"Not as good as Albert or Freddy."

"Or you."

"You live in Middlesbrough?"

"Well, sort of. We go to boarding sch…" Mike shot me a look and I shut up.

"I've got a place just near there, at Redcar?" Peter's gentle eyes probed ours to see if we knew it.

"Yeah, Redcar!"

"I've got a farm called Albatross."

Suddenly I loved the song. The car was pulling over and we were climbing out.

"'I'll be there in a fortnight. Come and stay for a week. You'll have to work the land. Everybody pitches in. You won't get any money, we don't use money, but we'll feed you and... stuff."

"Thanks man."

We stood sadly upon the grass verge. It all sounded marvellous.

"Be sure to come."

"Sure man."

Mick was trying to get his knee out the way of first and set off.

"Peace."

And there went our Green Maharishi, offering us Utopia. We hadn't dared tell him we'd be back at boarding school that week, where we were being turned into Soldiers and Cabinet Ministers and Merchant Wankers.

Except it didn't turn out like that. Here I was now taking Mike through his pre-flight drill as he twinkled with amusement, before hitting the stage to face an incoming meteorite storm, armed only with a hairdryer, an electric guitar and a cry of "Goodness gracious, Great Balls of Fire!"

One matinée towards the end of the run, I strode into the pre-flight bar and there awaited Jon Miller, who you may remember produced Café Society's doomed second album, and reappeared in my narrative when he offered me the free studio time that led to Rick Wakeman. This time, Jon had appeared in my life to offer me a job. He worked as second-in-command to impresario Bill Kenwright these days and had come to reel me in for their next production: 'Are You Lonesome Tonight'. It was a theatre piece about the last week in the life of Elvis Presley and was written by none other than Alan Bleasdale. Jon offered me the role of Assistant MD and it was a sign of improved times that this was not enough to entice. But Jon pitched: the show would star Martin Shaw, the current MD was moving on after 6 months, then the job would be mine and the money go up.

"Will there be a show in 6 months?" I'd never done anything for that long, except a 4-year stretch at boarding school.

"Oh yes, we're planning a national tour – and I'm sure it'll go West End."

"But none of that's definite, right?"

"Well… no. The initial contract is for 6 weeks rehearsal, then a 4-week run at The Playhouse."

"The Playhouse where?"

"Liverpool."

"Of course."

So, Merseyside reclaimed me and it was a strange, rather unfaithful feeling to be working not at the Everyman this time, but the other theatre down the road. Equally strange during the rehearsal period was to watch Martin Shaw going through his lines with the other actors and try to imagine how on earth they were going to transform him into 'Fat Elvis'. There wasn't a spare ounce on the guy.

The world back then knew him as one half of Bodie and Doyle, a perm-haired, fist-swinging cop from The Professionals. Soon, apparently, it would know him as a heavily overweight and weighed-upon Elvis Presley. The actor I watched rehearse was a vegan, the first I ever knew (well, apart from my 9-year old boy Jody, who I had traumatised out of ever taking another mouthful of meat). He also had a candle-lit shrine in his dressing room to his own personal Indian guru. He was 'new age' before the term had been invented.

Once, Chinese takeaway and young son Leon in tow, I knocked on his dressing room door. We found him upside down on his head and bollock-naked, with his ankles crossed above him.

"What have you got there?" said his face, somewhere near the floor.

"Dim Sum."

"Oh I wouldn't say that, he looks quite intelligent to me."

"Yeah, but you're upside down."

He was yoga-toned, chakra-aligned, alcohol free, fit as a whippet and just as skinny. But come the 'first dress' where I observed the costumed entry of the cast from my vantage point of a pink Cadillac suspended above the stage, I saw Martin emerge from the wings in a purple crushed-velvet romper outfit. The fat-suit he wore underneath had inflated him like Michelin Man. The scrawny neck I thought he never would disguise was draped with a towel. He dropped his chin down into it and dropped his voice too. Add aviator shades and a great wig and whadaya got? Uh huh huh, Fat Elvis!

He used to dip the two ends of that towel in Olbas oil. When the moment came for him to cry, he turned towards me and my electric guitar in the Cadillac behind, and dabbed at his eyes. Turning back towards the audience, his eyes streamed with tears.

"I can't believe you're gonna take away mah little Lisa Marie."

Give that man an Oscar.

Inside his fat suit, Martin would sweat two to four pounds during a performance. And on Thursdays and Saturdays there were two shows. So he wasn't impressed come matinée day, when there was a plumbing problem at the Playhouse and no hot water. He politely informed the staff he needed a shower he could actually step under at the end of a performance.

Next evening, same problem and a sharper reminder from the star of the show.

Crashing, wrenching and roaring emanated from his dressing room the third time the problem remained unaddressed. He emerged like Doyle from a cop fight, wearing a huge grin and wiping his hands against one another, as if applauding himself for the scene. There were pipes torn away from the wall, fittings and tiles smashed – and next day, hot water.

He didn't take crap from an audience either. A camera going off and he was going off. Elvis would push the aviators further up the bridge of his nose and step aggressively on to the very lip of the stage whereupon he would glare, long and hard. That was the first time. Having observed the shower cubicle exercise, I detected a rule of three.

On the second occasion a flash distracted him, he stayed in character and worked the incident immediately into the scene, much to the bemusement of Peter Marinker, his fellow actor across the pill-strewn smoked glass table.

"Did you fuckin' see that?"

"See what El?"

"Fuckin' flash goin' off."

The third time I saw a flash go off in the audience from my pink Cadillac, I thought delightedly: 'here it comes!' Over went the table and everything on it, a cascade of clattering pills and spilt booze. Then Martin marched off. Had Elvis left the building? Actors remained coolly in position as if unplugged, waiting to be reactivated. They were there a long minute – and there's nothing longer than a minute on stage when the play's stopped. Above, we members of the band in our gleaming chrome roadsters barely dared breathe. In the unblinking dark, the audience could be heard shifting about uncomfortably in their seats. There was a cough or two.

Martin returned, the upended table was set back and the scene reconvened. I don't recall a camera ever going off again.

During the run in Liverpool, Alan Bleasdale nudged up to me before the show one night and said: "Fancy coming down the Adelphi later? There's someone you might like to meet."

A grand Edwardian hotel is the Adelphi, a landmark to rival the Liver Building.

From a table at the centre of the large lounge, Alan rose in welcome. He ushered me over to an empty seat next to a quiet-looking bloke with a beard, nursing a pint and introduced the two of us.

"Hereward, Elvis."

We nodded at one another and my heart sank. It had been a long night and now he'd dragged me out and sat me down next to an Elvis obsessive at 11 o'clock in the evening. Did Bleasdale think my life revolved around his fucking show? Did he think, just because he'd written a show about Presley there was nothing I would like more in my life after a long night servicing one song after another, than to meet a super-fan who even changed his bloody name to Elvis? I could hardly hide my derision as I brooded in silence. I mean, what kind of twat does that?

Conversation flowed up at the other end of the table, with Alan describing his life-long passion for collecting press cuttings that appealed to his sense of the ridiculous.

"Honest to God, I've got one from Marjorie Proops," he told the table, adopting the voice of the celebrated agony aunt: "I'm sorry to return to the subject of premature ejaculation… but my postbag's full of it!"

Ribald laughter, then Bleasdale turned his attention to my quiet end of the table.

"What you been up to Elvis?"

"Well," said weirdy beardy, "I've got a new album coming out and I've written about 40 songs towards it. So I've been in the Australian Outback, playing the working men's clubs. I figured if those guys couldn't tell me which ones were shit, no one could."

Hang on, I sat thinking, new album? And flying all the way out to Australia to road-test, how many… 40 songs? No one's that prolific. No one's that dedicated. No one. Except…

I looked at him again. He'd put on quite a few pounds and grown a beard, but there was no doubting now it was Elvis Costello.

"I must've sung 'Alison' a hundred times in London wine bars!" I gurgled. "I love that song!"

"I'm glad someone at least's singing it."

Now I was the twat, making up for lost time with garbled conversation when offered the chance to hang out with a great artist. He was pretty gracious in the face of my graceless disinterest followed by intense interest in his every word. At the end of the evening he even saw me out to the door – where I tripped up on the mat.

All these decades later, I wish I could have told him it was reading his memoir 'Unfaithful Music and Disappearing Ink' a couple of years ago that inspired me to write my own.

Are You Lonesome steamed out of Liverpool and sailed into Manchester, Birmingham, Plymouth, Bristol, before berthing in London at the Phoenix, where it ran for the next year and a half.

Six months into the run, just as Jon Miller had predicted, the MD departed, I was promoted and my money went up. What he didn't tell me was that half the band would be leaving too. It fell to me to magic up three new musicians and train them up for a West End show in mid-run, which was about to be secretly visited anytime now by the *Evening Standard* awards judging panel. Drummer Dave and keyboard player Rod were not such a problem to replace – I simply picked up their 'deps' who had covered for them in times of absence. The drummer proved trickier. That I managed to land legend Clem Cattini was something of a coup. This guy had played on no less than 45 Number One hit singles.

Clem had a pigskin snare, which thrilled me. Previous drummer Dave had been playing an electronic drum kit that was the authentic sound of the Eighties at that time (think of the theme tune to Eastenders), whereas I was determined to replicate the authentic sound of all those classic early Elvis hits: That's Alright Mama, Jailhouse Rock, Heartbreak Hotel. This would be the signature of my stewardship, now I could proudly call myself a West End Musical Director.

Trouble was, I was an MD who couldn't read a bloody note of music – probably the first one in history! Anticipating my promotion, I had hurriedly begun music theory lessons with Jody's recorder teacher. She'd insisted on beginning from the beginning, so now that I was in the hot seat it was all a bit 'too little too late'. By morning I was trotting along to Mrs Stevens in Kneesworth-Cum-Bassingbourn to learn Waddling Ducks. By evening I was running a band of highly competent readers of music at the Phoenix Theatre in London's West End.

But I have to say I felt pretty happy after the first three performances with the new band – that is, until Alan Bleasdale and Director Robin Lefevre collected me for an emergency meeting in Martin Shaw's dressing room.

Three men with long faces sat before me, shaking their heads from side-to-side instead of up and down, as I passionately defended the new drummer.

"He actually played on records back in the '50s and '60s. He's the real deal!"

"We don't want the real deal, we just want Dave," Bleasdale apologised.

"We want it to sound exactly how it did before," explained the director.

Martin was saying nothing but was surely the architect of this little dressing room dressing-down. It was a bit of a coincidence that this was the third performance with the new band. And if the star wasn't happy…

So I had to sack Clem Cattini, a musician who had already achieved more in his career than I could ever hope to accomplish. I was the apprentice, he was the master. Clem could see my discomfort.

"Don't worry mate," he said. "I played on a remake of the old Tornados hit 'Telstar' the other week. The producer said to me 'can't you sound a bit more like the original drummer?' I said 'don't be a silly cunt, I am the original drummer!'"

You never knew exactly when the awards panel would drop in to see the show, but I like to think it was during those few performances when Clem was whacking the pigskin and bringing closer to life the true sound of those original Sun Record recordings, as recreated by my little Lonesome band.

Anyway, with or without Clem Cattini, Are You Lonesome Tonight won the Evening Standard Musical of The Year Award in 1985. And that, with a MD who couldn't read a note of music!

Chapter 9
Ba da da daa
- 1986 -

Tom Robinson and Debbie McGee were beside me on the BBC Breakfast Time sofa. Francis was at his weather map. Frank Bough's avuncular tones were quite soporific, after such an early start. Then the camera swung full face.

"So it's Cramp without an 's'"

"Yes, absolutely."

"And not 'Clamp'?" He was toying with me.

"Absolutely not."

"And it's on at the…?"

"Bloomsbury."

"Sure?"

"Absolutely."

"Been doing this musical lark long have you?"

"Absolutely Frank," I replied earnestly, "ever since A Midsummer Night's Dick."

Unsurprisingly, they cut straight to the news desk. Exotically attired male models began forming up for the fashion spot, which was next up. They were very beautiful and Tom's eyes grew quite moist. Frank leant across at him, conspiratorially.

"I wish I could wear clothes like that but Nesta won't let me."

When we came off the air I rang my mother. "How was I?"

"You looked very effeminate somehow. Like a homo."

I tried Pat instead. "You said absolutely a lot," she said. "Your hair looked a bit thin darling."

On my way into the theatre that afternoon I bought a hat.

A mysterious message awaited at the stage door: 'Ring Rick Lloyd'. I didn't know him but apparently he knew me from my Café Society days. What's more, he wondered if I'd be interested in joining the Flying Pickets. The lead singer had left – the one with the sideburns – taking the bald one with him. They'd already replaced the one with the sideburns…

"'Fing is, how would you feel about coming in and having a little chat wiv the boys?"

He was one of these people who adopted a cockney accent when it suited them.

Chat meant audition, obviously. They'd had a Christmas Number One, I remembered, a couple of years back. That nice one. How did it go? 'Ba da da daa'… what was it?… 'all I ever knew…'

Poster for Hull Truck Theatre's production of Cramp, 1986.

Only You.

"Sure Rick! A chat sounds great."

I parked up in the multi storey and made my way along Wigmore Street to the rehearsal rooms. The corridor was a gauntlet of cacophonous sound. A lone trumpet gave way to a practising cello whose bowed lament was stolen by a soaring soprano. I knocked and pushed on door number eight. The hot, weary room contained four thin men, middle aged and some would say, rather unattractive (more than some, in fact. They were voted 'ugliest band in the world' in 1984). Each wore the same glazed smile on his vaguely recognisable face.

The Flying Pickets. Like, er wow.

A pock-marked type with greasy grey hair came casually towards me. The handshake was limp, a touch almost, as if he eschewed bodily contact. His white T-shirt could not have been more wrinkled if the dog had whelped in it.

"Rick," he said, with a rictus grin. I grinned back. His eyes slid sideways and he turned away.

The next handshake was better. Vice-like, in fact.

"David," he intoned mellifluously, eye contact secure and twinkling. He was very small and looked a bit like Dudley Moore. But not as much as the next guy looked like Neil Kinnock.

"Gareth." The voice was deep, designed for sermons. The smile kept coming, long after we'd shaken hands. The vicar was stoned. He looked too old for that sort of lark. He had brimming eyes and thinning red hair.

The fourth one wore a glossy suit, smart tie and brogues, completely at odds with his hair which was straining in every direction, stiff with soap and dyed platinum blonde, a colour which argued violently with his pepper grey beard, though at least his roots agreed. His eyes were flirty and dancing with humour. He looked like some awful northern club comic, but I liked him immediately.

"Ken," he said. Ken! Perfect.

Five weeks at Number One had bestowed upon them a certain aura.

"You know we're left wing?" blurted Ken, excitedly.

"Sure, that's cool." I didn't like to say my eldest had just been accepted on a scholarship to a private school (despite the fact I'd accompanied him to the interview in a pair of purple pixie boots). Instead, I crossed to the piano and played Stevie Wonder's 'For Once In My Life'. I vocally busked along with them to 'River Deep Mountain High' and tried not to ruin 'Only You'. I put on my latest demo. A bit of a chat later, they asked me: would you like to join the Flying Pickets? I was pretty elated. This was pop music after all and they were a name; actually quite famous at the time. I'd love to, I told them.

Before I could join, I had to finish paying my dues to musical theatre with Hull Truck's national tour of Cramp. Tom and I had co-written the songs, which had led to our appearance on Breakfast Time, and I was appearing in it, too. But I commuted from wherever the show was playing at the time, to Wembley. There we recorded the Flying Pickets next single: 'Take My Breath Away'. They gave me the lead vocal, an early test.

"Think sex and money!" whispered Ken as I entered the vocal booth. "And left wing", I muttered to myself. I was hopeless at politics. Trouble was, I could always see both sides of an argument. I wasn't Chairman Mao and I wasn't Genghis Khan, but I was everything in between, with many truths, often complete opposites. I blamed it on one too many tabs of acid and one wise old man: George Lyward, founder of Finchden Manor. Back when I was an impressionable 17-year-old burning with revolutionary fervour, he told me: "never go left wing or right wing, a bird needs two wings to fly." It

The Ship Hits the Fans

has been my mantra ever since. "Music is my politics man," I would conveniently say in moments of fierce political debate, to cover my ineptitude. With the Flying Pickets that was never going to wash. This lot were hotter to trot than Trotsky.

The other new guy was there, Gary. He did trumpet impersonations on Esther Rantzen's 'That's Life'. He looked like a cross between Max Headroom and the front end of an E-type jag. He was handsome in a Sherlock Holmes kind of way and laughed a lot, though the eyes were watchful. His hair was prematurely grey and he smoked his cigarette like a girl, narrowing his eyes as he did so. The eyes were bedroom and the voice smooth. We were as different as two new boys could be, but we had our new boy status in common and were younger than the others, so we bonded.

First publicity shot of the new Flying Pickets line up. Left to right: Hereward, Rick Lloyd, Gary Howard, Gareth Williams (foreground), David Brett, Ken Gregson.

I went on a diet and bought myself a black kohl eyeliner pencil for our first group photo session. Cramp was drawing to a close and I rang Rick every couple of days to reassure myself I had a job to go to.

"Oh hi man," he would say, casually, "Listen, can you see if 'River Deep' suits you in A? What else? John Sherry's got the photos back and they've come out well – Sherry, our manager? He's picked one out. What else? Good feedback on the single. I'm sure there was somefin' else. Oh yeah. Spain. It's a TV is that okay? For your first gig? Clashes with an Amsterdam TV date but it's better money…"

Last time I was in Barcelona it was a dingy pensione with bickering women and howling babies in the corridor. Now it was a double room, TV remote, fridge, massive mirrors and marbled bathroom. We ate in the Plaza Real off the Ramblas. Then Gareth disappeared into the red light district. Rick went off for three minutes and reappeared with some dope. They were behaving like proper rock stars.

I was here to lip-synch for the first time in my life, to Only You, of course. Playing it safe they'd given me the vocal snare drum part – 'Ker CHU!' I had to go, 'Ker CHU!' over and over, for three and a half minutes. It wasn't very difficult. We were supposed to pretend it was Christmas day. Amazingly, that was when this would be going out in Spain. The cameras started rolling as a nubile blonde slipped into the seat in front of me and a waiter filled our glasses with champagne. The camera honed in on us. Blonde babe beamed dreamily, as if we were starring in a toothpaste advert with a champagne mouthwash. I knew what was required of me. Ker-Chu! I went into her beautiful face, Ker-Chu! I was tasting pop stardom. Don't ask me what she was tasting.

Next morning, Ken was all of a lather. We were waiting for Gareth, who could not be revivified in his room. Ken didn't drink and we were about to miss our flight.

"I'm held to ransom by people's drunken personalities, everybody's so selfish," he ranted. "It makes me want to shoot you all, that's my dream. I hope you all fucking die and the human race is eaten by the leopard and the square taken out of nature."

Brian – our tour manager – decided to save time by settling the extras himself on Gareth's room: £150. We'd only been there for one night. Mine had come to £4.50. I would try to do better next time.

For our second excursion, miming got even easier. We were lip-synching on the radio! Yes, such a thing exists. Work doesn't get any easier than miming on the radio – especially if it's Belgium, a country that is right next door. We fell out the van late and, not knowing where to go, pushed through the nearest entrance, only to find ourselves on a stage in a room combusting with applause. Happy faces shone up at us.

"Here at last!" crowed the presenter.

A track immediately began playing: 'Only the Lonely'.

'Only The Lonely'? We don't do 'Only The Lonely' do we? I looked uncertainly across at Rick who nodded minimally in answer. I had no idea how the arrangement went. "Dum dum dum dumbeedooah" I sang, walking towards a dead mic. glaring at the Picket next to me. It was David, too busy to notice. He was preening himself for a lead vocal, I could tell. "Woah woah woah – yay-yay-aah". I scrutinised the rest of the group for clues as to what the hell I was supposed to be doing, feeling like Eric Morecambe, crossing the back of the stage with his shopping bag on the way to the bus stop.

From there we drove to Holland for a residency in a small theatre in Amsterdam. Wives arrived. Suddenly it all became rather cosy. Domesticated would be the wrong word. Mo, Ken's girlfriend, was an avant garde performance artiste more at home talking about drum machines than washing machines, and Bunny – Rick's girlfriend – seemed to have blown away the back of her throat in an avalanche of coke. Only Pat was normal, and Pat's not normal. But at least Pat and I were abroad together for once. We visited Ann Frank's house and by way of contrast the Museum of Sex with its photographs of men with unfeasibly long penises. We got stoned in a Bulldog café, emerging beatifically into the street, sending cyclists colliding. We trod in dogshit, crossed a square with more mime artists in it than pigeons and headed into the theatre for my first gig.

We Flying Pickets hit the stage in front of a good crowd and two girls leapt to their feet to dance. A bouncer tried to remove them. Ken stepped forward, mid-song. "Leave them alone, you fascist bastard!" he stormed. Cheers. A prolonged stamping of feet. The show was easy after that.

Gareth was responsible for most of the banter and very good at it he was too.

"I'd like you to imagine you are standing on an English pier," he said. "Lord Whitelaw, for preference."

My first lead vocal – 'Young and in Love' – came and went.

"For those of you interested in sartorial elegance," said Gareth pointing to my woolly green jacket, "the rest of the carpet arrives on Tuesday." He gave a nod towards my skinny jeans. "Those trousers are also available in his size."

During the performance Gary pinched Ken's arse on stage and got a laugh. Ken found it an offensive gesture. He berated Gary after the show.

"I felt patronised. It assaulted my dignity. I also found it offensive to gays."

"Bullshit!" Gary and I exploded in unison.

"No, no, I agree with him," said Gareth.

I went off to forage for food. Fourteen members of the audience followed me and sat around the big white table watching my every mouthful in silence. A woman next to me spoke in Dutch to her friend, touched my cheek, and laughed.

"What did she say?" I asked the friend.

"She says on stage you are beautiful and off stage you are ugly."

Obviously, this was the kind of thing I was going to have to get used to.

And so it came to pass, one failed single, one Spanish TV appearance, one Belgian radio fiasco and a few gentle dates in Holland later, that we were ready. The great British public awaited. We unveiled the new line up on the stage of The Hackney Empire, over three nights in December. I had dyed my hair purple for the occasion and borrowed Ken's black leather jacket. We had a backdrop of the Leningrad skyline. During 'Space Oddity' a hardboard Karl Marx flew across it, hammer and sickle in hand, dressed as Santa.

I don't know how we compared musically to the previous line up, but I do know that, looking down from the balcony, former lead singer Brian Hibbard – the one with the sideburns – got up and left, halfway through the show. 'You can't watch your old group' he told Gareth on the phone.

Rick wasn't pulling his punches when we met later to analyse the gig. "The act is in very bad shape; fucked, in my opinion. People have caught up with the Flying Pickets. We need something new."

"I've got a new song!" I chirruped.

"We need a new concept before we start looking at new material."

So we sat around glumly trying to conjure up a new concept out of nothing. After several yards of oppressive silence, I suggested they hear my new number. None of them had the will left to disagree, so I put my demo on.

Our house is small, let's all celebrate…

Here was an anthem to the healing power of positivity and togetherness. Just what these surly Marxists needed.

Belongs to us all, let's all integrate…

The boys ingested the wicked aural trifle I had prepared for them. A long fade out, then silence. Rick was the first to speak. "I'm not standing on stage" he raged, "at the age of 38 and singing those words."

He was apoplectic, though the Alexander Technique, acupuncture, a gluten-free diet, Ginseng and Royal Jelly had dulled the edges slightly. "Neither should the Flying Pickets," the miserable bastard added, before signing off with his usual three word flourish: "in a way…" It was a technique he had of taking a verbal hammer and sickle to you and then watering it down with the qualifying phrase at the end of it, delivered in a drawn out, self-declamatory fashion. It was accompanied by a sliding away of the eyes, as if to deny he'd said what he'd said.

"What's wrong with the words?"

"They're Swingles, they're" – he smirked meaningfully at the rest of the group – "John Benz…"

"Who's John Benz?"

"Just someone who supported us in Australia."

His smirk was replicated by every other member of the group – except Gary, who had no more idea who John Benz was than I had.

"You don't like my lyrics, then?"

"They're wally. They don't cut it and the Flying Pickets shouldn't be looking at stuff like that. It doesn't mean anything, in a way."

"Oh I quite like it" said Gary, "although I agree with Rick, in a way."

Nobody else expressed an opinion.

Due to their original working relationship, Rick absolutely held the whip hand over the rest of the band. Here's why: David, Gareth and Ken were actors originally, members of a theatrical troupe called 7:84 –a reference to the fact that at the time the left-wing theatre group was formed, seven percent of the population of England owned eighty-four percent of the wealth. John McGrath and Rick Lloyd wrote a musical for the theatre company called 'One Big Blow' in which a group of miners form a brass band. They can't afford the instruments, so they sing the brass parts instead. As well as composer of the piece, Rick was also musical director – hence his tendency to refer to David, Gareth and Ken as a 'bunch of fucking actors' and their tendency to think of Rick as 'management'. Having just come from musical theatre I knew things would never change. Our trademark was acapella singing – an extension of the acapella musical that had brought them all together and put them all on Top of the Pops. As such, Rick was the band's musical midwife and master.

Now I was part of the mix, Rick found himself no longer sole songwriter in the group and it wound him up something terrible. So setting my own songwriting ambitions aside, I went home and created instead an acapella arrangement of Billy Joel's 'Goodnight Saigon'. If my life now depended on a great song, this one was it.

"Twenty years out of date," decreed Rick, "and Billy Joel's a wally."

I went home and rattled off an acapella arrangement of 'Sledgehammer' by Peter Gabriel. Surely that couldn't fail? It could. This time Ken was the saboteur.

"The Flying Pickets can't sing that second verse!"

"What's wrong with it?"

"'Show me round your fruit cage'?" gasped Ken incredulously, "And I'll be your honey bee?' It's sexist!"

Rick was forced to agree with Ken, which hurt. The only thing they usually had in common was mutual loathing. They took an oppositional stance as a matter of principal.

"David?"

"Mmm. Aahh…"

"Gareth?"

"Yes, I mean… no… I mean… mm."

"Gary?"

"I'm sorry, I have to agree…"

So I went home, said 'fuck 'em' and celebrated Christmas.

The Flying Pickets set out upon their 1987 New Year tour of Great Britain. Gigs piled up like mashed potatoes. One of them was an 'end of the pier' show. 'Tonight, The Flying Pickets' was emblazoned across the front of the theatre, and underneath:'Next week, Sooty!'

Interminable hours were spent in the van. At one point it broke down in the snow.

"Chaps," apologised Brian, turning from the steering wheel. His sentence had started well, but there was always a bit of a wait for the rest of the words to emerge. Brian wasn't the dour Yorkshireman those who didn't know him judged him to be. Outside of the group he was delightful. He just wore a permanent scowl and became tongue-tied in the face of this lot. "We seem to have a temporary breakdown of power." Brian looked back at us in anguish. "If you could simply take a moment…"

"You're saying we need a push-start," came a voice from the back.

"Yes," admitted Brian, after a dramatic pause.

I looked around the van. Gareth was skinning up and giggling. Rick was dead under his blanket. David was trying to tune his radio to the world service. I'd pushed the van last time so I wasn't doing it and Gary was far too selfish, so it was down to Ken.

"I'm not fucking pushing unless everyone else pushes." Ken glared round the van. "You're like the ruling class" he steamed, "fucking fascists!"

"Take another pill grandad," purred Gary, "where's your calm tablets?"

At the hotel, a television crew turned up for an impromptu interview. Whilst I obediently trotted down to reception, Rick was furious at the promoters for dragging us all from our rooms. "It's so tacky" he railed at the director, as the rest of us stood about. "We're a class act, we don't have to put up with this."

"Fucking bollocks!" yelled Ken, leaping into life. "You're either in a group or you're not. You want people to see us don't you? We're a product aren't we? I can't stand all this fucking negative moaning. I'm sick of fucking talking. The picket line's been crossed. The time for arbitration is over. Now then. You're the cameraman aren't you? You must be, you've got a camera. Where do you want me to stand?"

Ken won the day. We climbed trees; stood at a bus stop. We were wacky.

"Smile!" our director implored.

We 'smile'.

"What I'm looking for," she smiled back anxiously, "is a little bonhomie."

With Ken and Rick mere feet from one another, locked in a marital dance to the death, this was a non-starter. One was scowling and the other muttering through fixed teeth: "I'm going to go round his house. Throw a petrol bomb. Kneecap him."

These guys were becoming too much like hard work. I yearned to be part of something welcoming again, to do something creative outside of this troubled band that had taken over my life, on a tour that never seemed to end, where recognition of my own compositions never came my way. I longed to return to the Pat I hadn't kissed, the sons whose birthdays I'd missed. To sit in my studio and create music that would be embraced instead of rejected. But the diary perpetually filled with Pickets dates to keep me away.

Home became a place where I visited rather than lived, as one tour ended and another began. If we were in a country in which the band were famous, I can't deny I experienced privileged times. Australia was a six-week daisy chain of five star hotels, sold out concerts and TV appearances. In other countries – territories we were yet to conquer – touring was a slog of chilly Ibis box rooms and sticky-floored clubs. Home visits were a succession of romantic reunions and departures. It was unsettling to be in the living room, my family all about me and a memory being shared of which I had absolutely no recall.

"I don't remember that?"

"Oh, you weren't there." It almost felt like an epitaph, that phrase. Upstairs, I stared into my open suitcase, about to be filled again with the socks and pants going round in the tumble dryer downstairs. I had a sense of occupying a space I would soon be abdicating, almost as if I had no right to be standing in it. The clock was ticking and the feeling in my heart was one I hadn't felt since I was a 12-year old boarder at public school.

Three Sundays a term you were allowed to go home and spend a few hours with your parents. After morning service they'd be waiting by the car, your mum and dad. You came over the bridge and there they were, waving up at you. You were gargling with gratitude at the very sight of them. You had your grey Sunday suit on and you saw them seeing you. You wanted to bury your face into the folds of your mother's skirt. You wanted to throw your arms around Dad. When you got next to them you found you couldn't anymore and you didn't know why. Pulling away in the car, euphoric as you were to see that chapel bell receding, you knew it stood waiting to toll once more, calling you back to Evensong. At home, you could sense the clock ticking, wiping away the hours and minutes left. The ticking grew louder as the day wore on. You wore your home clothes self-consciously, knowing the time was fast approaching when you had to change back. Like a condemned child you ate forkfuls of sawdust – your favourite meal. With every mouthful you knew exactly how long to go. Nunc dimmitis was calling. You choked on your apple sauce. You ran out of conversation. You felt tiny and tearful. You were even glad to get back.

* * *

Following a band meeting, where we workers decided to walk out on management and grasp the levers of power, we bought a van, financed our own album and sold it on a merchandising stall manned by Brian, in a Flying Pickets baseball cap, worn backwards. We became a slimmed-down cottage industry. Instead of flying everywhere we took the Dover/Calais ferry and drove, Gareth and Ken in the back enveloped in a pall of dope smoke, Rick with a blanket over his head to avoid contact with the rest of us; David asleep. It was to be a long tour – eleven weeks of Europe to fill the Pickets coffers. We were heads-down for the motorway.

At one point we based ourselves for six weeks at the Quentin, a 'muso' hotel in Amsterdam. We were cohabiting with three bands: Massacre, Shaved Pig, and They Might Be Giants. Bob Geldof was passing through reception when the third of those bands arrived and on hearing their name, uttered sotto voce: "They Might Be Giants? They might be cunts!"

Whatever they were, they looked pretty dodgy across the cornflakes. Another time Wishbone Ash was in reception, checking out. Dinosaurs of Rock don't die – they just tour Europe. We circled warily, like two dogs of the same breed. They inspected our tour bus. We inspected theirs. Ours was bigger. Theirs was better.

Mick Ronson was resident too, David Bowie's wingman. Over an exotic cigarette or two, he and I watched the last ever Ziggy Stardust gig on video in reception. There on the screen was Mick in his loons at the Hammersmith Odeon, long hair swinging. The man beside me looked far more sensible. "My God, what was I thinking?" he muttered, observing himself.

Band meetings were a regular feature on the road. They were always tortuous affairs, given that no one could ever agree on anything. Killing time at a radio station, item one on the agenda was a proposed trip to East Germany. We would be paid in Ost Marks, a currency unacceptable anywhere else in the west, apparently. We would have to leave our earnings behind as we exited the country, or else translate them into goods to bring back home.

"What goods can we buy Brian?"

We waited.

"There is no shopping."

It was a statement imbued with the kind of finality that only a Yorkshireman like Brian could imbue. There was more, we knew it, but we'd have to wait.

"I've been to East Berlin many times." Brian snagged up on another pause.

"Brian?"

"And…?"

"There's one record shop that only sells Russian LP's."

"So we can't buy anything?"

"'Ten Years After' went over there and played for five tractors."

"I don't want commodities," snapped Ken. "I don't want rattan chairs or fucking dustbin lids."

"I think you're being very unprofessional Ken… in a way," ventured Rick.

"Bollocks! If you'd been more professional in the first place we wouldn't be in this shit."

And so it went on – and on – until it was all over. Holland, Belgium, West Germany, East Germany, Austria, Switzerland, Hungary, Yugoslavia. At one stage, we slept in six different countries on six consecutive nights. That's a lot of driving, performing, raving, room partying and next-day hangovers.

Coming back exhausted into London, there was a pecking order to being dropped off, though Brian insisted it was purely geographical. Rick happened to be first of course. His house in Streatham was a large building, bought with the proceeds of his self-penned B side to 'Only You'. In those days, you were paid as much for the B side of a single as the A side. Vince Clarke of Erasure had written 'Only You', but Rick contrived to have one of his own songs on the flip side. Consequently, whilst Ken passed a tolerable existence in a small rented flat in Hackney, Rick owned a three storied detached property opposite the wide-open acres of Streatham Common. It was crammed with lodgers – wild Australian hostesses and black exotic boyfriends.

David romped home a close second, wandering off into his own mysterious world of newsprint and muesli, invisible birds and butterflies settling upon the arms of his coat. Gareth was poured across the threshold of his own front door, a desperately ill man delivered into the forgiving arms of his wife, who took over from here. Gary doggedly harangued Brian every inch of the way to drop him off in Northfields, even if it was too far out of the way, because that was where he lived and that was Brian's job.

Ken, meanwhile, was festering murderously on the back seat, outraged at being dropped off second last. It was all a plot and the government was probably involved, sending Brian secret information via the pylons.

Last amongst equals was my privilege; tipped out in a dishevelled heap on the concourse of King's Cross at dawn, with two hours to kill before the trains started up again. Much as I could have wept for home life, it would take some adjustment to become a normal family member again. "You're always somehow different when you come back, it's never quite what I want," Pat had told me once, a funny expression on her face. She was only being honest. We both changed in so many minute ways when we were apart. Reunited, we found ourselves locked in a love dance around an invisible bomb that took two days to diffuse.

I once dropped in on a member of the band, a day or two after we'd all come home. I knew it was wrong, but he'd gone to earth with something of mine I needed to retrieve.

"I'm in re-entry!" he yelped on the doorstep.

"Can I not come in?"

"I feel a bit funny about letting a Picket into my hallway. You've caught me in my pupae period. I'm changing into the me that lives at home."

That was me now, hoping I could make that change, hoping Pat would give me the time, patience and understanding. Much as I craved to be a loving husband and father, all my molecules had been rearranged. I felt like a stranger.

Several shows ago, we'd all been presented with bouquets of flowers. The rest of the band had thrown theirs to girls in the audience, but I'd saved mine. Now I sat in the ghostly glow of Kings Cross Station waiting for the first train, clutching a dried-up bunch of tulips. I hoped she would like them.

Chapter 10
Alf

Wrenching open our front door I heard Pat cry out "Darling! Guess what I've discovered?" She didn't wait for a reply. "There's a bloody great research centre less than a mile from our house and half the village work there!"

"Gosh… let me just get in the house."

"It's the biggest vivisection lab in Europe. They experiment on animals!"

"Hello," I said pointedly, "how are you?"

"They torture them!"

I had yet to cross the threshold and set my bag down.

"Some medical research is important? Like trying to find a cure for cancer?"

"Cosmetic testing more like. Just so people like me can wear fucking make-up for people like you! Every six seconds an animal dies in a British lab."

This didn't sound like Pat at all. What did she mean, people like me? I was her husband!

"Little animals probably. Mice. Rats. Vermin." I didn't know a hell of a lot about the subject.

"And monkeys! And beagles! Right on our doorstep; your doorstep, when you're actually here." She turned her back. I followed her in. "I've learnt all about it," she said over her shoulder.

This was violating all protocol of re-entry. Back then, in 1989, international travellers law clearly stated that a 24 hour grace period was active upon a Flying Picket's homecoming. Where was my welcome in the valleys? Pat was mugging me the moment I was through the door.

"Well darling, I'm sure they know science better than you or I. They are, after all scientists."

"It's bad science. Human beings and animals are physiologically different. A product proven safe on a rat may be disastrous on a human being. Look at Thalidomide. That was tested on animals."

She'd gone from animal lover to animal political. "Great to see you too," I sulked.

"I'm sorry darling, I'm so sorry!" She turned all her attention upon me. "How was it?"

"Hmm."

I moved into the living room where Pat's mum Dorothy nested in the corner, draped in dogs and surrounded by newspapers. She rolled her eyes at me, instantly conveying she had plenty she could say too but wouldn't – yet.

Pat on tour with the band in Vienna, 1990

"What are you going to do about it?" I probed glumly.

"I've formed a pressure group" Pat stated, "Huntingdon Animal Concern. I've met loads of new people and I've gone vegetarian. You need to go vegetarian too." She smiled playfully. "If you want me to kiss you darling…"

"What's that supposed to mean?"

"I refuse to kiss a meat-eater."

I'd come home to discover aliens had abducted my wife and replaced her with a good likeness, though wirier, who only spoke in slogans and – as I came to discover – dashed the bacon sandwich from my hand before it could reach my mouth.

So I went down to Huntingdon Research Centre (HRC), to witness Pat doing some picketing of her own. She stood comfortably at the centre of her group, licking the gum on her hand-rolled cigarette. Someone offered her a light and she leaned into him, cupped her hand around his. She was looking good in her tight black leggings; thinner than last time I was home, purposeful, more alive than she'd seemed for a long time.

The activists were a strange cross section. There was Janice who co-ran Huntingdon Animal Concern with Pat. A London-commuting career woman, she was a civil servant who worked in Westminster, expensively scented and immaculately presented, her red hair coiffured and sensitively set off against soft cashmere. Janice owned a dream home. The builders were always in, adding a conservatory, converting space above the garage, landscaping the drive. Cats were her downfall, as was her inability to say no to a rescued animal. Consequently, as her house was being redeveloped, it was correspondingly being trashed by any number of four-legged friends, clawing away at the Laura Ashley wallpaper and dumping on the woven Axminster. Janice seemed oblivious to the vandalism, not to mention the feral reek. Serenely she introduced more and more cats and dogs to the household as the cause overtook her life.

There was uneducated Lee, almost her exact opposite, though both had kind hearts in common. Animal Rights was his education and he itched to become a hard-line activist. He'd recently gone it alone and stolen ducklings from a really nice couple who'd hatched them from eggs and were nurturing them for their duck-pond. In his devotion to the cause, Lee liberated them and delivered them to the group, who didn't have a clue what to do with them. Pat and Janice passed them on to a wildlife park, who released them into a duck-pond.

Then there was Angie, who didn't believe in household pets and loathed the very phrase 'animal lover'. Her caravan was stuffed to the gunnels with rescued dogs. There were no curbs or sanctions on their behaviour and no training applied. So they barked dementedly all day long and crapped all over her caravan.

Now she was going round chaining everyone together. "Er, no thanks," I stammered politely as she approached, "just a spectator." I sounded exactly like my father.

Angie threw back her head: "What do we want?"

"Animal liberation!" came roaring back.

"When do we want it?"

"Now!"

I attempted to stifle a disastrous impulse to giggle. What unnerved me though was the fact Pat had been part of this tribal call and answer. She'd never done anything like it in her life.

"1.2.3.4!" someone yelled.

"Nail the bastards to the floor!"

"5.6.7.8!"

"Smash the labs and liberate!"

Pat stole a guilty glance in my direction. Just then, the convoy of coaches carrying HRC workers, many of them members of our own village, rounded the corner. Enraged, the animal rights activists charged at the buses shaking their chains.

"Scum! Scum! Scum!" They hammered at the windows as the vehicles slowed at the gate, the workers only a glass-width away. Then this many headed Cerberus-in-chains surged ahead of the first coach and lay down in its path.

A policeman strolled over and spoke to them all on the ground. "I'm afraid you'll have to stop obstructing the road," he said sheepishly. "However righteous your cause and however much I may personally sympathise, these people have a right to go to work and it's my job to protect that right."

"Bastard!"

"Fascist pig!"

"Rapist!"

No one in the chain moved, so the policeman leaned over, unlinked Pat and scooped her up into his arms.

"You're light, love," he observed.

"Yeah! I'm vegan!" she crowed, wild with adrenaline.

To a chorus of boos the coach was waved through at the gate, followed by the two behind. The show was over. The police drove off. Stranded on the grass verge with no one left to terrorise, the group sagged. What they needed was another fix of direct action.

"McDonald's?" suggested Angie.

"Yeah, they do great chips!"

"I don't mean to eat. To activate."

"Yeah, let's put a brick through the window!"

"Meat is murder! Meat is murder! Meat is murder!"

Then a voice of reason piped up. "We'll explain to the customers exactly what's in their burger, how many deaths it takes," said Pat. "We'll explain the chopping down of rainforests for fields of McDonald's cattle." With a look of apology towards me, off she went with her merry band and off I went, to mine.

I travelled up to Sunderland, where we were to perform before hundreds of shipyard workers about to be laid off. The event was being filmed as part of a TV documentary:

10. Alf

'Tell Them in Gdansk'. Footage of our gig and the soundtrack of our voices would later be juxtaposed with heartbreaking images of empty shipyards and queues of redundant men. Other songs we performed would be accompanied by black and white newsreel footage of great ships sliding down the ramp and into the coal black North Sea. As a child in Middlesbrough I had been taken to witness these launches: the bottle of champagne that took three swings to break across the prow, the groaning and clanking of the monstrous metal construction on its backward slide. The cheering of fitters and welders and flatcaps flung skywards. Good men were being thrown on the scrapheap – this entire audience facing the six spotlit mic stands on stage, awaiting our entrance as we stood by in the wings.

I identified with these men; my job had never felt less secure. Little did the audience know, our group was in as much danger of extinction as the shipyards. Ken had informed us the dates in the book for this month would be his last with the group. He was emigrating to Australia to be with his beloved Mo. Furthermore, his nemesis, the mighty Caesar of The Flying Pickets had fallen. Rick had been the recipient of silent treatment for a while now and things had come to a head during a meeting at his house, where the band had been largely unresponsive to whatever he said.

"I feel the vibe in the room is against me" said Rick. "Maybe I should go."

"You can't go," Gareth said, "you're already home."

"I will go unless anyone can persuade me otherwise."

We had concentrated on our feet as the deafening tick of the clock wiped away the seconds and our silence screamed out the verdict loud and clear. "Well that's it then," admitted Rick, facing up to the moment.

Now here we were stage-side in Sunderland for Rick's last ever gig with the band. Compére for the night was a northern comic of the old school, Mike Elliot. He gave us a classy introduction; one of the finest we've ever had: "Our lass leaned over our backyard and said to the neighbour: 'is your shithouse working?' 'No' she replied, 'he's down the betting shop.' And now brothers, The Flying Pickets."

We leapt out on stage and in honour of our fallen leader, laced into one of Rick's songs. His words had never rang truer:

Remember this, nothing is sacred, we live life beside the abyss…

Feeling more emotional than usual after the show, I phoned home. My youngest answered.

"Hello darling boy! What have you done today?"

"I went to the circus!"

"That's lovely Jody."

"Joe."

"Oh. Okay. That's lovely Joe. I wish I'd been there to take you. Who did you go with? Mum?"

"Vera and Grace."

"Those two old animal rights nutters? What the hell did you go with them for?"

"Direct Action!"

"You're 12 years old Jody."

"Joe."

Then the story emerged. He'd gone to the circus with Vera and Grace, two highly principled, terribly British Quaker ladies – who'd once read Peter Singer's 'Animal Liberation' and correlated the oppression of animals with their own feelings of female oppression at the hands of men. At the ages of 80 and 71, you wouldn't have thought they'd have had much of a problem with the hands of men to be honest. As Jumbo the elephant entered, the ringmaster brought out a football and cracked his whip. Jody rose to his feet, urged on by his two escorts. "What are you doing with that ball? What are you doing to that elephant?" he called. "She should be bathing in a river in Africa, not being forced to do stupid tricks for stupid people!" – at which point a circus thug came hammering across. "Remember!" shouted Jody as he was evicted, "an elephant never forgets!" This was the tale so proudly related by my son and in the stunned silence that followed, he waited for words of praise from his father.

"Put your mother on."

* * *

Pat met me off the train from Newcastle and as we followed other commuters out to our cars, she was fishing about in her shoulder bag. She pulled out a sticker. Then she leaned forward and gently pressed it to the back of the fur-coated woman walking in front of us. 'All fur coats are second hand' the sticker read. The woman continued for a few steps then paused, before turning and confronting us.

"You touched me!"

10. Alf

"Do you realise the last owner of that coat was murdered?"

"Last owner? I bought it brand new at Harrods."

"That coat's had at least 90 former owners."

"How could you people possibly know anything?"

"I know that coat's real fur."

"Of course it's real, it's Chinchilla!"

"And I know how many chinchillas were murdered to make it. Ninety. Gassed, to protect their beautiful pelts. Gassed."

The two women glared at one another until the lady turned and stalked off, nose in the air.

"I really wish you wouldn't do that," I said, "It's excruciatingly embarrassing."

"It's not my fault," Pat shrugged, "it's hers."

A few days later, I was up to Edinburgh for the second of my band obligations that month, a corporate show for a hi-fi company. The organisers had booked a private room in a Chinese restaurant after the performance, so they could show us off to their wives and girlfriends. Thirty or so of us thronged a table that ran the length of the room. I had a drunk Gareth on my right. Opposite me was David's wife Angela, six feet of uncompromising feminism. I think we'd done almost as many bottles of wine as spare ribs when the lights suddenly dimmed and a stripper sashayed through the door. David blanched and stole a glance at his wife. The rest of us blanched and stole a glance at his wife, too. The 'dancer' swayed her way down towards our end of the table, tickling the backs of corporate necks and stroking the tops of bald heads, her bosoms swinging like lighted lanterns. Before me, Angela was losing it fast. I tried to engage her in eye contact to drag her gaze away from the stripper, who was almost upon us now.

"Tell me Angela, how's your little girl enjoying the Montessori?"

Just then, I experienced the frisson of a breast brushing my neck. Angie's mouth was open and it might even be that she was answering my question, but I wouldn't have heard her, because the stripper had clapped a tit over each of my ears. Angela's face twisted in rage and with a roar that I definitely did hear, she hurled the contents of her glass at us. I was drenched – only my ears remained dry. Orange juice was plipping from the stripper's nipples, fluorescent lights were on and there was outcry all around. "Ah'm no tekkin' that, yu fuckin' bitch!" the stripper was screaming, being bundled backwards from the room.

Publicity photo for Flying Pickets, UK tour, 1988.

"Marvellous," murmured Gareth in the seat beside me, "fucking marvellous!"

In a huff Angela upped and left, trailed by a subdued David.

From Edinburgh to Bratislava. Such is the glamorous life of a minor European pop star. Queueing to show my passport at the other end, I clocked Bob Geldolf in the line behind me. He was wearing a white frilled shirt, and white is being kind to it, though the frill made up for it, being exotic. I encountered him again 24 hours later as we both boarded a courtesy coach from the hotel to the TV station – it looked like we would be appearing on the same show.

Slovakia's press corps were camped out at the entrance to the studios. Rather like Pat's pack of activists, our coach turned the corner and the media made for us. Saint Bob emerged and was immediately engulfed. At the epicentre of a blizzard of flashlights and a clamour of jabbered requests, he made it to the main doors and passed into the quiet of the station's corridor. It was my first real glimpse of a world-famous star under siege.

Turned out we were sharing a dressing room with him too. Bob slunk in and draped himself sulkily against an opposite wall. He was wearing the same frilly shirt as yesterday, I couldn't help noticing. Now even the florid fronds of the frills were tinged grey, they looked the colour of net curtains in a squat. He didn't get much of a breather either – a female assistant ushered in a TV crew and a mic was shoved under his nose. "What was the best bit about Live Aid?" asked the reporter in her heavy accent, eyes burning into him.

"Walking out on stage," he said, becoming more animated, "and knowing that everyone in the world who had ever known me was watching me at that moment."

"And tell me," inquired the reporter, with a slightly disarming change of direction, "what is it you dislike most?"

"Cheap TV shows." Geldof shot a meaningful look our way.

A few moments later we were all called for and each act recorded their own contribution to Slovakia's version of Top of the Pops. I didn't see him again till a couple of days later, when we shared the same flight back to London.

Guess what Bob was wearing?

There was one final Pickets show to see off that month, Ken's last ever. East Berlin. Yes, we ended up doing the gig where we had to transform 'Ostmarks' into goods. And I think Ken enjoyed it. We were in a communist state after all and we were followed everywhere by the Stasi, which appealed to his sense of paranoia.

Our movements were closely monitored. When I came off the phone there would be two clicks, the first from the person I'd called, the second from whoever was listening in. I also hailed a taxi on the street and, instead of taking me where I asked to go, the driver wordlessly drove me back to my hotel. This was alarming, as I hadn't told him where I was staying. Before I could reach for the thick bundle of notes in my pocket, he sped off.

Much of our money we gave away. The wad of Ostmarks each of us were carrying round burnt a guilty hole in our consciences, as we realised what a fortune it was to these inhabitants of East Berlin, with its dingy interiors, its aura of frugality. As if in mockery, the bright lights of the West lit up the sky not a mile away. In these final days before the Berlin Wall came down in '89, residents on this gloomy side of the great divide were still living half-lives repressed by authority. Those that could afford it, nevertheless had to wait seven years before being allocated a vehicle – a Trabant, the only make of car on the roads. You'd hear it coming, clacking round the corner like a little pedal-powered Singer sewing machine. It felt as if we had time-travelled to the 1950s.

Backstage pre-performance at the Palast der Republik (which was closed down a year later, due to the 5000 tons of asbestos used in building it!), I asked our tour manager the usual question:

"How many out there Brian?"

"Five thousand."

"You're joking!"

"No. Mind you," he said, "if they make an announcement – 'would the owner of the white Trabant please move your vehicle' – the whole audience is going to get up and leave."

It was the night before we were due to fly home. After the show we chose the most expensive restaurant we could find, as we were still trying to get rid of our currency, worthless once we were back in England. The food was tasteless and so were we, flirting shamelessly with the star-struck waitress. Before we left, we tipped her about three months wages. She was so happy she burst into tears.

Coming through customs at Heathrow the next day, each of us was pushing a wobbling mountain of goods. Knowing where we'd flown in from, the customs officers just waved us through; life was too short to add this little lot up. Gareth had raided a classical instrument shop, his laden trolley topped off with a highly-polished violin of virtuoso quality. Mine was loaded with all manner of photographic equipment, tripod sticking out and somewhere within the folds of a Persian rug, a top of the range camera, the best I had ever owned, the best that could be found anywhere in the DDR outside of the Stasi.

I walked into a living room full of very tall men with beards and army fatigues. They glanced at Pat quizzically as I entered and set my bags down. I might as well have had 'You Weren't There' tattooed to my forehead.

"Hello darling!" she breezed much too brightly, without making a move towards me, "how's the band?"

Bob Dylan was whispering in my ear: *Somethin' is happenin' and you don't know what it is, do you, Mr Jones...*

"Aren't you going to introduce us darling?" I inquired.

"This is my partner," Pat told them. As I had carved out 15 years at the marital coalface, this felt like a downgrade. I felt my blood pressure instantly skyrocket.

"Right, breakfast," I decided. "Sausages! Bacon! Black pudding! Just popping to the butcher. Coming Pat?"

At this Dorothy, cowed into silence in her corner, made a sound. "Hrrumph!" she guttered. Dorothy had two 'hrrumphs' and this was the triumphant one. Like a coded communication passed between members of the resistance in times of war, this sound told me all I needed to know. I'd struck a low blow for the *Daily Mail* reading public.

I stormed into the village and returned home with a monumental T-bone steak. Then, under watchful eyes I whacked the gas up full and shook the pan like a violent stepfather on baby-sitting duty. Blue flame flashed and the living room filled with black smoke. Bleeding wedge of flesh on plate I trotted over to my favourite armchair.

Occupied.

There in my sacred seat, eyes twinkling with amusement, sat. . . let's just call him 'Alf'. He'd been in all the papers after he'd skinned over a churchyard wall one drunken night and dug up a Master of Foxhounds. Here he was now in my living room. He had my armchair, he had my wife's rapt attention, he had a cause. When I weighed it up, what did I have? A tantrum. Suddenly I felt a little foolish and rather angry with myself for losing control. It was undignified behaviour. I needed to demonstrate a little more grace under fire.

I set down my plate and went in search of my new camera. A magnanimous gesture was called for. I handed it to this rival for my wife's respect. "It's yours," I said, "you can use it on one of your raids."

For a moment I'd almost surprised the terrorist bastard! Pat was nodding furiously somewhere in my peripheral vision. With one of her 'other' 'hrrumphs', Dorothy subsided back into her cushion defeated, sending up a cloud of dog-hair. At her feet, the six dogs she wore subsided into the same abject posture of defeat. Did I say six? There were seven, counting them now. There was a new one scrabbling about at her feet, displaying highly neurotic behaviour. The moment I looked at her, she shot under Dorothy's seat and cowered in the dark, only the anxious whites of her eye visible.

A beagle…

It was with heavy tread and heavier heart I climbed the stairs that night. Climbing into bed, I stubbornly avoided eye contact and snapped off the light.

Pat and I lay side by side and worlds apart, staring into the dark.

"What's your problem?" came her voice eventually.

"It's this… bloody grave robber of yours."

"He went to prison. He regrets it. He was drunk. I'm not going to defend him, it was a disgusting thing to do."

"You hero-worship him."

There was no answer.

"These, these… people who think an animal's life is just as important as a human one. I mean, we all love animals…"

"An animal's life is as important."

"They can't just go around lobbing bombs."

"They don't lob bombs."

"What about that fur shop in Portsmouth?"

"An incendiary device."

"That's different is it?"

"Look, I don't condone anything," she said wearily. "I've told all of them, violence is the wrong message, it only alienates people."

Pat turned over on her pillow. "It's animal rescue. It's animals in distress. Somebody's got to fight for the animals."

Then she was asleep.

I lay a long time in the dark that night. Animals were all Pat had ever cared about; they meant every bit as much to her as music meant to me. She was doing this from the goodness of her heart. She had not been emotionally cauterised at an earlier age by boarding school as I had, she was a kinder person than me and, as was becoming very much apparent, every bit as rock 'n roll.

Did I dream of a scientist with a syringe coming towards me that night, chanting 'Meat is Murder'? Maybe, for I awoke in a different frame of mind. I determined to be a more supportive and loving husband. I would lay down my guns and, in a clear demonstration of commitment to our relationship, I would renounce animal flesh.

Becoming vegetarian wasn't so difficult as it happened and in time, to align myself even more with my warrior wife, I went the full hog and became a vegan. That was tough though, out on the road. In 1989 it seemed half the rest of Europe had never heard the word. Exasperated chefs would emerge from the kitchen and stand before our table, as the rest of the band sniggered.

"So, you don't eat ze meat. You don't eat fish. You don't eat eggs. You don't eat cheese. What do you eat?"

It was a bloody good question.

Chapter 11
Firebomb

Scud missiles rained down on Tel Aviv. It was 1990 and Saddam was attacking Israel. For the first time, war was live on TV. Enthralled and appalled, a whole world watched riveted, sitting on the fighter pilot's shoulder as he focused the crosshairs of his machine upon the target on his V.U. Boom! – fathoms deep, a smoky flower bloomed. It was so similar to playing a video game, you had to remind yourself of the actual havoc the firebomb was wreaking down below.

I think I must have been the only person in the world who wasn't watching that night. I was downstairs in the garage. It didn't have a car in it of course – I don't think we'd ever quite managed that trick. The garage had been converted into a carpeted home studio, it was full of recording equipment. I had new gear and lots of it! After long hours pouring over manuals, all my machines were now in communication with one another. Here I was in the middle of the night in my dressing gown at the age of 36, nursing a cold cup of tea and succumbing to wriggling worms of delight. From here in my swivel chair, at the merest touch of a button with fingertip or toe, I could set tape rolling and watch columns of lights dancing up and down to the music.

All I needed now was the perfect project with which to test-drive all this new equipment, and I believed I had the very thing.

It had been three years since I last saw Robert. He had waylaid me as I arrived in our Flying Pickets tour bus at The Mayflower Theatre in Southampton. He stepped out of the shadows, a big beam on his face.

"My dear Robert," I said, wringing his hand.

"Moby Dick!" he said in reply. "we need to turn it into a smash-hit musical."

"I could not agree more!"

We found somewhere we could be private and in a heartbeat I was back there with Queequeg and Starbuck and all the other quirky inhabitants of Herman Melville's tale.

"We need a number for Ishmael," said Robert. "Here." With a flourish, he thrust sheathes of new lyrics into my hand. Last time it had been 'Knucklehead Meadow'.

This time it was 'I Live and Breathe':

I remember cuddling pygmies and the leaps from spar to spar

And the witch-like liquor potions we drank when under par

I remember making blood pacts with the heathens from afar

And the devil ever grinning, holding every door ajar

It was good. And the tune I had put to it was good. But somehow, another production had failed to materialise and I hadn't seen him since. Now, however, three years later Robert had been back in touch. He was on the case again with Moby Dick and needed a tape of four or five of the songs to firebomb Producer-land.

What a perfect maiden voyage for my new studio! I could play with my machines and revisit the tunes from Moby Dick at the same time. They came swimming into my head and heart: 'Heave Away', 'Building America', 'A Whale of a Tale'.

If the world didn't end tonight, I would start tomorrow!

* * *

I slid into Finsbury Park station. I had Robert's cassette tape ready. With three minutes to spare before my onward connection, this was to be a hand-over of military precision.

I looked around. No Robert. I swept a gaze across the tracks. An inflated man in a suit was waving at me from a distant platform. Him, God, yes! It had been so long since I'd last seen him and in that time, he'd gone from Stan Laurel to Oliver Hardy. I watched him duck down the stairs on his side and rattle up the ones on mine very quickly, in a light-footed, prissy way, as we do when we're overweight, to show people we're not. Almost immediately, my connecting train approached the platform. Hurriedly I pressed the tape into his hand.

"Fab!" he said.

"Luck Robert!"

11. Firebomb

"I'll be in touch."

Somewhere in Europe with an idle hour to fill, I zapped through the cable channels. Steffi Graf winning a tennis match. Larry King interviewing the Duchess of York. An episode of Love Boat. Two 50 year old men on a hillside in traditional costume with an accordion. An American couple raving about a potato peeler. The opening credits of Bonanza; Hoss Cartwright shuddering to a halt on his horse and grinning cheesily above his name. I flicked off the TV and phoned home.

Leon answered. "Hi Dad."

"Hi darling. Is Mum there?"

"No."

"Where is she?"

"On a demo."

"For?"

"Against. The decapitation of turtles."

"Ah."

"But Dad, listen. Robert Longden rang."

"Yeah?"

"He said Cameron Mackintosh wants Moby Dick!"

"No!"

"Yes!"

"Cameron Mackintosh?"

"Yes!"

"*The* Cameron Mackintosh?"

"Yes!"

Chapter 12
Ship ahoy

The phone shrilled to life. "Robert."

"Hello dear."

"You liked the tape then?"

"It was fantastic. I sent six of them out with six scripts to six different Producers."

"And?"

"Five of them didn't even bother to reply. I still don't know if they got them. Then on Monday I called home for messages and a voice said 'This is Cameron Mackintosh calling from New York. Would Robert Longden please call me back on this number."

"Wow! You rang him straight back?"

"Well, no…" He giggled. "I just thought it was one of my friends pulling my leg so I didn't do anything about it."

"Then?" I prompted.

"A couple of days later he rang again. 'Look, this is Cameron Mackintosh calling from New York. Would you please get in touch?'"

"So you did and what did he say?"

"Well, he said he thought it was a really funny idea that deserves a shot. Contemporary, next Rocky Horror… stuff like that."

"What about the music?"

"He said he receives thousands of tapes and this was better than any of them."

I was speechless. I was dreaming. I wasn't listening properly. "…200 hundred seater in Oxford,' he was saying, 'ten nights, Howard Harrison, Martin Koch…" I tried to keep up with Robert as he recounted his conversation with the big 'CM' calling him from the only slightly smaller NY.

"He's giving us £10,000 to put it on at the Old Fire Station in Oxford so he can have a look at it. It's his own private theatre, you see. He wasn't going to take on any more new shows but I'm sure he'll change his mind when he sees it. He told me to go to his offices in London and make myself at home. He hasn't got time to produce it himself so I'll have to produce it."

"Who's going to direct it?"

"I thought I would. I'm the only person who understands it, you see."

"Well, that's true."

"I'll put you a script in the post. You've got lots of new songs to write."

"What about…"

"I'll try and send you £1,000. Be in touch."

Each time I came home I picked off the new Moby songs I had to write and fired them off in the post to Robert at Cameron's office. It would take a day to write a song and two more to arrange it on the Atari music system. When I had developed three numbers up to this status it was time to call on my in-house singers. Leon I could generally find in his bedroom with girlfriend Mhairi; Pat was usually struggling through the mire at the end of our garden on the end of a barrow wobbly with bales, trying to make for the stable.

"I need you to sing!"

If it was anything after 4pm: "Do me a Martini!" she'd turn and holler, the wheelbarrow shedding half its load.

The three of us sang everything, all the 'Leads' and the backing parts for 'The Swarm' – as the Moby ensemble were now called. I would track us up several times till we sounded like a squadron of von Trapps. Then I'd stick my guitars on and all the other overdubs – piano, bass, strings, whatever the arrangement called for. Finally, I'd balance everything up and finalise the production of the track. Then it was on to the next one. Down the road in London, Robert was similarly going for it. We had our tails up! The two of us were busier than a dog burying a bone under a marble floor.

Extract from Robert's programme notes:

> 'I woke up like a human exclamation mark, vaulting over breakfast trays and bulleting towards the foggy joys of Bedford Square, the Cameron Mackintosh offices! I remem-

ber crossing over the threshold and entering the grand reception with its elegant staircase. I was like an elephantine Annie stepping into Daddy Warbuck's mansion. I was suddenly gripped with not unreasonable panic. I couldn't breathe with excitement.

I contacted a number of art colleges and awarded Worthing College of Art the job of painting, constructing and modelling a set and props (designed by my friend Paul Farnsworth) as work experience. All executed for less than £2,000. Paul was an even bigger friend now.

I had to find what seemed to be the vast creative team of unutterable brilliance who wouldn't charge me anything!

Two ex-dancer friends from 'Me And My Girl' came to the rescue. Howard Raynor designed and handmade over 60 original costumes for £700. Anthony Lapsley, who because of a leg injury had become a reluctant ticket seller at the Comedy Theatre box office, suddenly became the choreographer of a potential West End show.

I had earmarked Antonio Rossario Monopoli (aka Tony Monopoly) for the lead. I met Earl Tobias in a sports car driving through a snowstorm to a matinee, when I was playing Dorothy Parker in a musical about Tallulah Bankhead. Discussing the difficulties of reinventing Hollywood legends, Earl began to unravel his talent at impersonation. He went through a grand repertoire of voices and slowly it occurred to me that I should weave him into the fabric of Moby Dick.

I visited various stage schools and the 3rd year students from Arts Educational (14 in all, girls and boys) created the show's Swarm of wildcat schoolgirls. I had foolishly suggested that I could present Moby Dick with 12 artists and a musical comb, but that wouldn't do. I was, after all, the deMille of the Fringe. I couldn't cope with a company of less than 30, and I certainly didn't want to charge a jaded public half a nicker for a black box and two Steinways evening…'

Life became a succession of expensive phone calls between the two of us; Robert at Cameron's offices in London and me, somewhere in Europe. He told me he'd asked for twenty grand instead of ten – and got it. And he faxed me a photo of a shifty looking chap. 'This is your agent' was scrawled across the bottom. I called the number and scrutinized the picture as the phone was ringing. "Mark," I muttered.

"Hello?"

"Hereward Kaye. Hi! Robert says you're my agent?" I was radiating enthusiasm.

There was a slight pause. "Your tapes seem to be very successful." Diffident. Disinterested.

"Do they?"

"Well Cameron seems to like them, doesn't he. And Martin Koch."

"Who's Martin Koch?"

"Don't you know him? Musical director of Les Miserables, Miss Saigon, Jesus Christ Superstar He does all Cameron's big musicals. He's agreed to arrange your music." He waited for me to say something. "Can't be bad, can it?"

"No," I had to agree, "It's probably a good idea."

"And you've heard about Polygram?"

"No?"

"You're getting a two single deal. They'll choose the songs and place them with in-house artists."

"Wow!"

"Deal courtesy of Robert Mackintosh."

"Where did he spring from?"

"Cameron's brother. He's married to Jayne Collins, who's in your show. He's trying to get her signed to Polygram." Dry. Ironic.

"Does that mean we'll get any money?"

"Possibly, if it happens. Cameron doesn't seem very keen. I think he wants his brother to mind his own business, but he can't keep him out because Robert's cast Jayne in the show."

"What sort of money?"

"Not much, I shouldn't think. Nobody buys singles these days. Especially singles taken from musicals. And who's heard of Moby Dick the Musical?" Sarcastic, amused.

"So no money?"

"Oh I wouldn't say that. It could mean advances and a publishing deal. Robert's on the other line, must go."

Chapter 13
Wham bam wallop

The moment I came through the door, Dorothy's face took on an expression of enlightenment. "I knew there was something else!" she said. "Robert's in the studio, waiting."

He leapt up as I entered, the blessed Robert, the bullying Robert; he of the great tensions within and the blue skies and slapstick without.

"Hello dear!"

"Robert!" I cried, ridiculously pleased to see him. It was the first time we had come together since Moby Dick had combusted into life. This long-dormant project was suddenly active, and the adventure that lay ahead filled us with creative hunger. We had work to do – we were still several songs short of a full musical.

"He wants the same stuff, but huger!" Robert told me. "Wham bam wallop intros and finishes, and incredible journeys in between. And a great big musical 'button' just in case people don't know it's over. The arrangements simply aren't theatrical enough. Cameron likes the camper stuff. He says if it makes him smile, it'll be a winner. That's how he judges a song. That's our task now. We just have to make him smile."

"Let's get on with it then!" I crowed, eager as a wet spaniel on a beach to begin.

"What's first?"

"Well…" he considered, grinding the thumb of one hand into the ball of the other, "we have Ahab's version of 'Heave Away' to think about."

"Right…"

"Just think of Dracula or Fantasia or the wicked witch in Sleeping Beauty… we have got to give the audience what it imagined it was going to get when it bought a ticket, anything less will lead to disappointment. The key is unabashed melodrama."

"Uh huh… and?"

"I'd like to reinstate the sexy chord sequence in 'Gypsy Dancer' from the Cornet."

"Oh right, 8 years ago…" I tried to remember.

"Also, you need to add six or eight melodramatic step down chords at the end, while Ahab is screaming from the tattoo being burned off."

"Gotcha…"

"Your 'Building America' demo was very nice but I need a stronger home stretch, some Holst's Planets… clanking, chugging, ship moving-off music with a heavy duty melody to cross the main melody, giving it drama and resonance. Think of the 'Bolero' violin motif."

"Ah."

Robert snored lightly on my studio sofa in the mid afternoon sun, his stomach peeping from his ridden-up shirt, hand resting self consciously upon it, even in undulating sleep. He'd been forced into oblivion by long hours of me and my mouse, clicking away. We'd been holed up for days and nights – a couch potato and a mouse potato. Awoken by my 'hurrah!' he jumped to his feet.

"Is that it?"

"On the computer, yes. Now I've got to transfer it all onto tape. You should know by now."

Robert damped down his frustration and set off to the off-licence for supplies. A total insomniac, he needed two videos to get him through the night and half a bottle of scotch. He was one of these people who never actually bothered a bed. He slept on the living room floor in the upright position, back against the sofa, in his underpants, a violent video flickering against his upturned eyeballs. Sometimes the dogs and I found him like that, coming down in the early morning for the garden.

Alongside his other formidable talents, Robert also wrote songs. Good ones. He was already in the habit of rewriting all my lyrics and I hadn't wanted him doing the same with my tunes. I set one very important ground rule right from the outset: I write all the music. He readily agreed. But one morning our agreement was breached and it was my own doing. The song we were addressing was 'Pequod'. Robert had constructed the lyric upon the bones of an old tune of his own.

"Hang on," I said, listening to his lyrics, "'Pequod, with sails that touch the sky' – didn't that used to be 'Kibbutz, not quite Jerusalem'?"

He nodded.

"That's a great tune. I can't improve on that. It deserves to go in."

"Well, if you're sure…"

Two songs later, I was struggling to come up with something – anything! – for 'Clamfish Chowder' with its almost impenetrable lyric: 'Pound up the biscuit into powder, mix up the salted pork with butter…' I shook him. "Robert, wake up!"

He sprung from the sofa.

"'Pep up the steamy sauce with pepper'" I quoted, "'where's our Clamfish Chowder supper… what the hell?'"

"This one needs to be a cakewalk." He frowned in concentration, thumb gouging away at the hole as I winced. "A simple-minded minstrelsy sort of thing with a table-thumping chorus."

"The trouble is Robert, the lyric's so dense. It only seems to work with your tune."

"We'll go with that then, shall we? Might as well. Almost done now. Eighteen covered in Act One and fourteen in Act Two."

It was a newly-minted morning, but I was giddy. "What next then?"

"Ship Ahoy?" He scrutinised me. "No," he decided. "You should wake up and tackle that one when you're feeling bright, joyous and uncomplicated. I have to get back to London."

My spirit soared. Suddenly I felt perfect for 'Ship Ahoy'.

"I'll do it when you've gone. Then what?"

"Two overtures and a dance-floor version of 'Heave' for the radio stations."

"We didn't do the start of Act Two, did we. What does that involve?"

"Melodrama and mystery sounds… something highly imagined… for a start, you need to have distant island drums… then the Ahab motif, Hammer Horror style and weave it like a wasp through the next sequence. Remember the different countries each sailor comes from – Dagoo from Africa – Feddalah from India – Flask from France – the best way to tackle it is to create a silent film piano underscore in your mind and change course each time a new character surfaces, focusing the melody to fit the precise detail of how they say a sentence, but with the flavour of the country they come from. You've written all the tunes for it already. They exist elsewhere in the show. They just need putting together here in the correct way. It's not a song as such, there's no chorus. It just needs atmosphere and colour. I'll look at it with Martin Koch. You get on with the entracte and overture."

With that, thank Christ, he was gone. I staggered out of my studio, dizzy from concentration. After days and nights of big intros, incredible journeys and great big musical buttons, I was wham bam walloped. The fat lady was probably singing but I couldn't hear her; tinnitus was drowning her out.

Chapter 14
Romance

- 1991 -

Cameron crossed the carpet, hand outstretched. "At last," he said, drily, "we meet."

"We have met before," I said.

"I know," he replied, visibly racking his brain, "but I'm trying to remember when."

"Rocky Horror Show, German tour, 10 years ago. I was an understudy."

"God, yes."

"You, me, Richard O'Brien and Ziggy Byfield singing 'Alma Cogan' in the back of the bus."

"My God, we were pissed for a week – do sit down."

There were three sofas to choose from, framing a giant coffee table. I sunk into one of them, though not quite as deeply as Robert, who was drowning in a quicksand of cushions next to me. Our agent Mark and our solicitor Tina grabbed another, shuffling pert buttocks to accommodate Nick Allot, Cameron Mackintosh Limited (CML's) affable second-in-command. Cameron was left with no option but to sit next to his brother, something he managed rather ungracefully.

"Tee?" he called.

"Coffee," I replied.

Tee Hesketh, Cameron's Private Secretary entered.

"Tee," said Cameron, "would you see what people want?"

I sunk deeper into the cushions.

"Coffee anyone?" twinkled Nick.

"Tea!"

The Ship Hits the Fans

"Coffee!"

"Black!"

"White!"

"Thanks!"

After this clumsy conversational ballet, an awkward silence.

"Seen the poster?" chirped up Cameron.

Before us upon a sheen of green glass, lay the most expensive poster I had ever seen or had my name upon, the poster of our new show.

"I think it's rather good, actually," said Cameron. "I put a lot into it. I'm pleased as punch."

He sounded as if he'd designed the bugger himself, but then, he probably had, he was clearly creative. As well as his interest in our show, he was also currently collaborating with movie mogul Steven Spielberg on a musical adaptation of Kipling's 'Just So Stories' and with Oscar winning director Bruce Beresford on a movie of 'Les Miserables', as well as revising a musical version of Arnold Bennet's 'The Card' and God knows how many other projects beside. He was surfing a fantastic creative wave.

On the walls, Cameron and members of the Royal Family. On the great mantelpiece, statuettes. Behind us, the Steinway. Do you think... Andrew... Ll... Ww..?

Enter Tee, bearing bone china.

As I stirred dreams into my coffee, I was all too aware of the company Robert and I were now keeping. At this moment in time, Cameron Mackintosh Limited had eight shows in 44 productions in a dozen languages, providing employment for over 10,000 people worldwide. Five of their shows were running in the West End and four on Broadway. Three of their shows – 'Cats', 'Phantom of the Opera' and 'Miss Saigon' had grossed more than one billion dollars in the US alone. Cameron had recently been in the paper quoting the song 'Hello Dolly' and the line which says: 'money is like manure, you spread it on the ground to make little things grow.' After years spent mired in the shit and years more spent painfully extracting myself, his manure was the kind of shit into which I longed to dive headlong.

Then we were talking percentages. And West End. And Broadway. And fuckin' Japan. And the coffee table book rights. And secondary royalties from amateur productions around the world. I gazed into a chandeliered future. Headlines swirled like the cream on my coffee:

'Kaye & Longden Storm The Musical Stage!'

'Kaye The New Lloyd Webber!'

'KAYE & LONGDEN FLOATED ON THE STOCK EXCHANGE!'

'ARISE, SIR HEREWARD!'

"Of course," he added sternly, snapping me back, "I may see it and say very nice chaps, but it's not for me."

And before I knew it I was back on the street.

Chapter 15
Sweet mango

We loitered in a Hilton hotel lobby waiting for Brian, who was parking up. We Pickets were lost children without him. Outside of this group, two of us at least had mortgages, children, motorcars. In this world we stood waiting helplessly to be handed an aeroplane ticket, a gate number, cash, an itinerary, a room key.

Brian burst through our ranks cascading pens in his dash for the desk. Manicured and poised, the female receptionist pushed forms toward him.

"You will each need to fill in one of these, with your passport number."

"S' okay, s' okay," gabbled Brian and, over-mouthing every syllable, asked rather too loudly: "avez-vous BAIN or DOUCHE?"

The receptionist looked slightly alarmed, possibly because she was German and we were in Germany. Realising he was not making himself clear, Brian upped the decibels. His hands described a small boat about his hips: "BAIN? or…" his hands went up above his head and performed an aerial flower arrangement "DOUCHE? BAIN or DOUCHE?"

She was mesmerised.

"Yah, Mr Wilcock" she managed eventually, regaining her composure, "all the rooms come complete with bath and shower."

But it wasn't over yet.

"Also," said Brian, "Do you have a room LOW DOWN? Not at all HIGH UP?" He jabbed a finger at Gary, who wasn't there any more. He'd nipped into the Patisserie next door for one of the cakes on the revolving glass stand.

"HE cannot get in A LIFT."

"I think we have one we can change to the first floor" she mumbled, very un-German now, and took refuge behind the computer.

"Right chaps," said Brian, Mainwaring once more. "We have to be ready to leave at half five for the soundcheck." Sensing rebellion – "OK, call it six."

* * *

With two days off, I splashed out and flew myself home to Huntingdon, to rendezvous with Pat at the 'Darjeeling', a kind of halfway house where we would become reacquainted over the Mateus rosé and poppadoms. We had a big decision to make. My Flying Picket schedule for the next seven months had come through and it meant me missing out on all things Moby Dick. Next month I was meant to be going to Vienna to start work on our new album. The band, aware of my conflict of interests, were apprehensive about having me all over a new CD when I might bail out at any time. They wanted a solid commitment for the rest of this year and the whole of '92, to promote the new album. That was a long time and a lot to ask, but they were holding a gun to my head. Should I leave the band? Should I miss out on Moby? Leaving the band would mean goodbye to my monthly retainer; direct debits would be bouncing around our cringing bodies like hailstones. Poverty was the taste of lime pickle, for all eternity.

"But Pat," I argued, "how long am I going to miss out on everything? You know what I'm referring to."

"Dancin' Thru the Dark."

Two years before this poppadom tête-à-tête, Willy Russell had given me four newly-written songs to arrange. No doubt he gave them to four or five other people to have a go at too, this was how he liked to work. Then he rang to say he was coming down to London and could he pop round my studio to hear what I'd done? My studio was actually my garage and my home was 64 miles out of town, but that didn't seem to put him off. Then, watching the Olivier Awards on TV the night before he was meant to arrive, there was the great man himself booted, suited and graciously accepting yet another statuette for 'Blood Brothers'.

"He's coming round our house tomorrow mother," Pat informed Dorothy in her armchair, draped in liberated dogs.

"Fancy!"

I was less than sure he'd arrive. But as if by magic, there he was the next day at our front door. "Put the kettle on Trish," he shot at Pat, displaying an easy familiar touch striding through someone else's living room, following me through to the garage.

Willy liked what he heard. Before he left, almost as an afterthought he said: "Hey, while I'm here, dunno if you can do anything with this? They're making a film of 'Shirley'. I've written a song I want to go in, if Paramount will accept it."

I groped for the record button on my dictaphone, as Willy's fingers groped their way across the keys of my synth. Like any songwriter, he was excited about his new composition: 'Shirley Valentine' – the song.

She just grew tired staring outside

Watching the rain that falls on suburban walls

When the furthest she'd been in search of her dream

Was the end of the Northern Line in '69

It was Russell magic and I arranged to the very best of my ability, with love in my fingertips. When it came to recording the demo, Pat delivered a stunning lead vocal. And then of course, goodbye and straight on a plane for another tour. But the next time I phoned home…

"Willy rang."

"Did you explain I was away?"

"Yeah, but he didn't want to talk to you, he wanted to talk to me," she laughed.

"Oh… did he mention the arrangement?"

"Don't think so, he just went mad about my vocal, raved about it!"

"I'm not surprised."

"He offered me the part of Mrs Johnson in 'Blood Brothers'."

"In the West End?"

"Yeah."

"That's just about the main part – you've got to do it!"

"I've already turned it down."

"Oh for God's sake! Why?"

"The children" she said, as if I was bonkers.

The Ship Hits the Fans

"I'll look after the bloody children!"

"No you won't," she declared emphatically.

Then Willy took the tape to LA to play to studio bosses at Paramount. It was too much to hope Hollywood was beckoning, but it was hard not to. A few weeks later I came off the phone to him. "The good news or the bad?" I asked Pat, not waiting for an answer. "Paramount loved the song."

"But...?"

"They want Marvin Hamlisch to arrange and Barbra Streisand to sing."

We just looked at one another and laughed. We were laughing about it now over the Mateus and pickles in the Darjeeling. We'd thought we could skin all the way up the ladder on one throw of the dice, but quelle surprise, we slithered down a snake instead.

"You'd never have got on the plane anyway, Pat."

"I would! They'd have had to pay for my children and animals to come with me, but I would."

So no Tinseltown. Perhaps as a gesture of consolation, Willy offered me a peach of a job on another project instead: Musical Director of his film 'Dancin' Thru the Dark', featuring all four of the songs I had recently arranged. "You can be in it as well if you like H?" he offered, rather thrillingly.

I went to see the film's director Mike Ockrent. My heart sank as he took me through the shooting schedule. It was a direct clash with a month-long Flying Pickets residency at Stratford East Theatre, where we were unveiling a new show. I had tried to talk the group into allowing me to put in a dep, but the band went ballistic.

Reluctantly I turned the film down.

"I don't think Willie's spoken to me ever since," I told Pat in the Darjeeling, probably snapping a poppadom a little too violently.

"And you missed out on 'Forbidden Planet'."

The show I had helped develop over three productions in Liverpool and London had gone West End, where it beat Cameron Mackintosh's production of 'Miss Saigon' to Musical of the Year without me on board. It had been both joyful and painful watching from afar as it succeeded, seeing all my friends performing in the awards show; watching Bob's acceptance speech.

I wasn't there...

"You're missing your kids growing up" – she was piling it on.

"I want to come home, I desperately do." The poppadom was probably pulverised shards in my fist.

"God, I don't know," said Pat. "Just don't do anything I'm going to regret."

And now I was back on the road that thundered endlessly beneath the tyres, taking us from the last gig to the next one. Gazing wistfully out of the van window as Austria slid by, suddenly I didn't want to be in this van any longer.

I began to grow euphoric. Had I reached a decision? I think, maybe I had… this time, I would be there! I began to inwardly rejoice as the road thrummed and the band around me snoozed. Pat and I would place our future in the lap of the Gods and should Moby Dick win, success would be the taste of sweet mango pickle forever after.

* * *

"Any calls?" Pat snapped at her mother, coming in from picking me up at the airport. She was pissed off, having just discovered I'd left the group and cancelled all our income.

"No."

"None?" she asked incredulously, removing her wax jacket.

"Oh, Liz Pinder. She says she cannot do anything about the turkey with the dislocated leg."

"Oh no!" Pat reacted as if shot.

"At least it made it through Christmas love," I said tenderly.

Pat had made the vet open up on Christmas Eve to try and fix it, which didn't exactly fill him with seasonal goodwill. The vet's gaze went from the turkey's damaged leg to me, to her.

"Why don't you just put it in the oven?"

"Cambridge Radio rang," recalled Dorothy, warming to her task. "I'm trying to remember. I think they're phoning you back for an interview in two minutes. Glen rang. He wants you to make a speech for somebody or other. Who else?…We really must get a piece of paper for the phone…"

"Hurry up!" snorted Pat, pawing the floor like a horse about to take a fence.

"I'm trying to remember. A couple of people on motorbikes turned up but they went when I glared out the window…"

"Mother!" Pat admonished. "Anyone else come round?"

"Lee came round with a friend. His ear was bleeding, well what do they expect? They'd been out sabbing and a huntsman had attacked him with a whip."

"Is that it? Hurry up, I've got Radio Cambridgeshire putting me live on air in about thirty seconds!"

"I'm trying to remember. Ah yes, that's it. Alf and Angela called."

I finished it for her, unable to keep my facetious streak at bay: "they'll be popping round with a few friends at three in the morning. Just a social visit. It doesn't matter if you're not in, but could you leave the stable light on?"

The phone rang. "It's them," said Pat urgently. "Turn that TV down. Darling, you wouldn't nip to Greaves for me, get me a pouch of Old Holborn and a bottle of Martini… hello?… Slimline tonic, darling, slimline… Hello! Speaking…"

Then it was Helsinki and my last ever gig with The Flying Pickets. Feeling sentimental on the plane home, I went and joined a couple of the guys in smoking.

"What's happening on the old musical front, then?" asked Rick's replacement Nick, "sit down here, old son."

"Yes, how's your panto?" inquired Gary, chortling up his sleeve at his devastatingly derogatory term.

"Have you signed anything yet?" asked Nick.

"Next week. Possibly." I was embarrassed. "Publishing. If it happens."

"Advances?"

"Set off by inbuilt triggers. On release of single, five thousand between me and Robert. On release of album, forty thousand between us. If there's a US album release, twenty-five grand each. If they ever make it into a film, fifty grand each. Course, it's not the money I'm bothered about." We laughed at that one.

"Have you got some kind of contingency plan?" asked Nick, "In case none of this comes off?"

"No." Another laugh. "Yeah," I agreed, "obviously it's too much to expect any of this'll actually happen. But I'm not gonna lie; things are looking good. We've got a whole episode of Wogan."

Gary pulled a face. Nick pondered. "Are you doing a cast album, then?"

"Yeah."

"Nomis?"

"Abbey Road." That really did feel a touch too grand, however true it might be. I attempted to deflate my own bubble: "It was time I put myself out to grass anyway," I told them both. "My sell-by-date's coming up."

What a lie that was! As my train inched ever closer to my local station of Huntingdon, I was 10 years old again, squirming in my tip-up seat waiting for the Beatles.

I was coming home, where a whole fresh adventure awaited, with 'Composer' written next to my name.

Moby Dick the Musical?

Bring it ON baby!

Part Two

A Whale of a Tale

Chapter 16
The Old Firestation
- 1991 -

The rehearsal room in King's Cross, London, was a harem of beautiful girls and androgynous boys. Self-possessed dancers, models and drama students threw shapes and ran after them. They jabbered and posed, trilled to the ceiling or recited aloud. Five muscle-shot men practised raising Jayne Collins – our Mr Starbuck – above their heads. These were the Bodyguards, here at St Godley's to guard the school's most exotic pupil, an African princess. Robert slung them in for good measure to perform a strip at the end, just in case we didn't already have enough powder to our keg.

Head tossed back like Freddie Mercury before the mirrored wall, moustache meticulously manicured and peacock-fabulous in his leggings stood Anthony Lapsley, our silver-haired choreographer. He should have been singing "I want to break free" – but no, for some mysterious reason (mysterious to me at any rate), he was shouting out numbers at his reflection. Thoroughbreds in leotards stretched out at his feet and dance routines combusted all about him.

Around the perimeter of all these fabulous creatures loped the less attractive production team: Martin Koch the Musical Director, two wardrobe persons, two Assistant Stage Managers and Robert, who's directing. Meanwhile, hovering by the door, ready for the speedy getaway lurked the gangsters, the 'Suits'. They were well placed to nip off to hastily-invented meetings, should there be nothing to get excited about.

It was a lot of people for one room.

I'd stride up York Way of a morning and the sound of my tunes, lustily delivered, rolled down the road towards me. Sidling in, I'd find the company shiny-faced, seated in semi-circular rows around Martin Koch who was teaching them the songs. They sang in the mornings and 'blocked' in the afternoons.

Lawyer Tina and agent Mark popped in and out from thrashing deals with Nick Allot and CML's lawyer Michael Rose that may or may never happen. Tina walked back with me to King's Cross one evening, fired with enthusiasm.

Show poster for the try-out production of Moby Dick, September 1991. Designed and printed by DeWynters PLC London.

"It's so exciting, it's such fun" she exclaimed, "they're such great tunes! I'm not just saying that. I wish I hadn't seen it; now I'm desperate for you to get your deal."

Ten days later we relocated. Oxford University was closed for the summer and the student population gone. Along with the majority of the cast, I slept on campus at one of the deserted colleges in a tiny cell, with the roars of the Bodyguards and screams of the Swarm echoing down the corridor as they rioted around the empty building. Meanwhile, Robert stayed in a swanky house up the road with his most favoured principals. Should I not have been staying there instead of here? Excluded from the royal court, it felt like a snub. I made nothing of it anyway, though I was a little lonely in my room at night, a prickly grey blanket pulled up to my chin and the shrieks of the Swarm ringing round the deserted campus.

We worked in The Old Firestation, Cameron's try-out theatre. It was busier than an anthill before the rain. I was aware for the first time of other tugboats joining the slipstream of our ship: a lighting designer, a sound design team, Martin the MD and his band. All went through their paces as Robert and the cast went through theirs. Meanwhile stage management raced around plugging all the gaps, fetching and carrying, buying or creating props on the hoof and catering to the cast in all their needs. A low undercurrent of urgency underscored everyone's work.

Lamps were focussed and lighting states re-examined, throwing the auditorium into a variety of moods. "Can we have some light on the stage please?" called Robert, plaintively. Sound effects cascaded from the ceiling – deafening surf, violent storm, cracking mast and crashing wave. "Can we have some quiet please?" Robert appealed.

Smoke machines vented, like fire hydrants. The band went through their paces at the expressive hands of Martin. Dance routines were clattered through and the Swarm swarmed in a sea of dry ice, as all around them construction went on with instructions yelled, metal welded, and the set percussively hammered together.

Into the midst of this seething firestorm, Daniel-like, walked Cameron, or 'Romance Hologram', as he'd dubbed himself. Stephen Sondheim came up with Romance, a clever anagram of Cameron, and the anonymity of it suited Cameron in this instance, till he knew whether he wanted to be associated with the piece or not. As for the Hologram, Robert used to tell the cast: "he doesn't exist. He just hangs over us, a spirit, unseen."

Well he was sure as hell here now and, if I wasn't very much mistaken, that was Melvin Bragg walking alongside him, discerning presenter of 'The South Bank Show', a programme that took a forensic scalpel to all things artistic. Oh Christ, the game was up.

We ran the first act, horribly prematurely, and Cameron sat next to me to watch. He jabbered into my ear incessantly. "Cut the overture," he hissed. "It's ordinary. It's 'Joseph'. Give us thirty seconds of piano and into the School Hymn. Save the real music for the musical."

I furiously scribbled down his ideas in the dark. Then: "Why is she singing this? I don't understand. You haven't taken us with you. Bring on a blackboard to set her up. Who is she?"

Then he started to get into it. Before long he was sniffling and snorting with suppressed mirth and not long after, openly weeping and shouting out uninhibitedly, like one of those odd kids at a bus stop. When it came to the Bodyguards stripping off and a schoolgirl parading before them with a sign – 'The Chipolatas' – he was halfway under his tip-up seat emitting gurgling noises.

At the end he stood up and announced to the cast, "I'm a friend of Romance Hologram's – and I know…" he paused for effect, "…she's going to love it!"

Everyone applauded him as he exited. I stayed where I was, grinning beside his vacated tip-up seat. We'd not run the act till now and I really hadn't known whether it was going to be any good or not. But now I knew. It was rougher than a tramp's chin, but it worked!

Extract from Robert's programme notes:

> 'A strange man swept into the theatre smelling of Concorde. Bang Wallop – I walked straight into Cameron. What followed was for me the best part of the experience. Here was a massively enthusiastic, relentless bully who was so excited by the whole thing, and so bombarding me with notes, I thought I might have to buy a box of earplugs. But I rose to the occasion, as did my drinks bill at the bar, and each day I sat rewriting, creating reams of notes and demanding pre-show changes which continued until the matinee of the final day of the run'.

Cameron never let us alone. As Robert worked with the actors and I worked with Martin and the band, he was in your face, spittle flying, cross-eyed with enthusiasm. He turned up with someone different every time, anyone who's opinion he trusted or valued. Some were wildly enthusiastic, others not (most notably Philip Hedley, artistic Director of the Theatre Royal, Stratford East).

Opening night was upon us. Virgin Sewing Kits awaited on every other seat, alternating with condoms. Tasteful. Pat turned up, dressed as a schoolgirl, as if my blood pressure wasn't high enough already. We members of the team gave one another cards, as you do. Dewynters – responsible for the artwork – presented me with a huge lifebelt, bearing the legend: 'The Ship Hits The Fans'.

I watched the show tucked away on the balcony with Robert, laughing hysterically at bits that weren't even meant to be funny, as he gurgled into a very large whisky. The sound engineer hadn't had time to learn his cues and had far too much to do. After about the tenth missed sound cue I went into shock and remembered nothing more about the performance.

As they filed out at the end, each member of the audience – and there weren't that many – was given a badge: 'I'VE BEEN DICKED!' I wore one myself, with some feeling. Then Cameron introduced me to his mother Diana as "the Composer" and I felt a whole lot better. Nobody had ever called me that before and I found I liked it a lot.

As his back receded Barbara Windsor scuttled over. "I didn't understand a bleedin' word of it!" she declared, "But I had a lot of fun."

And so the run continued, and continued to improve. So did the audience. After a while they were walking in wearing 'I'VE BEEN DICKED' badges.

Extract from Robert's programme notes:

> 'As we worked relentlessly on the show in front of paying audiences, their friendly bemusement turned into enthusiastic focus. By the end of the second week I witnessed my first queue around the corner and promptly had a photo taken of it.'

Still Cameron wasn't sure. "I've never produced a show in the West End," he told me, agonising in the bar, "that didn't have a following first. Who's going to come and see it?"

"All those people who go and see Cameron Mackintosh musicals in the West End."

"This isn't a Cameron Mackintosh Musical!" he exploded. "That's why I like it. It should have a following first. It should be a best kept secret. It needs to become a

16. The Old Firestation

Dear Hereward,
Thank you for letting me tune up your Dick.
Long may it be stiff competition for other shows.
Much love, Romance
CAMERON MACKINTOSH

Producer's first night note, signed 'Romance' – Sondheim's clever anagram of Cameron's name.

cult at somewhere like Stratford East and then I could bring it in. But I brought Phillip Hedley along to see it and he hated it!" He fixed me with an accusatory glare, like I was a kid of ten.

"All I know," I said, fixing him back, "is that there's only one producer in the world for this show, and that's you."

He nodded gravely.

Despite Cameron's misgivings however, word of mouth was good and the audience continued to grow. At the end of the first week of the run, I saw the first ever mention of our show in the national press. Baz Bamigboye's Hot Gossip page in the *Daily Mail* had this to say:

'Watch out for Moby Dick, also known as A Whale Of A Tale, which is running at the Old Firestation studio theatre in Oxford. Don't expect a straightforward version of Herman Melville's classic novel. What you get is a piece of nonsense in the manner of (well, sort of) Rocky Horror Show and Hellzapoppin' with half a dozen very good songs by Robert Longden (who also directs) and Hereward Kaye. The premise is that a bunch of St. Trinian-like schoolgirls who would very much like to lose their virginity, put on a production of Melville's tale. To work, it must be highly polished disarray, which it isn't yet. If it works Cameron Mackintosh, who is very much behind it, will bring it in in the New Year.'

Cameron kept turning up with friends of great repute, dragged along for their valued opinion. His own reputation was too valuable to sacrifice upon the black-candled altar of our show, however much he may have grown to love it. Whilst Robert and I turned inside out wondering whether the adventure was to continue, however, it seemed that Cameron's trusted confidantes were telling him that it should. Either that, or despite himself he ignored their advice. For at the end of the second week of the run, CML took the plunge and picked up the option.

My agent Mark grabbed me as I walked into the little theatre and ushered me through the bar to an alcove where Robert sat, bemused, before an ocean of vellum. Men in suits stood over his shoulder. The worsted sea parted to let me in. I took the proffered fountain pen and side-by-side we signed. Since Robert and I had first worked on the show a whole generation had passed. I'd gone from spring chicken to rock dinosaur. He'd gone from 10 to 19 stone. Now he had the glorious task of visiting the three West End theatres vying for 'Moby Dick, A Whale Of A Tale', as it had now been rebranded. We were to open in the West End in the Spring of next year, with the most successful Producer on the planet behind us. The game had opened up beautifully; after years of desperate defending at the wrong end of the pitch, here we were inside the opposing penalty area, the world at our feet and a great open goal before us. All we had to do was stick the bloody ball in the net. We couldn't miss. Could we?

From Cameron's notes:

'For the first ten days in Oxford we grabbed people off the street to make up an audience, then suddenly word of mouth got going and the show took off with queues down the street. The exuberant girls of St Godley's were ready to chase Moby Dick to London.'

Robert wrote:

'On my 40th birthday my agent informed me that Cameron had decided to take up the option of producing the show in the West End. I had been given a break by a seriously serious impresario; I had been writing for 25 years and for the first time in my life someone was genuinely interested in it. That's a long wait. I was in a prolonged dream. The iceberg of neglect and indifference to our 20 year old writing apprenticeship was beginning to melt. Like the whale, I felt I was on my way to being saved.'

And then I received a letter from old Café Society band-mate Tom Robinson:

'Just a note to drop you a few lines of heartfelt congratulations after seeing Moby Dick at the Firestation last night. I went with Colin Bell (Head of London Records) and a friend of his called Jane who's a high-powered casting director and already had an idea of how good the show was from the West End grapevine.

Herry, I was stunned. I was prepared for something good, but the show exceeded my wildest expectations. Everything about it – script, casting, design, direction, lighting, production values, musicianship, but above all THE SONGS – left me completely floored. My only first-hand experience of musical theatre is 'Cramp' – and comparing that with Moby Dick in terms of a vehicle for your talents is like comparing a Datsun Cherry with a Boeing 747.

These are not only your most potent, focused songs ever, but they hit the bullseye time and again. And 'Love Will Always' is a hit if ever I heard one.

I always thought your talents were a key that would sooner or later open the right doors for you, and last night I heard the unmistakable sound of locks turning in the latch. Unprompted, Jane ranted on about the show's wild originality and great, great songs, while Colin was willing to bet money on it being a resounding smash within weeks of opening. The last time I smelt impending success this tangibly was – gulp – just before the release of '2-4-6-8-Motorway'.

I'm jealous as fuck and pleased as anything at the same time. May success come thick, fast and furious. I can't think of anyone who deserves it more!'

Chapter 17
Hope

A West End theatre was chosen: the Piccadilly, just behind Piccadilly Circus. It was big! Too big if anything; 1,200 seats on three levels. The theatre's souvenir brochure upon its opening in 1929 averred: 'If all the bricks were laid in a straight line, they would stretch from London to Paris'.

Setting out our stall for the Piccadilly, I started writing 'Happy Again', a song to replace 'Clamfish Chowder Supper', which Cameron declared a dud at the last night party in Oxford. I phoned Robert, to let him know what I was doing.

"It's alright," he said lightly but tightly, "I'm already writing something."

"I thought I'd write something" I managed.

"You just get on with whatever you're doing with the Flying Pickets and when you get back I'll have a new musical for you to write."

"I left the group remember? To concentrate a hundred per cent on Moby?"

I replaced the receiver and inwardly seethed. I had to stop Robert from diminishing my role in all this.

The phone rang and I snatched it up immediately.

"Hereward, are you vegetarian?"

My mother.

"Mother, I've been vegetarian for more than a year now."

"Yes, but do you ever eat meat?"

"No!"

I tried to collect my thoughts. Robert. What was the bastard playing at? We were partners, we shook, 50/50. Together we'd given hard yards of endeavour to the project.

Without either of us, it simply would not have existed in its present form. He asked for a number and I went away and created music, lyrics, arrangement, demo. The demo had done its work. The lyrics he had reconstructed, each and every line, into similar ones of his own. Now he was beginning to renége on our agreement that I wrote the music.

I phoned him back. "Hold fire on Clamfish, will you? I've got a great tune, sassy, brassy, Latin. I want to have a go at it."

Sullen silence at the other end of the phone. When I realised he wasn't going to say anything, I replaced the receiver gently in the cradle. It rang immediately, making me jump.

"What I mean to say is, do you ever make exceptions? I mean, what shall I give you on Sunday?"

"Mother, I'm militant."

"Millet?"

* * *

I was working on arrangements with Martin Koch in the basement at Bedford Square as Cameron met with the Polydor moguls in the room up above.

"You've heard about the Royal Variety, at the end of this month?" asked Martin.

"No?"

"God! Doesn't anyone ever tell you anything?"

"No."

"The Royal Variety this year is to be a tribute to Cameron, the overture ending with a few bars of 'Save the Whale', as Tony Monopoly crosses the stage."

"Wow!"

"You like that, don"t you? As he crosses the stage, he whispers: 'Moby Dick, I'm coming!'"

"So am I!"

"Spooky, eh?"

"Yeah! Are you conducting?"

"Not this year, no. I'm doing the Oliviers."

Just then we were interrupted, as a message came down from above: don't let Hereward leave without seeing Cameron.

I waited in his drawing room, toying with the ornaments, examining the miniature London bus with the projected Moby advertising on the side, until in he bounced and flumped down on the couch beside me, very close, arm along the back, eyes locking on.

"Polydor have pulled out, the deal's off."

He watched for my reaction.

"You're joking."

"Unh – unh. It's all over. Andrew's put the boot in."

"Andrew?"

He just looked at me. Obviously there was only one 'Andrew'.

"You mean...?"

"He's brilliant in many ways, but terribly jealous and possessive. He regards Polydor as his own. He's the one who has chart success from musicals, no one else. And you had his team."

"But he has everything and I've got nothing!"

"He keeps hearing about Moby Dick, you see. I was with him at the awards last night. Martin Levan came bouncing up. 'Moby Dick has the best pop score I've heard for years,' he said. Andrew's face was thunder. He's got at them. They shuffled in this morning, made several lame excuses and left. Which means your publishing deal's off as well. How much did you stand to make in advances?"

"Fifteen grand. I left the band, I thought it would all be okay."

"I'll pay it. Tell me how much you want and how you want it paid and I'll pay it. You can pay me back when the show's a huge success."

* * *

Open auditions at the Royalty Theatre. The foyer clamoured to the sound of over 150 out-of-work singers, actors and dancers abuzz with nervous anticipation, exclaiming greetings and air-kissing, stretching, warming their voices, or chomping on apples sitting on the floor. We had them up on stage in batches of 30 to learn the dance routine from Anthony, who was strutting about in his legwarmers, barking out the numbers: "ANd one, two, three, CHAnge!" They were put through it five at a time. It was a meat market.

The principals, safe passage already booked, lolled laconically in the stalls: Tony Monopoly, Jayne Collins, Leigh McDonald, Mark White, Earl Tobias. They were the A-team and they knew it. At the back of the stalls, Robert Mackintosh and record producer Martin Levan hung around for an opportunity to talk about the upcoming cast album.

The dance routines were followed by music auditions. A steady trickle of wannabes and haftabes passed before our eyes singing the same few tired songs from the same handful of American musicals. Normally I would have glazed over pretty quickly, but Cameron sitting alongside me ensured the adrenalin kept pumping.

Sandwiches came and went. I went for the egg mayo, but it had bacon in it. I pounced on the avocado, but it had shrimps in it. So I starved, made notes, stepped in to play piano when called upon. When the final performer had been and gone, we knew that in amongst the dross, the average and the really-quite-good-but-not-quite-right, we had enough thoroughbreds jockeying for position to fill all the stalls for the race.

All bar one. One birth remained empty. We still hadn't cast Ahab's wife – we still hadn't 'found an Esther'. Well, Robert and I thought we had – a fabulous, husky jazz singer in the Billie Holiday mould, but she wasn't what Cameron wanted at all.

"I want someone loud! Brash! Funny!"

"Oh, then you want Hope Augustus," I said, matter of factly. "She'd be perfect."

"I've never heard of her." Cameron rounded on me. "Who is she?"

"She's been on the same bill as us at a few Labour Party benefit gigs recently."

Cameron smirked.

"She's exactly what you want, I can assure you."

Cameron made up his mind to believe me.

"Where can we get hold of her?"

"I don't know."

"What do you mean, you don't know? Who's her agent?"

"I haven't got the faintest idea."

He snorted and turned away from the stage, to face the human debris draped across the stalls at the end of a long day.

"Get me Hope Augustus!" he thundered.

We waited.

Thirty minutes later, there was a commotion at the back. I turned to see Hope Augustus stagger in backwards, tottering on her heels, clearly not having the slightest idea why she was there. She'd been beamed down and materialised within half an hour of Cameron's call going out. I was seriously impressed.

"You!" she exclaimed as she passed me on the way to the stage, understanding for the first time why on earth she might be here.

I followed Hope up to the piano and taught her 'her' song. She sang it brilliantly. She flounced about and made everyone laugh.

"Well done, Hereward," murmured Cameron, as I returned to my seat in the stalls.

Our team reconvened at CML's to compare notes. Unsurprisingly, the choreographer wanted the best dancers and thought the singing placed an unfair burden upon the dance routines. The musical director wanted the best singers and thought the dance routines seriously affected the quality of vocal delivery. Everyone else wanted the best actors. We found two of the requisite abilities present in most of the auditionees, but rarely all three. Some of the dancers were good singers but hopeless actors. Some of the actors were good singers but couldn't 'move'. Meanwhile, Cameron wanted charisma and Robert wanted 'sex on sea-legs'. There were further considerations: Full Equity or Non-Equity; suitability for doubling as understudies; availability. Those with the most obvious talent were often otherwise engaged. They didn't actually want the job, they just wanted to be offered the part.

Casting compromises were thrashed out between us late into the evening, until finally we had our full company, on paper at least. I noticed the endless supply of chilled rosé we had been quaffing was Cameron's own, from his vineyard in France.

Organised!

Training it home to Huntingdon the following morning, I sorted through the *Sunday Times*, jettisoning sections, disgorging half a ton of rainforest onto the carriage floor. Suddenly, I came face to face with a full page Cameron Mackintosh interview about Moby Dick. Two pages later, a huge advert and a pristine logo I'd never seen.

Moby Dick – Coming March 11th

The Ship Hits the Fans

Advert in national newspapers, in the weeks before opening night.

It had started!

In the days that followed, a really quite scary advert began to appear in every major paper and glossy magazine. It was a strip of six logos, five of which were famous musicals with instantly recognisable images: 'Miss Saigon' with its scribble of chopper-blades against the rising sun, 'Cats' with its black blur of a dancer in each cat's eye, 'Phantom of The Opera' with an upturned ghostly mask against a blood red rose, 'Five Guys Named Moe' with a jazzman's horn held high, 'Les Misérables' with the hungry face of a downtrodden girl peering at you from the poster. Then came ours, the sixth in this police line-up and surely the dodgy one who did it: our grinning sperm whale, leaping for life through a loop of school tie.

The seven-piece pit band rehearsed together for the first time. Now I had a live percussionist called Matthew, best in the business, to replace the shakers and tambourines from my HR16 drum machine back in the garage. So huge were his timpani, builders were expanding the Piccadilly pit to accommodate him.

"Look, I understand that we have to have live percussion," Cameron had grumbled at me, "but do we have to have kettle drums?"

"I'm afraid so."

"Why?"

"Because it'll sound better."

"Well I can't argue with that," he agreed.

We had a real drummer behind a real kit. We had a slick guitarist and two keyboards armed to the gunnels with dangerous musical samples. And with the magisterial Martin Koch leading the line, everything I heard coming back at me was a glorious extension of my home studio demos. Long hours of clicking away at a mouse in step edit mode, doggedly following the music in my inner ear, came back at me now in sparkling Technicolor, as I goose-pimpled up against the back wall.

A Sunday Times magazine special, to fanfare the arrival of Moby in the West End, March 8th 1992. © Times Newspapers Limited

Then we were in Abbey Road; who'd've thought it? I've got that album emblazoned through me like the lettering in a stick of rock. What's more, at the end of a hard day's night, I was crashing out at the house next door, owned by the studio. It was where they'd all stayed, apparently. John, George, Paul, Ringo, Andrew.

John Craig, the head of First Night Records (who were putting this out) was there on that first morning, sat smoking one of his revolting little cigars. I wished he'd put that out instead. Also present and correct was Maurice Day, fixer to the musicians of theatreland.

The band began with 'Parents Day', Robert's replacement for the opening scene. He hadn't bothered mentioning the fact that he was replacing the first scene, let alone with a number of his own, he just went ahead and did it, then bypassed me and took it straight to Martin Koch to arrange. Now it was in, it was an undeniable fact. I was livid of course, but I had to lock the feeling up, keep it all within. Negative vibes were the last thing anyone wanted.

Once we were beetle-browed over the Abbey Road mixing desk, Robert arbitrarily decided he wanted to record every inch of the show, instead of just the numbers. This meant a significant extension to both budget and schedule. Where was Cameron to run it by? Beyond contact, away looking at whales in Antarctica – a deeper level of immersion in the subject than most on the planet would surely contemplate, or be able to afford.

There being no one stronger-willed around to stop Robert, fiddly bits of underscore began to eat up time as the musicians in the booth rubbed their hands and phoned their stockbrokers. A three-day session expanded into a full-blown album scenario. This might have been okay if the show was already a hit. It wasn't. We had a show as yet unexposed to critical gaze, a show that had only travelled this far already thanks to the patronage and approval of our absent benefactor.

We were half way through a new bit of underscore I had never heard before, when Cameron burst into the control room, Nick Allot in tow. Both were fiercely tanned. Cameron listened for a moment and then, unable to recognise anything, turned and hissed in my ear: "what's this music?"

"Underscore for a new scene."

"What new scene? Why haven't I heard it?"

I attempted to defuse the bomb. "How was Antarctica?"

"Stunning."

"Did you see any whales?"

"Lots. Why haven't I heard this music before?"

"It's a new bit."

"This has got to stop, now. You're not recording another note till I know what's going on. Robert!"

And so the band was sent home and a lengthy confab ensued as to what kind of record we were supposed to be making. Cameron got his way of course and the day ended with us going through the script ruthlessly, paring down the links from one song to the next, until they were just a couple of lines here and there, a mere word even, if it would suffice.

The year was almost done. CML had their office party, an annual bunfight with the staff of DeWynter's. The two companies had gone from strength to strength on the back of this huge resurgence of interest in musical theatre, for which they themselves had been largely responsible. As both organisations grew, so the festive battle had escalated. I imagine it once started with a food fight. Over the years it had developed into all-out war. This year they'd put a marquee up on Regent's Park, nice and close to the lake, so they could refill their homemade water guns instead of using up all the champagne, like they did the year before. Everyone wore clothes you could hose down.

Before the fight was due to begin, both parties sat down to Christmas dinner, with Cameron sitting in his throne at one end of the table and Robert DeWynter sitting in his throne at the other. They didn't know it but this year, both thrones had been wired to explode. Cameron was Santa, of course. He'd customised the traditional uniform somewhat, introducing thigh high scarlet boots and a whip. No doubt the presents he dispensed to his team were sensational – he was in the habit of sending them off on safari as a surprise, if he thought they deserved or needed it.

I was in the studio that day with Martin Levan, cracking on. No Robert. He was at the party, primed to explode from a cake in full drag, with a set of fairy lights up his arse probably. But he turned up in the middle of the afternoon, when he should have been at the party, looking extremely disgruntled.

"What happened?"

"I waited and waited in the dark, in my fucking silly costume, waiting for them to come and get me. I could hear the party going on. I must have waited an hour. I've got better things to do. I'm not going to be made a fool of."

Robert went home for Christmas. Martin Levan and I got our heads back down over the faders. An hour or so later, a half-cut Cameron turned up. The child in him had taken over.

"What happened to Robert?" asked this little boy lost trailing a teddybear. "He was meant to be at the party and then he wasn"t. What are you doing?"

"Overdubs."

"What overdubs?" He sobered up in a nanosecond. "Play me it."

Martin pressed play. It was 'Building America'. Cameron came alive.

"This reminds me of the old Gang Shows. You know what we should do? You'll like this…" He chuckled at the scale of his new idea. "We should arrange to have hundreds of Boy Scouts marching past Bill Clinton singing 'Building America', at the Inauguration!" Sounded bloody good to me and I wouldn't have put it past him.

Before he left Cameron took a phone call and came off the line laughing. "Robert Maxwell's estate. Do I want to buy his yacht for nineteen million?" The infamous owner of the *Daily Mirror*, had recently plummeted overboard. "I said no."

Then Robert Mackintosh's private secretary arrived with my Christmas shopping. I hadn't had time to do it myself and she'd offered.

"I went to Debenhams on Oxford Street in the end" she gushed, flushed with success, setting my shopping down. "I got Pat a camera – it is Pat, isn't it?"

"Yes, Pat."

"I hope she likes it."

"I'm sure she will."

"Do you really think so?"

I'd never had someone else do my Christmas shopping before – but it had been that kind of year, and a bloody long one at that. It was time to go home and see if anyone still loved me.

Chapter 18
Carve up at L'Escargot

Before we had even begun rehearsals for the West End production of Moby Dick, *The Observer* predicted the show would be the first flop of the year and the biggest of Cameron's career. In the *Daily Mail*, Douglas Slater assured us Cameron was 'reviving Moby Dick, which he first put on in the Seventies to distinctly muted acclaim'.

A revival from the Seventies? This time last year Cameron hadn't even heard of our show and we certainly hadn't written it back in the '70s. I rang Baz Bamigboye, the *Mail's* showbiz editor, to complain. "For that to be true" I told him, "Robert and I would have to be a couple of failed tossers turning fifty. And we're not. We're a couple of failed tossers turning forty."

Agent Mark called me in to update me on the financial side of things. I needed reassurance. The cheque for £700 he owed me from Oxford had not arrived.

"You will receive only two and a half percent of the box office instead of three and a half, until Cameron has recouped all his costs. Then it goes up to the proper rate, plus the extra one percent you are owed, backdated. All minus my ten percent, of course."

"I'm sure. So, two and a half percent of the Piccadilly box office. How much is that?"

"Depends how full it is."

"If it's full, how much will the cheque be on my doormat once a week?"

"Minus my ten percent and Cameron's one per cent until he breaks even?"

"Yeah."

"Just a moment dear." Mark gets out his calculator and punches a few buttons. Then he looks up.

"Three thousand, nine hundred and thirty seven pounds, fifty pence."

"Four grand?"

"Almost."

"Every week?"

"And that's not counting merchandise…"

"How much of that do I get?"

"Five percent. I've told you all this before."

"Yeah, but it wasn't real then."

"Then there's album sales, coffee table book rights… you'll be able to take me out for dinner, dear."

"Four grand a week!" I tried to calm myself.

"And don't forget that'll go up by another one percent."

"But only if it's full."

"It'll be full, don't worry. The show has already taken one and a half million in advances."

He had to be either joking or lying.

When I got home, Pat grabbed me at the door. "Have you got the cheque?"

"Sorry Pat," I said, sagging under her incredulous gaze.

"How could you?"

"I was so freaked out by what he told me, I forgot to ask him about the seven hundred pounds!"

"What did he tell you?"

"Well, how rich we're both going to be."

She rolled her eyes.

"It's the first day of rehearsal on Monday darling," I said. I'll ask him then."

Pat sighed the sigh and turned away.

* * *

18. Carve up at L'Escargot

We gathered at Soho Laundry at 10 a.m. for croissants and coffee, with all gangsters present. New members of the cast sat in nervous isolation as old Oxfordians swapped anecdotes and flexed their hierarchical 'pecs. Robert made a nervous welcoming speech. He hadn't slept. People kept asking me if I'd slept. I felt guilty that I had; no one else seemed to have done. Designer Paul Farnsworth talked us through the show, using a little model of the set to demonstrate. His assistant deftly inserted pieces of cardboard at strategic moments, like swords in a Lady-in-a-Box routine.

Cameron gave a short speech. "I hadn't intended producing another show" he told the company, "it's just that Robert and Hereward have created something so magical that has the strongest urgency on an audience since 'Godspell'…"

I gulped. Robert flushed, serenely.

"It's the complete opposite of all those big boring musicals that some producer keeps bringing into town, what's his name…"

Cameron grinned. We all laughed indulgently.

"So long as you can all say 'Stuff Art, Let's Dance'," declaimed the great producer, "then it will happen. And if the audience don't like it… fuck 'em!"

He surveyed the sea of beaming, upturned faces and resumed his seat to rousing applause. I alone looked like I was sucking on lemons. This was because the front page of every script on every lap read: *Music – Hereward Kaye and Robert Longden. Lyrics – Robert Longden. Arrangements & Musical Direction – Martin Koch.*

Robert had grabbed the billing for his bits of music, how come I wasn't credited for my bits of lyrics – the few bits that were left? The words to the last number, 'Save The Whale', were mine alone. The chorus to 'Whale Of A Tale' was mine – and the title of that song even provided half the show's title! Agent Mark was supposed to have sorted this out, but being Robert's agent too (and half of the rest of the cast's), he was dealing with a massive conflict of interests. Furthermore, the arrangements entirely credited to Martin Koch were half mine. If this show was to go around the world with the wrong billing, I'd be harbouring a sense of injustice every time I spent my filthy lucre. I wanted to be rich and happy, not rich and resentful. As the cast settled down to film-footage of whaling, I went to phone my agent.

The following day, conveniently close to lunch, Nick Allott, a regular geezer, slid on to the bench alongside me.

"How are they singing?" he whispered, after a dutiful pause.

I gave him the thumbs. He returned his gaze to the singers.

The company broke and Nick, Martin and I chit-chatted as Nick scuffed the floor thoughtfully with his Gucci loafer.

"Um, chaps, have you discussed between you the billing for the arrangements?"

"No we've never discussed it." We laughed in unison.

"At the moment it simply says: 'Arrangements and Musical Direction, Martin Koch' but we should sort it out," warned Nick, "it's getting pretty close to the wire."

Silence.

"I think it would be fairest," said I evenly, "if it read: 'Arrangements by Martin Koch and Hereward Kaye' in that order, Musical Direction, of course, Martin Koch."

"That's fine by me," said Martin, amiably, "put it however you like."

"How's the Piccadilly coming along?" I asked Nick, changing the subject.

"Have you not seen it? It's the most expensive front of house we've ever done."

So I strolled across central London to take a look. At Oxford Circus I stood open mouthed as London buses trundled by. 'Coming Soon, Moby Dick!' they proclaimed, giant replicas of the little model double-decker bus in Cameron's office. And every other London bus that came along seemed to have our school tie logo on the front and 'Stuff Art Let's Dance!' emblazoned along the side.

As I turned the corner to the theatre, a huge red and yellow school tie hove into view, all lit up. Chase lights glamorised the title, the theatre, and the legend: 'Moby Dick Is Coming!' Life-size pictures of the girls of St Godley's suspended all the way round. A giant Splash, frozen in time, topped-off the building.

Inside, workmen clambered all over the auditorium and welders, like giant flies in their masks, buzzed in the eerie half-light of their own sparks. A sea of blue paint had transformed this corner of Central London into our very own theme park.

Cameron found me outside, scrutinising my name in tiny gold lettering, tucked away in a doorway.

"I thought our names were going to be big and in lights."

"When I've quadrupled my investment you can have your name in lights," he said. "And what about the billing? Are you happy now?"

So my agent did make phone calls.

Cameron said: "I've never seen a more complicated billing in all my life: *Music – Hereward Kaye and Robert Longden. Additional Lyrics – Hereward Kaye. Musical Arrangements Martin Koch & Hereward Kaye.*"

18. Carve up at L'Escargot

"It's fine."

"It's what you wanted."

"It's the truth."

"Hmm," he said.

We set off for the Soho Laundry.

"How are the advances?" I ventured.

"Awful, pathetic, sixty thousand, we'll last about a week. But I don't want to hype it. I don't want to put the girls in *The Sun* or the *Mirror*. This one's got to be a best-kept secret. So long as we get the first fifteen minutes absolutely right, the critics and the public will discover it for themselves and it will be a cult."

* * *

I was late arriving at The Prince Edward theatre for the 'Sitzprobe' – a mysterious title given to the joyous occasion when band and cast come together for the first time. There they all were, brilliantly arrayed, band and company united, on a day trip out to another theatre, one of Cameron's own. It was closed to the public, being in the process of a million pound refurb.

The cast were necklaced around the band on six mikes, belting it out, shrieking with the joy of it. All the rest of us were up there on stage with them too: Lights, Sound, Creatives, Stage Management, CML top brass. Cameron was in my face the moment I arrived, change this, change that while Robert sat like a bad tempered tent in toytown, son Blair under his overcoat.

Cameron stood up at the end and said: "Hereward and Martin and Robert have created one of the most brilliant scores I have ever heard in 40 years involvement with the theatre."

Whilst I heard the cheering of shipyard men and saw the bottle of champagne breaking over the bows of the good ship 'Moby' as she slid serenely into the waters, Robert heard only his name mentioned last and Nagasaki went off in his breast. He slipped grimly out through a side door and didn't re-appear that day. But there was a phone call for me later, from Mark.

"Robert's been in Cameron's office all afternoon, in tears," he said darkly. "He says you're claiming the credit for all his work."

"That's bloody ridiculous! If anything, it's the other way round."

Silence.

"What's his problem?"

"He's under a lot of pressure. And he had to look after Blair, so he felt a bit trapped while you stole his thunder."

"I fucking didn't!"

"You know what Robert's like. If you could just apologise, everything would be okay again. He's very sensitive."

You could almost hear his eyes rolling heavenwards as he added: "Someone should write a book on this bloody show."

* * *

I watched the run from the dress circle. It should have been the first preview, but Cameron had cancelled the audience. I could see why. Something had gone badly astray in the move from rehearsal room to theatre. The final run at the Soho Laundry had been anarchic and fun, a law unto itself, a winner, and it wasn't just me who thought so. The 'Wogan' team; the people videoing the run for rehearsal purposes, the production company privately commissioned to film four one-minute 'bites' from each act to sell on to the TV companies, the creative team and assorted gangsters; all left that room with adrenaline pumping. The film director next to me wrung my hand at the end and said it would be huge.

Without props and a set, it had looked so right. After all, this was about a skint St Trinian's-style school, staging a production of Moby Dick with absolutely no resources save a hotbed of teenage hormones and a do-or-die attitude to make it succeed. It was a paean to the power of the committed amateur. But when we switched to a fabulously kitted out West End theatre, with its newly-installed hundred thousand pound set and state of the art sound and lighting systems, it became apparent that our homespun show harnessed to the glossy look that propelled Les Misérables around the world, made for uneasy bedmates – like Quequeg and Ishmael.

Robert was an explosive presence in the centre of the stalls, stretched like a giant tortoise over his table, casting a shadow like a plane over a control tower of telephones, plots and stage plans. I made the mistake of whispering an idea to him once, in the middle of a run. Like a child startled from sleep who finds himself spinning in the middle of his room shouting at shadows, Robert grabbed his microphone and, corkscrewing his head to take in all interested parties draping the Royal Circle, the Grand Circle, the Stalls, the cast on stage – everyone but me next to him in fact – stopped the show dead with one great bellow:

"NO ONE TALKS TO ME! DON'T ANYONE TALK TO ME WHEN WE'RE RUNNING!"

There are few feelings worse than public humiliation. I clattered my way along the row of seats and shot up to the Royal Circle. There I stayed, a four-pack at my feet for the rest of the runs. Now here we were at first preview night with the audience cancelled and a dark foreboding overhanging all. At the end of another unsatisfactory run I found myself next to Cameron in the gents.

"I enjoyed you on Radio 4 this morning," I said politely, staring at the wall.

"Well it was a damn sight more entertaining than this evening," he growled. "Are you coming to L'Escargot?"

My agent had already informed me there was to be an emergency meeting at L'Escargot to which I was not invited.

"I'd love to" I said, making my excuses, "but I'm already booked. In fact they're waiting for me now."

On my way out of the theatre, Cameron and Howard Harrison intercepted me.

"We really think you ought to come," said Howard.

"Okay" I agreed immediately. "I'll just go and tell my friends I won't be joining them." I dashed over the road into the bar and bolted down a glug on Jonty's Guinness.

"Can't stay, guys. Cameron's holding a carve up at L'Escargot."

"How exciting!" beamed girlfriend Nicky.

In a private room, over delicious food and fine wines, he wielded the theatrical butcher's knife like a mighty surgeon.

SLIT!

"The directing of this show is completely amateur. It makes less sense than it ever did. Half the time you've got an empty stage and someone tucked away on the balcony delivering a vital piece of information where you can't see them. The whole of Act One needs re-blocking."

SLICE!

"You keep throwing props at it, hoping it will make it better. You can tell if a show's in trouble by the length of the props list, and I've never seen a props list like it. And the rewrites! You've got Earl Tobias crawling all over the first half like a second-class drag act. Quite honestly, I'm ashamed to have my name outside the theatre."

In the dining chair next to him, the sweat was dripping from Robert's greasy, queasy countenance and plipping into his celery soup. This was the face of a desperately tired man, crushed by pressure. I felt for him in this moment. Despite everything, I saw a friend in trouble and resolved to leap to his defence at the first opportunity.

"The leading lady is a disaster," glowered Cameron. "She doesn't appear to want to sing. Can she sing, has anybody heard her?"

"She's got a throat infection," mumbled Robert.

"And Jacqui's personality doesn't cross the footlights."

"I think that's terribly unfair," said Mark coolly.

"Another of your fucking clients, I suppose?" glared Cameron. She was, too. Mark had snapped up most of the cast – and me! – on the assumption the show would be a success.

"I want to cut the Spouter Inn scene. What's the new number you've put in there?"

"'Tiger Under Table'" I said proudly.

"Well it doesn't work. That bit never worked. It didn't work as 'Clamfish' in Oxford and it doesn't make any more sense now. Has anybody else got anything to say?"

Silent waters lapped portentously.

"This is the show you saw in Oxford," I proclaimed. "This is the show you loved and bought. You must have known what it was like before you decided to bring it in. It wasn't like your other musicals, you said. You loved it for its amateurism!"

The four pack, the slug of Guinness and the second glass of chilled Sancerre combined headily with the moment. I felt like I was on the eve of Agincourt.

"I think that's a rather emotional point of view," cautioned an avuncular Nick Allot, though atwitter with amusement.

"You got the show you wanted," I crowed at Cameron. "If you don't like it, you shouldn't have bought the fucker!"

I had come down recklessly on Robert's side. I could've just as easily come down against him, but what the hell, loyalty under fire and all that. My agent looked faintly appalled. Robert stared at his soup. Had he located a fly?

18. Carve up at L'Escargot

Cameron glared.

"Hereward, you're wrong," he said, finally. "You're just wrong. Anyway, (*SLICE!*) I've decided to cancel the next four previews and start again."

After being forced to fall upon his fish knife, the ordeal was still not over for Robert. The following day he endured a humiliating meeting with the cast, as a supportive Cameron at his side explained in humorous terms to the company why Robert was herewith banished to the Circle (which was where I had been sitting in self-imposed exile ever since Robert roared at me. Now I'd have to move one circle further up!) and why choreographer Anthony Lapsley was taking over the blocking of Act One.

A gift from DeWynters to the creative team behind Moby Dick, with their heads superimposed onto the bodies of the cast. Cameron Mackintosh (second from left); Robert Longden (third from right) with Hereward directly below.

* * *

Dinner ladies, office girls, car park attendants and unhinged loners seemed to make up most of the 'Wogan' queue that snaked into the TV studio. As I hadn't received an invitation I had to queue too, along with the rest of my family. Sister Ros was wearing a mangy fur coat, which rendered Pat taut as piano wire for the rest of the evening, so we had that in common. As we settled into our seats, the great performing Irishman himself sauntered out, lobbing desultory peanuts to ironic cheers. Then it was 'for real' and he instantly switched into the genial Irishman we all knew and loved.

Tony Monopoly (our Ahab) did an interview, followed by Robert and Cameron. In between, the band and company crashed through four of the songs. By the time we dashed home to watch it on telly, I was smiling widely, for Robert had earlier told Terry and the watching nation that he had "nine years working on it with Hereward Kaye, collaborator and co-composer, who wrote most of the music." I heaved a silent sigh and a week of tension fell away. I could be proud of Robert, and us.

The Wogan show was deemed a great success – well, this dinner lady I know – and the new date for opening night was settled upon.

As March 17th grew ever-closer, amidst all the buzz and anticipation I began to feel I had finally drawn level with the person I was in my EMI heyday. Back then it had been Head of A&R Brian Shepherd cast in the role of Nero, as I nervously waited for his thumb to swing up or down to decide my fate. It couldn't go that wrong again, surely? After all, who was it arriving this time to sit in judgement on opening night? Why, a highly discerning and fair-minded group of professionals from whom I felt sure I had nothing to fear.

The good old British press.

Chapter 19
Knobsworth

Preview number one was upon us. Cleaning, notes, cleaning, notes, all day long in the theatre. Before the evening's performance by way of a warm-up, the cast formed a clapping circle and took it in turns to leap into the centre and rattle off a highly-dubious joke. Leigh jumped in: "Why do Greek men have moustaches? To look like their mothers!" Leigh danced out, Tony arrived: "D'you hear about the three gays assaulted a girl in Hyde Park? Two held her down, the other one did her hair."

The company went back to their dressing rooms to change. I sat in the upstairs bar where I sighted my first ever paying customer at a West End performance of Moby Dick. Another four customers followed. I started doing sums in my head. For all I knew, this might be as good as it got. One of them headed for the St Godleys gift shop, resplendent with fine merchandise. He picked up a mug. Wise choice, I thought. More people arrived to see what was on sale and the hubbub began to build up at the bar. Within five minutes people were shouting their orders over the heads of others and booking drinks for the interval.

It was strange to hear the bells for the first time and stranger still to have my comp. checked and to take my place in a filling Royal Circle, a Royal Circle I knew only too well. Soon, every seat around me was taken. Then the lights were dimming and the din of a steam train sliding to a halt shrieked through the air, followed by a prolonged and flatulent hiss. I groped for pen and paper in the dark and wrote 'first tape cue too loud' as the second tape cue crashed in even louder. It was Robert booming: "Knobsworth, all stations to Knobsworth!"

There was no doubt about it; our inaugural performance was underway.

After the show, as Robert and I hunched over my notes, the rest of the creative team bore down upon our table: choreographer Anthony Lapsley, MD Martin Koch, lighting designer Howard Harrison, sound designer Martin Levan, stage manager David Ffitch – each with copious notes of their own.

The Ship Hits the Fans

The following afternoon I was spread-eagled in the stalls with the rest of the cast. Robert was centre stage with all our pieces of paper in his fist.

"Mark, Mark White, are you listening?" Shields eyes. "Oh, hello, dear. Yes, Cameron seems to object to: 'I don't like to think of you girls going down'. He seems to feel it's too modern, not music hall enough. Have you any ideas?"

"How about," offers Mark from the stalls, "It's more than my Knobsworth?"

After the notes, a vocal warm-up. Then another high energy clapping circle. That night, our second preview, we were sold out again. I watched a tighter first half before getting into a chinwag in the bar next door with Baz Bamigboye of the *Daily Mail*, missing much of the second half. He'd already seen the show three times. He'd been following it since Oxford.

"What do you think of it Baz then, really?"

He swirled his Guinness thoughtfully, then looked up.

"I don't like it."

"Why?"

"It has no classic love interest. Look at the great Musicals" – he reeled them off impressively – "they all have a great love story. I'm not saying they have to. But I don't know a good one that hasn't. I like that song, though, 'A Man Happens', it's a hit. Who wrote the music, you or Robert…?"

"Fucking me!"

I sneaked back in, insinuating myself onto the back rail behind the sound desk, where Cameron's investors gripped it like a safety bar on a particularly horrid white-knuckle ride. I adjusted my eyes to the swirling heaven of lilac and golden light playing on dry ice. Statuesque sirens in swimming costumes stepped through its whispering folds towards me, thrilling me with familiar melody. Then Cameron descended and the intensity of his observations forced me up against the back wall, discreetly dabbing away spittle.

On March 9th we had a Media Night. Sixty per cent of the audience was 'papered' (i.e. free), all of them radio and TV. It was an off-the-record night, to get a media buzz going.

Filing out from my usual seat in the Royal Circle, I overheard Gloria Hunniford declare it sexist. I was right behind TV A.M's work-out fiend 'the Green Goddess', Lizzie Webb, as she agreed. She branded the opening number 'Parents Day' one of the most offensive things she had ever seen. Pat and I had been apprehensive enough before

Daily Telegraph feature, in the run-up to opening night.
© Telegraph Media Group Limited

the show that many women wouldn't like it and this reaffirmed our fears. Acres of suspenders were distinctly out of step with the times. In the classic old St Trinian's films, the girls were dumpy, lanky, spotty, anorexic – there was the odd glamour puss and what power they wielded, but not every bloody one of them! Robert was adamant however: the sex stayed.

And so the previews went on. Songs were taken out, songs were put back in. Scenes were reblocked, scenes were re-written. A blizzard of notes rained down like ticker tape, upon a cast desperate to please, hoofing to hell on a wing and a prayer. After a while I couldn't tell what was bad or good anymore and I don't think anyone else could either. I decided to give the show a miss for a couple of nights.

On Saturday, March 14th, there was a feature on me in the weekend section of the *Daily Telegraph*. The interview had taken place in my conservatory and there were photos where I was surrounded by horses or draped in dogs. I can't lie, it put a spring in my step as I headed back down to London for a double preview day.

Cameron intercepted me the moment I entered the foyer, five minutes before the matinee began. "We had a fabulous show last night. You weren't there. We've done lots of work and sorted things out. I think you'll be very happy with what we've done."

The bells were ringing. Peter Roper, company manager came up. "Your sister's waiting for you at the stage door." An usherette stopped me. "Here's a couple of tickets for this afternoon's performance."

Entering the auditorium, Trevor from Lincolnshire days waved and grinned from three rows back. Mike, a radical left-wing friend who writes Mills and Boons novels under a female name, gave me thumbs aloft from the front row. The house lights dimmed. "Knobsworth, all stations to Knobsworth!" came Robert's booming voice.

The show had indeed altered. Tony didn't play Ahab now, he played headmistress Dorothy Hyman all the way through. It was like watching the exquisitely tasteless

'Springtime For Hitler' routine from Mel Brooks's tale of musical theatre disaster 'The Producers'. Captain Ahab with a compact… God knows what the critics would make of it.

And then, Lord help us, Judgement Day was upon us. I went in early, gift-wrapping my first night presents on the train. I'd gone for school victory shields, all inscribed. For Cameron, I'd moved slightly upmarket, buying a little gilt hockey player on an inscribed plinth.

Robert and I came together for a London Weekend TV interview in the stalls, then retired to the Grand Circle to pen messages of good luck to cast and crew. Cards and gifts were passing in the opposite direction too, from them to us. They built up at the stage door – a knitted sailor with my initials on his swagbag, a blackboard clock, posh champagne. There was a giant portrait with my face superimposed onto a schoolgirl's body from DeWynters and a towel with logo and date sewn into it from Cameron, accompanied by a specially commissioned print of a whale.

Feeling quite unreal, I set out for Covent Garden to buy a crisp white shirt and a smart pair of shoes. I was in suspended animation as family and friends turned up agog with excitement. I was dazed and removed as we took our seats in the auditorium.

The house lights dimmed. Clive Anderson shuffled uncomfortably in the seat before me. Pat gave my wrist an encouraging squeeze.

This was it then.

"Knobsworth, all stations to Knobsworth!"

Up came the stage lights, up struck the band. Moby Dick, the all-singing, all-dancing Cameron Mackintosh extravaganza passed silent and flickering before my eyes, like a black and white newsreel.

As we shuffled out at the end, I found myself alongside Cameron's mother. Normally effusive, this time Diana said nothing. I cast an eye back at the almost emptied auditorium. Shirley Bassey was the last one left in her seat, surrounded by cameramen now, riddling her in flashlight as she went through a succession of poses.

Outside, old fashioned double-deckers awaited with 'St Godleys' on the destination board, to take us to the Mystery Ball. Everybody who boarded was clutching their party invitation, a stiff gatefold affair, with the grinning white sperm whale leaping out of a school blazer pocket, with the motto 'Stuff Art Let's Dance' emblazoned across the badge. Opening it, Cameron Mackintosh invited you to the St Godley's Parents Day Annual Ball after the West End Premiere of Moby Dick, at the St Godley's Academy for Young Ladies. Dress: Splashy! Carriages: 2 a.m. £20 notes of monopoly money

19. Knobsworth

Front cover of the glossy Piccadilly theatre programme. Designed and printed by DeWynters PLC London.

fell out, each bearing Tony Monopoly's face instead of the Queen's. It could be spent at the St. Godley's casino from 12:15 a.m., straight after the midnight synchronised swimming display by the British Olympic Synchronised Swimming Team. That was the clue. The location for our Mystery Ball would be Seymour Street Swimming Baths.

Pat and I sat on a trestle table by the door, swinging our legs like kids, sucking champagne from school milk bottles through a straw. People funnelled through, not knowing who we were or how much this show could possibly mean to us both, intent only on hitting the food menu, which boasted Miss Hyman's sugar-glazed, overwrought hams, Captain Ahab's fish from the deep, not to mention the spotted Dick and custard, courtesy of the domestic science department. Pat and I didn't eat, we couldn't, we were more overwrought than Miss Hyman's hams. Anyway, it interfered with the school milk.

The Sunday Times described our celebrations thus, in their 'Style File' section:

> 'The party, which continued the naughty schoolgirl theme from the show, was a sullied extravaganza that resembled a bizarre cross between School Dinners, the London restaurant where waitresses wear gymslips, and a convention of gender benders. As guests trooped into the vast Seymour Leisure Centre near Marble Arch, they were greeted with Mumm Cordon Rouge served in school milk bottles with straws. Meanwhile huge banners proclaimed 'Stuff Art Let's Dance', and, charmingly, by the swimming pool, 'This is not a urinal'. Mini-skirts, school ties, fishnet tights and mortar boards were out in force, a band thundered out James Brown's 'Sex Machine', and there were hordes of beautiful young men, all saying 'I'm a friend of Cameron's.
>
> Mackintosh himself wandered about in short trousers, obviously feeling like the school swot, and donned his schoolboy cap for photographs. "I seem to do something that the public likes, for the moment at least", he volunteered, "and if my lucky streak runs out, I shall just be philosophical".

Susan George and Simon McCorkindale weren't philosophical, just tactful. "I have to say, Moby Dick wasn't really us," said McCorkindale. "We prefer something with more of a story, not just a loosely connected collection of songs and dancing."

Shirley Bassey, gushing and shimmering in a black tassel minidress, added: "I don't like musicals… period. They're theatre and I'm too much a part of that to really enjoy them, but this one had some songs I'd like to get my hands on."

Still, the lukewarm reception didn't appear to poop the party. The Mumm flowed – all had jettisoned their milk bottles in favour of glasses – as everyone breathed in the warm, chlorinated air and watched a display of synchronised swimming. As legs with their perfectly pointed toes thrust out of the water and the heads eventually surfaced, the File ruminated that 'their chlorine-bathed bodies were perhaps the only truly clean part of the evening'. *Sunday Times, 22nd March 1992*

Baz Bamigboye came by and I asked him if he had talked to any of the critics.

"Jack Tinker's given it quite a good review for the *Mail*," he said hopefully and lapsed into silence.

"And?"

"*Express* hated it, *Telegraph* didn't like it. *The Times*…"

"It's alright, I get the picture."

"*The Times* gave it a good one actually, but then they give everyone a good one."

At the stroke of midnight the national synchronised swimming team went through their grin and bare it routine for the drunken guests around the pool. Shirley Bassey danced with Robert's Dad. He was lucky to catch her vertical; by the time it was 'Carriages', she was passed out under a table. I talked for a long time with one of my heroes, Peter Cook. He was pissed and I was pissed so, tragically, much of it is hard to remember. But I do recall him saying his wife was a Moby 'angel' – an investor in the show.

Meanwhile, Pat was at the roulette wheel, gambling away the St Godley's banknotes that had been tucked away inside our invitations. She was gambling against Cameron and she was on a roll, ironically.

You had to be happy for her. As I ended the night hammering away at the piano casting sickly glances in their direction, it was beginning to look like Pat's pretend winnings were the only bit of Moby money she was ever going to get to spend.

Chapter 20
Waiving and drowning

Radio Cleveland, my hometown station, awoke me. "Hereward Kaye?"

My bruised brain broiled in the casserole of my cranium as I struggled to recognise whether that was actually my name or not. This had happened to me a few weeks before when my face had appeared at the top right corner of *The Sunday Times*, right next to the title. On a killer hangover I had racked my brains, thinking: I know that face, I really really know that face. Maybe the pressure was getting to me.

"Yes," I decided. "It is." I tried my name out to see if my rubberised lips still worked. "Hereward Kaye."

"If you don't mind, we're going to put you straight on air."

"Hang on now…"

But she'd gone. The sound of a live radio programme came filtering through.

"…Listeners will be aware the latest Cameron Mackintosh Musical opened last night in London's West End. We have on the line the Show's composer, who hails from Middlesbrough. Welcome, Hereward Kaye, have you had a chance to read any of the reviews?"

I croaked: "I've just got back from the first night party."

"Well let me just give you a rough idea!" bantered the dementedly cheerful jock: "'Schoolgirls Lost In A Sea of High Camp!' says one. 'Whale of a yarn drowns in an ocean of pointless mediocrity' says another."

"Who? Who said that?"

"*The Times*, I'm afraid. 'All At Sea With Males And Whales!' says Nicholas De Jongh, and what about this from Michael Billington: 'As people leapt to their feet all around me to applaud this garbage'…?" He waited for as many seconds of radio silence as he could bear. "And how about this! 'I don't want to be a Jonah, but I don't see what can save this whale. Perhaps the show's very awfulness could give it a cult status but I…'"

"As I say, I haven't yet seen the reviews."

A few moments further inquisition, a genial on-air goodbye and I was off the hook. I hung up and groaned, stole a glance at the clock. Good grief, it was afternoon! CML and DeWynters had booked a private room in Soho for a mass debrief over lunch. I was running seriously late.

Hammering into the station I grabbed a *Daily Express* off the newsstand and ran for the train. Squeezing into a seat, with morbid curiosity I opened the paper and there it was, on page three: 'SINKING FEELING FOR MOBY DICK'. They'd given the entire page over to the subject. I dragged shaking hand across tortured brow and read on.

> 'Let us fervently hope that the tourists who make their pilgrimage to the theatrical capital of the world understand the peculiar English obsession with gymslips. For their eyes and ears are about to be assaulted by the most extraordinary show in the West End. Herman Melville's epic novel has been vandalised by screaming harpies straight out of St Trinian's. This is the quaint story of how a group of disreputable schoolgirls, some of them played by boys in drag, stage Moby Dick in an empty swimming pool. I have it on good authority that this is a comedy.
>
> With over forty musicals in production round the globe, the philanthropic impresario Cameron Mackintosh can afford to take a risk. And this, chaps and chapesses, is it. Written by two unknowns, this no-star show is a camp and garish folly.
>
> …it begins with a chorus of lusty thighed maidens in mini skirts, stockings and suspenders. It ends with men in jockstraps and a boy dressed as a pregnant schoolgirl giving birth to a seal. It has the deliberately amateurish atmosphere of a shambolic end of term concert. Ex monk and Opportunity Knocks veteran Tony Monopoly is the bizarre choice for the lead role of the Headmistress who plays the one-legged Captain Ahab. Too adult for the children and too childish for the adults, it will be a miracle if Moby stays afloat'. *Daily Express, March 18th 1992*

Upstairs at the restaurant, key staff were gathered for the feast, about 30 of them populating long tables running either side of the room. The two Roberts – DeWinter and Longden – were either side of Cameron at the head of the top table, backs to the window and three sheets to the wind already. Nick Allott was on the top table too and beside him awaited my empty chair.

20. Waiving and drowning

"Hereward!" cried Cameron, a stage drunk as I entered twitchingly sober. "Have some wine!"

Jollity was the tone for the day. Wine waiters appeared and disappeared fuelling our attitude, till we could all see the world through a curved glass and call it straight.

"Whatever else goes," Robert averred, "the sex stays."

"The sex stays!" toasted Cameron, to my dismay. Unfortunately, what constituted sex to Robert and Cameron, was sexism according to the critics of our show. I felt as if I was trapped in a Brian Rix Whitehall farce, guiltily groping for my trousers.

One of the marketing team circulated a list of quotes from the reviews. I didn't really want to see them, being depressed enough already, and once I'd seen them I wished I hadn't. Drawn from ten or more different newspapers, they universally panned the show. Then Cameron breezily informed us that the show in question was not Moby Dick at all, but Les Misérables, now into its seventh year and playing in large theatres the length and breadth of Europe.

"The Sound Of Music" trumpeted Cameron, "received some of the worst reviews in history back in 1961."

It was encouraging. It was reassuring. It… didn't quite wash. If any of the other reviews were as scathing as the *Daily Express*, we were shipping water.

Whilst we on the top table were drinking but not eating, I couldn't help noticing that the employees on the other tables were eating, not drinking. They had jobs to protect. They were nine to five, something I've never quite managed. They were looking towards management for a lead, a management that were now hurling bread buns at one another in a wanton display of backs-to-the-window defiance, beyond which lay a world of spiteful newsprint and rejection that could scupper all their best laid plans.

"We enjoy ourselves as much as we like," said a red-faced Cameron with all his usual purpose, "but tonight, we ALL go to the show and ALL show our support for the cast. That's one thing I do insist upon."

We nodded our sombre agreement and under grey London skies wended our way towards the Piccadilly. There we made a morale-boosting tour of the troops in their dressing rooms, then yelled and hollered our way through Act One at every opportunity, though we never quite made it back from the pub for Act Two. Cameron and Nick Allott now sat morosely hunched over pints and I sensed the hangover from a disastrous first night had begun to take hold. But tomorrow I had no doubt, the fightback would begin. Seeing them in confidential communion as the second half played in the theatre next door, I suspected the seeds of recovery were now being sown.

Further reviews came out over the course of the week, not just in print, but on the radio too. I was actually in the dentist's chair with a large portion of Mr Miller's fist down my throat, when a forum of trendy young things on Radio One started attacking Moby Dick. "You can put all the girls you like in suspenders, it doesn't make for a good show," commented one hyperactive female voice. "Yah," agreed another,

"I mean, girls in suspenders, perlease!"

"Is this your show they're talking about?" murmured Miller.

"Yaargh!" I rolled my eyeballs.

"Rinse please."

I spat blood, with venom.

Walking home, I almost crossed over to the other side when the newsagent's hove into view, but then I went in and bought the lot. It was masochism on a grand scale. I didn't make it two steps further along the road before I felt compelled to leaf through the pages of the *Daily Mail*.

'As the West End's latest musical meets a chorus of disapproval' ran the byline above the headline – 'CAN CAMERON MANAGE TO SAVE THE WHALE?'

The article took up the whole of page seven. God almighty. It was only meant to be a bit of fun.

'Garbage!' cried the *Guardian's* Michael Billington, launching the following harpoon from the full might of his shoulder: 'Lacking logic, style, coherence or sense, it turns Melville's great Dostoevskian novel into a campy, vulgar, schoolgirl spoof'.

'Can't make up its mind whether it's a eulogy to gay culture, a girly show or a big West End musical' stated *Time Out*, concluding, rather crushingly, 'If oomph and pizzazz were everything this would be it – but it's not'.

'Like being sucked into somebody's very silly, very private joke' proclaimed Benedict Nightingale of *The Times*.

'An unholy, deafening mess' decreed *The Independent*.

'Hard to imagine this damp squib of a show exploding triumphantly around the world' said Charles Spencer in the *Daily Telegraph*, under a headline: 'SHAMBLES ON DECK', adding: 'Cameron Mackintosh admits he lives in constant expectation of waking up one morning and discovering that his taste has gone out of fashion. With the arrival of the £1.2 million Moby Dick at The Piccadilly Theatre, that dread day might just have arrived'.

After a critical mauling, carefully extracted quotes from first night reviews, appearing on a flyer for the show.

Then of course there were the 'Sundays'. Never have I approached our newsagent's with as much fear and trepidation as I did that Sunday morning. One of them liked the music but hated the book. Another hated the music but liked the book:

> 'Musically Moby Dick is outstandingly unmemorable, which is a bit of a drawback for a musical. The idiom is rock and ballad, with the odd touch of spoof blues and whatnot; there is a bouncy sense of rhythm; but such melodies as there are could have been turned out by a computer high on Babycham'.

I call that bloody rude.

A third hated the music and the book but liked the dancing and the staging. A fourth just hated it all.

The following morning the fight-back materialised, with our grinning sperm whale splashed across full pages of the dailies, rising up from a sea of quotes, pearls somehow trawled from the sea of bile.

'Sheer brilliance and uninhibited fun… so extraordinary you should see it at once!' (*Financial Times*)

'Lunacy on the high seas… The music is terrific… it's the most original, mad, wild, off the wall show!' (Jack Tinker, *Daily Mail*)

'It's fun, frantic and exuberant to the edge of delirium!' (*Jewish Chronicle*)

'A blend of The Rocky Horror Show and St. Trinian's… a raunchy pop musical!' (*Today*)

'Spectacular staging and stunning choreography for a company of dazzling hoofers!' (*Independent On Sunday*)

'A Whale of a Time!' (*The Sunday Times*)

'The most extraordinary show in the West End!' (*Daily Express*)

Daily Express? Wow! How the hell did they manage to put a positive twist on that venomous review? Clearly Cameron no longer walked on water, but it seemed he sure as hell knew how to turn water into wine.

The run continued and the audiences began to pick up. By Friday of the first week, Cameron's 'silly joke' had taken £310,000 in advance bookings. *The Sunday Times* had this to say about Robert, when they quoted his response to the critics: 'Nitwits! spat Robert Longden, the eccentric in lop-sided glasses who wrote and directs the work. 'Cameron Mackintosh is one of the few people who produces something new. This terrible greed to terrorise a new project is ignorant'.'

A couple of supportive reviewers crawled out of the woodwork. Sheridan Morley stated: 'This just could turn out to be one of those musicals that nobody likes except the public'. And John Peter, referring to his peers, said: 'you would have thought they were reviewing King Lear.' (Hallelujah! thought I, reading that one). Jack Tinker of the *Mail* attempted to be kind, decreeing that the West End would be a poor place indeed 'if it did not have room for such a piece of blatant and outrageous impertinence'. But he added: 'there were times when I felt the cast were attending a far funnier party than we were. And that does tend to freeze the smile'.

Cameron went public in defence of the show. 'We had the same problem with Les Misérables; while the critics weren't crazy about it, the feedback from the public was tremendous. Cats got mixed reviews and look at it now. The reviews of Moby Dick were bad. Obviously I'm disappointed, but all I can say is that they checked their sense of humour in with their coats when they arrived. I'm not surprised they've missed the joke. There's one thing this show isn't and that's pretentious. Moby Dick is a romp, and obviously their idea of a romp is not my idea of a romp. I believe in Moby Dick. I've always felt that it would become a favourite with the public, but not with the critics'. He concluded: 'like any musical, you don't see the final result till the twelfth night. There are always changes. It's my job to get shows right, even after they have opened. But the reaction at the first night was tremendous, and the majority were people who had paid for their tickets, they were the ones on their feet'.

20. Waiving and drowning

You would have thought as one of the show's creators I might have been adequately compensated for all the public derision I was being forced to endure, but not one cheque had come through our letterbox. As I turned away in disappointment from the doormat one morning having shuffled through the post, I recalled the conversation with my agent as he punched the buttons on his calculator.

"Three thousand, nine hundred and thirty seven pounds, fifty pence."

"Four grand?"

"Almost."

"Every week?"

"And that's not counting merchandise..."

"How much of that do I get?"

"Five per cent. I've told you all this before."

"Yeah, but it wasn't real then."

Well it was bloody real now, but – where was it? Surely a bit of the take on the show so far was for me? Obviously I didn't expect the theatre to be full after being speared so savagely by the critics, but I knew Moby Dick had sold £200,000 worth of tickets by opening night, and the box office had taken a whacking £140,000 the day after we opened, in advance bookings. Better a bad review than no review clearly, and God knows we were splashed all over the Press. I'd also seen plenty of people buying mugs and T-shirts. But I knew the show needed to take at least £80,000 a week to break even and run for more than 6 months with full houses, before it recouped its full investment. How did I know all this? I read it in the papers.

In the temporary absence of a cheque and in light of the stressful conditions under which we were prevailing, I tried unsuccessfully to contact Mark on several occasions. All I needed was confirmation that something we could live on was in the pipeline at least. For some reason my agent was incredibly hard to get hold of these days.

One morning, several weeks into the run, I arose to find an envelope from CML on the doormat. I wrenched it open only to discover it contained not a cheque, but a letter from Nick Allott asking us to accept a royalty cap. Pat was forking hay when I read it out to her. "What's that supposed to mean, a royalty cap?" she glared.

"I'm not sure. It just asks us to accept a capped box office figure of £37,500. I think it means we're waiving some of our royalties, but we'll get them back later."

"We haven't even had any yet!"

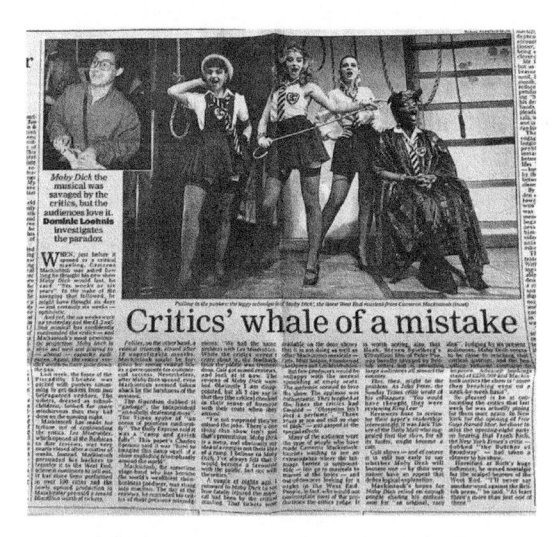

The fightback begins: an article in the Daily Telegraph a few weeks into Moby Dick's West End run, April 29th 1992. © Telegraph Media Group Limited

She turned to take it out on the hay, attacking it with her pitchfork.

Then out of the blue, Mark rang. "If somebody doesn't do something about this bloody show it won't be here in a month's time. I saw it last night, nobody could hear a word, the sound was dreadful. People were complaining loudly around me. Some people walked out. Robert's quite convinced the sound is being sabotaged by Lloyd Webber."

"No! How?"

"Through Martin Levan."

I was never a conspiracy theorist and couldn't believe Martin would do anything so underhand. I'd shared the house in Abbey Road with him, I'd bowed my head over the faders with him; this was a decent guy.

I'd taken to avoiding the show recently in the hope that, if I looked the other way things might improve, but it was clearly time to re-engage. I gathered up my young son Joe for comfort and headed down to the Piccadilly.

Robert Mackintosh grabbed me on arrival and extemporised upon the theme. "Martin Levan, I happen to know, spent all Sunday at Andrew's. On Monday he pulled out of producing the album."

"Oh no."

"And he's running the show so quiet. There's no dynamics. If you go and see 'Joseph', it really socks you in the chest."

The house lights darkened as I took my seat like a condemned man, condemned to watch a condemned show. Up came the lights on the cast, out rang the School Hymn from the company and in came the band, loud and clear. The theatre was sixty-five percent full and the crowd whooped wholeheartedly.

"What's all the fuss about Pa?" shouted Joe above the din of applause ringing out all around. A gushing well of hopeless optimism gurgled up in me as I joyfully bellowed back: "We can turn it around Joe, I'm sure we can!"

"Yeah Dad!"

"Yeah!"

I wasn't sure, but I wanted to be with all my heart.

Positive articles popped up in the papers, to make me think things actually were beginning to turn the corner. 'CRITICS WHALE OF A MISTAKE' was the headline in the *Daily Telegraph*, and beneath it: 'Moby Dick the musical was savaged by the critics, but the audiences love it. Dominic Loehnis investigates the paradox'. In another national, on the front page no less: 'MOBY'S REVENGE! – The show the critics harpooned is playing to packed houses'.

Tom Robinson wrote an article in the *Guardian* that was hugely supportive. Entitled 'Second Opinion', it ran:

> 'Last month I happened to attend and enjoy the opening night of a new West End musical, and the next day turned eagerly to read the reviews. There were one or two critics one might have expected to take a dim view of the antics we had witnessed on stage, but I was unprepared for the sheer ferocity of the onslaught. Nothing escaped – script, production, songs, cast, and audience were dispatched with savage efficiency. Audience? Was it me, or were these heavyweight columnists over-reacting just a teensy bit?
>
> Let me declare an interest. I went to see Moby Dick out of curiosity, having been in a pop group with its co-writer Hereward Kaye during the early seventies. This may have predisposed me towards tolerance but not masochism. Had the show been truly second-rate or even pedestrian I'd have left early without a qualm and fobbed my friend off with a few evasive platitudes. Actually I found it audacious, bewildering, vulgar and funny – a shotgun wedding of Melville's lugubrious epic with the traditions of ham-fisted amateur pantomime. Above all it featured some great new show songs – fresh minted and infectious. Don't take my word for it. Most of the audience seemed to think so too – for which it damned us as rampant philistines who'd never heard Mozart or Rossini.
>
> Now steady on. To measure the musical Moby Dick against Figaro is to compare Monty Python with Shakespeare. Who said you can't enjoy both on their own merits? The fact is, this lunatic extravaganza bears about as much relation to Melville as The Life Of Brian did to the New Testament. Both are uneven pastiches in the worst possible taste – hence the howls of outrage from devotees of the original works. In this case the sacrilege is cultural – 'trashing a masterpiece in the spurious name of entertainment' as Michael Billington put it – a charge Robert Longden and Hereward

Kaye would cheerfully admit. Yet they will have done Melville a service if even a dozen punters seek out his novel after seeing their show. I did, for one.

Maybe the critics erudition got the better of their discernment. Certainly the universal verdict that Moby Dick failed even in terms of entertainment was not only ungenerous but manifestly untrue, given the standing ovation. I've been three times now and each time people around me roared with laughter, cheered the songs and burst into spontaneous applause as the show careered from tacky opening to clapalong finale. Incomprehensible at times it might be, dull it ain't.

Moby Dick's problem is that it's essentially a fringe show shoehorned into a high profile West End opening. Some problem, you might think, but it has been measured by a very different critical yardstick from say, Rocky Horror's low-key debut upstairs at the Royal Court. It would have been fairer to judge it, not in comparison to classical light opera, but in the context of contemporary pop culture – Viz and Vic Reeves, Right Said Fred and Forbidden Planet – against all of which it comes off pretty well.

In the end what bothered me was not the fact that I enjoyed this daft piece of escapism and the critics didn't. It's simply that, going on their murderous reviews alone, I might never have found out'. *Guardian, April 22nd 1992*

Robert rang, to further buck me up. "We're doing good business," he said. "A five track CD went out to the radio stations yesterday. Robert Mackintosh has doctored them to make them more commercial, so you might have Cameron on to you, complaining, saying they're not representative of the show. What else…? The radio ads are making a big difference. There have been some good reviews…"

"Where?"

"All the provincial papers. They love it. I don't think you should worry about it coming off. Cameron says he's very happy with Moby and will now let it run. Copenhagen and somewhere else have applied for a licence to perform it. I think it'll happen in America. It's short you see, and it has your song 'Building America' in it."

"I guess…"

"And you've heard about the Oliviers?"

"No."

"Doesn't Mark tell you anything?"

"No."

20. Waiving and drowning

"We've got the cabaret spot; one number. 'Whale Of A Tale' with a thirty-piece orchestra. What are you doing now?"

"Waiting for the post."

"Because you've got two albums to write for, Jayne Collins and Tony Monopoly. I'll send you some lyrics. Baa."

Right on cue, the morning post dropped through the letterbox and one of the letters was from CML's royalty department. This time when I opened it, sunlight flooded into the living room and a choir of angels broke into the Hallelujah Chorus.

"Here…"

I handed Pat a cheque for £5,960.

"Thank God!" she gulped.

A week later another cheque. We went out and bought mountain bikes. The week after that it was a set of garden furniture.

The next time I ripped open an envelope from CML it contained not a cheque, but a long letter from Nick Allot under the ominous heading: 'MOBY DICK ROYALTY WAIVER'. I took the letter down the garden to Pat, who was mucking-out. Grimly I recited the title.

"Does that mean the money's going to stop?"

"No, but he's asking us to accept £350 a week for the foreseeable future."

"So that's it, a mountain bike and a set of plastic garden furniture?"

"Actually, we might have to give them back. It's to be backdated a month."

"Meaning?"

"Meaning we've already had several hundred pounds we're not entitled to and won't be receiving another cheque till it's paid off."

In a fury she turned and viciously attacked the hay.

"There's another letter," I told her sweetly, "a nice one this time…" No reply. "It's from Willy Russell?"

"What does he want?"

I cleared my throat. 'I was thrilled to note your success with Moby Dick. I hear from some people that it is quite appalling and from others that it is a truly wonderful show. The former have not put me off in any way and the latter only serve to whet my appetite further. What is it like to suddenly be staggeringly rich and what shape is your swimming pool?'

I didn't like the way she was looking at me. And she had a pitchfork in her hand. Judging it time to beat a hasty exit, I went in search of my mountain bike. I'd left it by the front door, leaning against a wall.

Gone. Stolen.

* * *

On June 16th, one month to the day since Nick Allot's royalty waiver letter, my agent Mark Hudson phoned. It was the call I had been dreading throughout all these long months of false hope and denial: the show was coming off. The cast would be informed tomorrow. The notice would be going up on Saturday. I wouldn't be receiving another penny. The cast album was shelved.

The following Monday, there appeared a small article on page five of the *Daily Mail*, simply headed: 'MOBY DICK SUNK'.

> 'Moby Dick is the latest casualty of the West End slump. Cameron Mackintosh's £1.2million musical will close on July 4th after a run of barely four months. The production was in trouble almost from its opening night at the Piccadilly Theatre. Critics panned the plot of a St Trinian's-style girls school which stages Moby Dick in its swimming pool to raise cash. Other shows closing include The Cotton Club, and Aspects Of Love, which both end this week.'

Cameron, Nick Allott, Martin Levan and a camera crew were all on the back rail, when I pushed past them to take my seat for the final performance of 'Moby Dick the Musical'. The Piccadilly theatre's stalls, royal circle, grand circle – all were chockablock and buzzing. I was up at the front wearing my green and yellow St Godley's school cap. And I was fine to start with, but when the School Hymn ended and two minutes of cheering to the rafters ensued, I was a goner, with the show barely begun. 'I Live and Breathe' choked me. 'Building America' killed me. By the final number I was up on my feet with the rest of them, fists clenched and tears falling. Several members of the cast were crying and singing at the same time, but they said it was the sight of me that set them off.

Cameron came scooting across in the bar afterwards.

"It's up to you and Robert to get your act together for once and make some sense of it," he said, rather aggressively.

"I think we'd make far more sense of it if we did Moby Dick for real," I said. "Let Ahab be Ahab instead of some demented Headmistress. It's a strong story. We should just tell it."

"In that case, why have the school in the first place?"

He had me there.

"It'll sell it," I said uncertainly. "Get people in."

"But it didn't, did it?"

Cameron Mackintosh turned his back and walked away, abandoning me to the rest of my life.

Chapter 21
Ba da da d'aargh!
- 1993 -

When Moby Dick came to the end of its West End run, £4,800 was still owing to me. It was an advance from Warner Chappell, the publisher of the show's songs. They assured me they had issued a cheque to my agent some weeks earlier and indeed, my collaborator had long since received his share.

"Haven't you had yours yet?" Robert sounded surprised.

So did Mark: "Well," he assured me, "it went in the post on Monday, give it a couple of days."

Three days later…

"Still hasn't come Mark."

"I'll look into it today."

And another three days…

"There's been a mix-up in accounts. It got lost in the upheaval of moving office dear. I'll send you another one."

A week or two more slid by.

"Still haven't had it yet? I shall see to it today and ring you straight back."

He didn't. Neither was he available when I rang. When eventually he did pick up…

"It came back because the cheque hadn't been franked. It's those wankers in accounts. But it's just been posted now."

"Really?" I sounded dubious.

"I've overseen it personally."

The cheque, it next transpired, needed two signatures: Mark's and the chief accountant's – who was away.

Finally, the Agency rang me, which was a first. It wasn't Mark, it was his fellow agent, Michael. He asked me to come in.

As soon as I sat down, Michael and another chap I had never seen before pulled up chairs and scrutinised me.

"Your agent is an embezzler. At this moment he's in Los Angeles on your money." He let that sink in. "With Robert."

A theatre in Herman Melville's birthplace in Massachusetts was looking to do our show Moby Dick, though this was the first I'd heard about it. Robert, who would be once again directing, was over in L.A. with our mutual agent Mark, to cast. I imagined the two of them together, Robert with his rightful share of money in his pocket – and Mark with mine.

"We prised open his desk," said Michael gravely, "picked the lock. Inside we found evidence of fraud on a grand scale including, on his bank statement, your cheque from Warner Chappell going into his personal account, followed by various withdrawals against the sum – back rent, a £1200 cash withdrawal, a return flight to L.A.… It was only your money he stole – well, you and a couple of other clients.

"Not Robert though."

"No. Two others on our books he stole from, but as he has highly personal information on each of them, neither wish to prosecute."

"Well I fucking do!"

"If you decide to bring in the fraud squad" Michael reassured me, "we will back you one hundred per cent. We'll furnish documentation and whatever else you need."

"Do you think I'll get my money back?"

"Not a chance. But here…" and he handed me photocopies of Mark's incriminating bank statement, the address of his flat and that of his parents up in Congleton. While we were still together I phoned my solicitor Tina for advice, on loudspeaker.

"You won't see a penny," she said flatly, the other two furiously nodding their agreement. "You should also consider that this will be a sexy story for the press and you might not come out of it very well. It will also take up a lot of your time. There will be documentation to go through, court appearances – between you and me, you'd be better off sending the heavies round, if you can find him. That's the only way you'll get any of this money back."

So I marched round to the local constabulary, where police officer Andrea took down my particulars and D.C. Hollaway asked me how I wished to proceed.

"I don't want to go through the whole rigmarole of a court case" I told them, "I just want a couple of coppers to go round his flat in London and drop in on his parents in Congleton."

"To what end?"

"Make enquiries! Confiscate his passport, put the frighteners on!"

He and the female officer looked at one another dubiously. "We're not really allowed to do that sort of thing," she said, "you have to start by pressing charges."

"I've talked to my solicitor. If I go down that route it'll just create a mountain of paperwork."

That seemed to do it. "Okay," sighed Hollaway, "I'll send somebody round."

Back from L.A. Robert rang to make light of it: "Isn't this business funny!"

"Hilarious."

"They won't find him. I bet he's sitting by the seaside somewhere, wearing a dress and sucking a piece of coal!"

"Well that narrows it down Robert, thanks. I'll pass the description on to the police."

In fact, Mark was back at his parent's house toughing it out behind the family solicitor, who wrote to the agency claiming defamation and demanding an apology in the *Telegraph*, *Times* and *Independent*. So I sent a photocopy of his bank statement to his parents evidencing his appropriation of my cheque and subsequent withdrawals against it.

I'd done all I could. I got on with the rest of my life.

I had three engagements in the book, that seemed somehow to reflect where I was right now with my career. My ex-Flying Pickets status had earned me an invitation to cut the ribbon on the new village hall. My recent Moby Dick notoriety had brought an invitation to judge the local Gala Queen Contest ("Ladies and Gentleman," crowed the M.C. introducing me, "a man who has brought joy to millions!" – cue waves of mirth at my table).

And thirdly…

Sitting in the DHSS I noted how much these places had changed since the last time I signed on back in Middlesbrough when I was an 18-year-old. What had happened to the grey-green walls and impenetrable pall of smoke? Where was the sudden eruption of violence at one of the booths? Now it was subtle lighting and first names. Now it was all plastic fronds waving in the air-con and Hank bloody Marvin twanging the tune to 'Bright Eyes' – none of which could disguise the sickening feeling of being out of work. As Primo Levi put it: 'To he that has, will be given; from he that has not, will be taken away'. That was me, him that 'has not', sitting in a moulded-plastic seat in a Job Centre. I kept my head down. I sure as hell didn't want to be seen. If anyone came up and asked me what I was up to these days, I would tell them I was in the Leisure Business.

What I needed now was my old job back, I decided. The Pickets weren't the Stones but it was a steady wage and gigs in nice places. I rang Brian, who greeted me so warmly I almost felt like I was being welcomed back into the bosom of the band there and then. Almost. He still had to run it by the boys. He promised to report back, which in due course he did.

"Uh firstly, the boys are absolutely devastated about your show coming off."

"I bet."

"They are! Devastated!"

"Thanks. All good things come to an end I guess."

"Secondly, they definitely DON'T want you back in the group."

"Right, thanks Brian, no problem. Something will come up."

"Sure?"

"Oh yeah."

"I'll let you know how the land lies."

"See you Brian."

Click.

I was out of work at 39, married with two kids, nine dogs and enough horses grazing under pylons to fuse the National Grid. That night I dreamt I had a bomb taped to my forehead. The next, I dreamt I was peeling vegetables, every one rotten.

It was some months before Brian called again. Unexpectedly, a member of the Pickets had left the group and with European dates looming, they had no choice but to turn to me.

"Thank you Brian," I said. "How sensitively put."

"They still don't want you to rejoin…"

"Why would they indeed."

"They just want to borrow you for three weeks."

"I'm touched."

The line-up had changed considerably. Rick had gone of course and also Ken, the only true anarchist in the original group I joined. Ken wouldn't have given a damn about losing his Flying Picket status anyway. At the height of his fame he'd been pursued into the Hackney branch of Woolworth's, where he'd shed all his clothes down to his underpants and thrown them at the fans, shouting: "now will you fuck off?!"

Sound man Nick had stepped up to the plate. Who knew? He had the voice of an angel. He was public school and cockney common, with no hair and fierce eyebrows. "Actually, I'm trying to comb 'em back over me head – you can't live the kind of life I've led without going bald baby!" And he'd throw a trademark laugh at the sky.

Nick had a pilot's licence, was into animation, had been tea boy on 'Bohemian Rhapsody' ("bits of tape everywhere, it was like: 'Where's Bismilla gone?' 'Over there mate, hanging from the end of the mixing desk'."). He numbered Tracey Ullman among his former girlfriends and his ex-wife was a witch. He was a born Picket.

Bass man Gareth had gone. I remembered him gusting through the door of our Amsterdam hotel, climbing up my leg and trying to snog me, grabbing the Genever gin I was drinking and downing it in one. He was talking in tongues. "C'mere, c'mere, c'mere." Shushing noises, fingers to lips, coaxing me behind a pillar. "I've just beenjust-been – you wantto know what I've just been doing don't you, doyoudoyou? I've just been to every peepshow in Amsterdam. It was marvellous!"

"Great."

"Not great. Not great. Fucking great!"

We looked out the window later that night and there was Gareth crawling about in the road beside the canal. And another memory… at the end of that tour, Gareth climbing the escalators at Schiphol airport, involuntarily letting go of his luggage at the top and turning to see it fall open and tumble to the bottom, wreaking havoc all the way down.

His bass replacement was Ricky from Washington D.C. who'd grown up singing acapella on street corners. Into the lap of the biggest bunch of impostors this side of Milli Vanilli had landed the real thing! He sang as sweetly as Sam Cooke and had a similar eye for the ladies. "It's just the dawg in me," he would say by way of explanation, when we finally managed to wrestle his attention away from the girl crossing our restaurant or the street or TV studio floor. Ricky came from a ghetto-past of gang warfare and running from drug dealers with guns. "Feel mah head man. That one there was the result of bein' hit with a chain, a fuckin' chain. Goddam!" He was straight out of Miami Vice.

David had finally hung up his acapella boots in Basildon. He was the last of the old band to go. David, who steered a clever course through the indoctrinated minefield of the early Pickets by being a card-carrying member of the Green Party. It was a smart move sideways. He was the nearest any of them got to actually being a politician.

His replacement was Kis and the name suited him. I'd actually recruited him to the group. A kind of Maltese Fozzie Bear, he was a big guy who got off to a great start with me on the first day of rehearsal up in Liverpool back in those days, when he sidled up with his conspiratorial grin.

"Hereward Kaye? **The** Hereward Kaye from Café Society?"

I was dumbfounded. Nobody had heard of Café Society. Nobody. "You've heard of Café Society? We only sold six hundred records!"

"My brother bought me a copy. He was your greatest fan."

"I didn't know we had one."

It was a show where all of the actors played all the instruments. Kis was playing Buttons, piano, bass, guitar, sitar and trombone. He was wide and warm and chock full of funniness. He was dark and serious when he played the piano, switching between Jazz and Classical. Or he'd be shaking the spit out of the trombone to try again, determined to master an instrument he'd picked up for the first time only days before. When he delivered The Four Seasons 'Rag Doll' to a sad Cinderella with a voice that was both ragged and pure, I observed a man equally poised between love of music and love of theatre, and dripping with talent. I mentally filed him under 'future Picket'. I knew he'd come in handy.

The jewel in the acapella crown was Mike, with dreadlock mane and a mighty singing voice, soaring like Pegasus. Whenever there was time to kill he would sit Ghandi-like, fingering his penny whistle and inviting you to name any tune. 'Captain Pugwash.' He plays it. 'Side Saddle, Russ Conway.' He plays it. 'Elgar's Dream of Gerontius.' He plays it. 'Belshazzar's Feast, William Walton.' He plays it. Mike composed classical quartets and operas for fun. He could actually complete the Guardian crossword. He was the smallest guy on stage but a powerhouse presence, sticking out his chest and producing a volley of improvised sound. Musically, he was so intelligent he'd vocally 'spot weld' all the flaws in our arrangements as he went along.

It was out with the old and on stage with the new. There was only Gary and myself left from those old days (not that I was in the band) and Brian, who had taken over the finances from David. Gary was very much ruling the roost.

The boys didn't seem to be in great shape, I have to say, during that first rehearsal. Nick had been dancing on tables at the Coconut Club with five Norwegian girls at three in the morning; Gary had hit a mate's wine bar and stayed there till dawn. Ricky was on some mysterious planet where no vegetative life seemed to exist. We sang like five tomcats with their balls in a mangle.

All a bit different to the theatre, darling.

At the airport Brian handed me a plane ticket, some foreign currency, told me my gate number. As I trotted off obediently to go through, Kis arrived and started going through his baggage. He was in a bit of a flap – he'd lost his passport. Later, I spotted him cruising the Duty Free shops and sidled along. "Where did you find your passport, Kis?"

"In my mouth" he replied, "I put it there when I was looking for it."

And then we were thundering down a German autobahn in the tour bus. It was almost as if the whole Moby Dick experience had never happened. Same old van, just a different bunch of Flying Pickets neutralised by endless grey road disappearing under the wheels. Nick was in the back corner looking like Widow Twanky with his scarf wrapped around his bald head and an inflatable pillow clamped about his neck. His face wore a pained expression. Mike had shaved his head for the tour and was wearing John Lennon 'granny' glasses. Now he really looked like Ghandi, pouring over his crossword and blocking out reality. Kis was grooving along to his headphones. Ricky had his newspaper open – Cindy Crawford, performing a catwalk pose. He'd been looking at that photo for a full ten minutes now; his eyes were quite glazed over. Gary sat in the front next to Brian, tooting on his pitch-pipes, disturbing the peace with annoying blasts of basso profundo and hooting falsetto. He broke off only to harangue Brian in a most disrespectful manner. There'd been a power shift clearly, but it wasn't my place to challenge.

We drew all the curtains and stuck a movie on. Gary clambered over and joined us plebs in the back. At the end of the film, we became aware we were stationary and had been for some time. Someone opened the little curtain through to Brian, who wasn't there anymore. The curtains in the side windows were pushed back. We appeared to be broken down and up on a ramp in a garage. Brian was down below, waving his arms about at a mechanic. Semaphore was the closest he ever got to a foreign language.

"I see we're still arriving the hard way, Nick," I commented.

"You're lucky you missed the last one."

"Oh yeah, what was that then?"

"Catapult from Dover to Calais, across the Alps by mule then submarine to Bangkok."

What with breaking down, we were late arriving for the soundcheck. It meant we had to rush through what should have been a leisurely routine. Brian hurriedly approached, to set the tambourine on stage. Elizabethan Pickets was all the rage and everyone was declaiming in Shakespearean cadences at the drop of a hat.

"Hark, a distant jingle of tiny bells! 'tis the Yorkshireman with the gaudy hoop."

Brian smiled in sickly fashion.

"Chaps."

"Chaps" echoed Gary.

Pained pause.

"Soft! Soft!" admonished Mike. "Our trusty man of York fain would speak! – a sorry tale methinks of doom and gloom – but prate on, Sir, for now doth thou have mine whole ear in thrall."

Pause.

"They want to open the doors."

We repaired to the dressing room. Brian removed the iron from his bottomless bag and dumped it on the table in front of Nick, who recoiled in horror.

"What is this infernal implement that doth flatten all in its wake?"

The 'rider' was all laid out, an orgy of joy – for a carnivore. "Aha!" growled Kis baronially, eyes drinking in the smorgasbord, "fine cheeses and hams, my Lord!" Grunting like a wild boar, he set to. Unfortunately for vegetarian me, the fine cheeses were wrapped up in the fine ham. But I was on best behaviour, wanting my job back; I didn't complain. I wasn't hungry anyway, I was nervous – it had been a long while!

I fell into the old dressing room routine of shit, shower and shave with supreme ease; unwrapping a pristine T-shirt, cramming myself into the faithful black leathers. A clean of the teeth, glug on the wine, gel in the hair, kohl under the eye. Sing and stretch, pull faces in the mirror.

"How many out there Brian?"

"Full. Two minutes chaps."

Such a familiar routine. Smile at your reflection, make your way down to the wings, touch each fellow Picket for luck and grin.

Hit the stage.

Afterwards, a radio man with a microphone approached us at the bar. Gary preened himself, the rest hung back. "Flying Pickets. It is an unusual name, yes? No? I have just one important question. Why? What does it mean? Why are you called this?"

"Well," explained Gary, "you know those fence posts that come to a point…"

"A picket fence?" The reporter looked puzzled. This was not the answer he was expecting.

"Yes exactly!"

So now we were named after a fence. Back in England half of all the coal mines were closing; 30,000 miners were being chucked on the slag heap. Ray Lynk, leader of the Nottinghamshire miners, was down a condemned pit refusing to come out. But here in Europopland, the Flying Pickets barely discussed politics anymore. They were a different bunch of people from the original band, all with different political alignments, if any at all. Ricky didn't give a damn. Mike was too cynical and too intelligent to vote. Kis's manifesto was love and peace. Nick probably secretly admired Margaret Thatcher. Gary was a champagne Socialist if ever I saw one. And me? As a constituent of John Major's, I'd just voted for Miss Whiplash in the last General Election. Only Brian truly grieved for the mining communities and what they were going through, but then, Brian was a true Socialist and one of the old lot, who'd been there more or less from the start.

As the discarded newspapers on the floor of the van showed crying at the pit-head, men clocking off for the final time, here we were, the rest of us, on the way to somewhere or other only-Brian-knew-where, discussing a proposal from the band's new European record company to do 'Material Girl' by Madonna. Admittedly, we weren't happy about it. "Still," said Nick, philosophically, "You never know what's going to be a hit, do you? For a million quid I'll sing anything, in bra and panties, live on TV with my head in a bucket of shit."

I was sitting next to Ricky. Aware he'd recently returned from the United States, first time he'd been back home for over four years, I say: "How was it Ricky? How was D.C.?"

"Shit, I saw friends I ain't seen in so long man, so long."

"Did they remember you?"

"Course they remember me! Everyone remembers me!"

"What did they say?"

"They said 'Yo Ricky! When did you get out of jail?' I said I haven't been to jail fellas, I've been in England. 'England?' they say. 'What the fuck ya doin' in England?' It was like, jail they could understand, but England man!"

Yes, this was definitely not the old band. I'll say this for them though; they were a hell of a lot more fun.

The venue in Berlin was a church. We changed in cramped circumstances in the vestry.

"I'm afraid there's no toilets" Brian said miserably, "but I've arranged a bucket by the back door if you're desperate."

Meanwhile, Nick was holding an inquest into his lost lighters. He'd bought a pack of five at Heathrow and one by one they had disappeared. He was not amused.

"Gary, come here," he commanded. Gary meekly stepped forward. Nick led him over to a crumbling statue of Our Lord with a decaying hand.

"Hold this hand and repeat after me: I swear by the hand of Christ…"

"I swear by the hand of Christ."

"That I have not taken, nor do I know anyone else who has taken…"

"That I have not taken, nor do I know anyone else that has taken."

"Nick's five lighters."

"Nick's five lighters."

"Well 'oo the Christ has got them then?" mused Nick sacrilegiously, stomping out to the back bucket. I was fishing round in my suit carrier at the time. Gary hurried over and thrust his fist under my nose, opening the palm like an oyster. Five different coloured lighters.

In a beer garden after the show we grew philosophical, possibly because we'd spent the whole evening in a church. Mike was talking about empirical truth and absolute truth.

"What's the difference?" I wondered, "what's an absolute truth?"

"I am born, I live, I die, stupid," scoffed Gary.

"An empirical truth one comes to learn through conditioning," Mike explained with some aplomb, "whereas an absolute truth exists beyond the condition of…"

"I 'ad one of them fackin' Jehovah's witnesses round my gaff," interrupted Nick completely off the subject, throwing back his bald head and laughing at the sky. "Bing-bong went me doorbell. I ask 'em all in me, Mormons, fuckin' what's its, get 'em to lay their plans out on the floor…"

"An empirical truth one comes to learn through conditioning," persisted Mike, slightly increasing the flow of air into his magnificent bellows, "whereas an absolute truth exists beyond the condition of…"

"So these Jehovah's come in. They give me their magazine right, so I says alright then!" Nick's synapses are inflamed with booze. "Who are these 150,000 people going to the Promised Land? Give me their phone numbers!"

"Nick" I said, "we're trying to discuss absolute truth, not absolute bullshit."

Brian appeared. "Two minutes chaps."

Suddenly, Ricky came alive.

"I know there is a God, right? Cos he came to me and he – he saved me man, and that's an absolute truth also."

Mike has been quietly waiting for a conversational lull into which he can insert the rest of his sentence. It's never going to happen. He cranked the volume up to eleven, knowing he possessed a bombastic boom to break the sound barrier.

"An empirical truth," he roared, "one comes to learn through conditioning!" He rose to his feet, clenched fists upon the table-top. "Whereas an absolute truth exists BEYOND THE CONDITION OF…"

"Come on boys," says Brian, "let's go."

Gary gently touched the shoulder of a passing waiter and raised his empty glass: "Haben zie noch ein Weissenbier bitte?"

Nick and I strolled over to the van as Brian tried unsuccessfully to round up the rest of the group. An attractive female made a beeline for us. "You were one of ze Flying Pickets!" she said delightedly, approaching me. I smiled indulgently and winked at Nick. She walked straight past me and locked eyes intensely with his. "This is my last night in Berlin," said Nick immediately, "shall we go?"

Together, they were gone.

"It's all in the lasers, my son," he confided over lunch the next day. "You give 'em a blast with the old lasers and if you get eye contact back, that's what's known in the trade as a 'Number One'. First contact. You go for another shot of the lasers – a 'Number Two' – and if she gives you one back, it means she wants it."

"How many numbers does it take to get her back to your hotel room?"

"Seven."

We were eating al fresco at the time. Moments later he gripped my wrist. His voice was low and throaty, as if his insides had just turned to water.

He said: "Number One just gone in."

"Who? Where?"

"Over there. Don't look, don't look, just keep talking normally; where were we?"

"Biggin Hill."

"Sunday mornings, dive-bombing the other trainee pilots, yes, ha! It's all highly illegal but everyone does it, giving it the old Red Baron, Number Two just gone in."

"…I'm sorry?"

"Number Two. Just gone in."

"Oh, you mean with…"

"Aryan babe in the corner, the one who's talking to her friends. Hold up, she stopped. Now she's looking at me. Look at that, H baby, a definite Number Three!"

"What number do you get up to before you start talking?"

"Four. Just you watch. I'll put another one in – a big one, mind; Number Four's got to be lasers on full power – and I guarantee she'll come over and talk to me."

He sent heat seeking missile Number Four on its search and destroy mission.

"Number Four locked onto target," he affirmed in a whisper, a low tremor of adrenaline charging his body, "and target about to approach table."

Incredibly, the second he said it, she unpeeled herself from her chair, gracefully set aside her napkin and excused herself to her companions. Now she was sashaying across the busy restaurant towards our table. Nick was setting his own napkin aside and settling back casually into his chair. I couldn't help noticing her flashing eyes, now that we had her at close quarters. Laser number five, six and seven seemed to be rattling through the turnstile in rapid succession. At this rate, if Nick's calculations were correct, they'd be having it off on the table in three laser's time, although examining her expression close to, somehow I doubted it.

"Vill you pleass to stop staring at me?" she exclaimed, loudly enough to stop conversation. "It is werry, werry rude. You are ruining my meal and making my colleagues extremely nervous!"

* * *

It was the last night of the tour. We ended our set as usual with 'Buffalo Soldier', marching offstage singing "Oh Yo Yo! Oh Yo Yo!" over and over till we were in the wings, whereupon the audience took up the cry. We waited a couple of minutes or so as you do, then marched back on, clapping at the back of the stage till the 'Oh Yo Yos' from the audience were back up to Gale Force Ten. The band were waiting for me to count us back in, whereupon we would rush the mics like the SAS and lace into the chorus.

"A-one! A-two! A-one, two, three, four!"

Piling forward, Nick noticed his lighters. They were taped to his mic stand in a neat little row.

We bade our goodbyes at Heathrow airport. Brian took me aside and informed me that following a meeting, I'd been given my old job back. I headed for the exit knowing in a couple of weeks I'd be passing through again in the opposite direction. I didn't mind – in fact I was pathetically grateful. I was a Flying Picket once more, back on the road, back on the retainer, singing on and signing off.

Back home there were two letters on the doormat. One was from Robert: 'I am about to inhabit the opportunity of a lifetime in America. I would suggest you watch this space. It was me who created the Cameron thing. We exist in a limbo of ineptitude and controversy. I am moving on'. I rang Michael at the Agency to see what was going on. All I knew was this new production in Herman Melville's birthplace was going ahead, with Robert directing.

"Robert's gone mad," Michael scorched. "He's spent all the money in the budget and they haven't started rehearsal yet. It's just a repertory production, you know what I mean? He's demanding a chauffeur-driven limousine, five star accommodation and he's flown his wife out as choreographic consultant. They can't understand Robert, they can't work with him. The lighting people asked him what he wanted for a certain scene and he said 'multiple clitorises all over the stage'. See what I mean? And he wants more money than you, says he should never have agreed to a fifty-fifty split. I think you need to find out what's going on."

"Okay Michael" I sighed, "I'll get on a plane."

I opened the second letter.

It was from Mark. It contained a cheque for £4,800.

Chapter 22
Pinkerton
- 1994 -

When I woke up on the first day of the year, I was 41 and had a 100 Flying Picket shows in the book. Time to get in shape! My New Year's resolution was to force the heart rate up for 15 minutes, three times a week. Faced with the choice of rising at dawn to run round the block (180,943 calories) – or having a horizontal jog (somewhere between 50,000 calories and 5 calories, depending on how long you've been married), I chose the easy option.

A few weeks later Pat and I gathered up our two adult sons. Sensible Leon, 19 now, looked glum. Dreadlocked, 17-year-old Joe looked spaced-out.

"I've something to tell you about me and your father," Pat began.

"You're splitting up."

"No! We're pregnant."

Leon winced. Joe giggled.

At St Thomas's, our baby was scanned. But no matter how hard the doctor squidged Pat's greased and burgeoning belly, the baby wouldn't budge. "It's one of mine," she said. "It'll never do as it's told."

We wrestled with names: Indiana for a boy, perhaps? Freya for a girl. The Indiana option was academic. We were convinced it was a girl.

Life settled into the old familiar pattern of farewells and reunions as new life grew. Now, as I regaled Pat with my Picket tales from abroad, uncorking the plonk as Puccini soared, Baby Freya kicked up a storm to 'Turandot' but blanked Eric Clapton's 'Blues Power'. "Only likes my music," said Pat.

I hadn't seen her so happy for a long time. She'd thought we were done with children. Now, at the age of 42 she was shocked and overjoyed to find herself expecting.

The Ship Hits the Fans

I entered the hospital carrying the first bag of nappies I'd bought in 17 years. Pat was carrying the baby, but not for much longer. I couldn't believe there would be a baby, or that all that body-ripping commotion was only hours away. Pat was brittle with tension, and well she might be. After two previous emergency Caesareans, she'd elected to have a Caesar by local anaesthetic. Who wants to be awake when they cut you open? My cowardly male brain could barely compute the horror of it.

Up on the ward, curtains were drawn as midwives, anaesthetists and nurses came calling, all of them younger than ourselves. Pat was monitored, scanned, checked and injected. I took to cooing like a dove; something I'm not particularly good at. With a conspiratorial grin, Diana the midwife eased herself through the curtains and perched upon the edge of the bed. She locked eyes with Pat, her voice a professional whisper: "What have they said?"

"They've said that they'll come for me in half an hour and take me through to the delivery ward to get changed," Pat whispered.

Diana turned up the grin. Now we were 96% radiant happiness, 4% concern. "I think we'll change in here now" she whispered, "then we'll take you through. It'll be more private."

"Okay" whispered Pat.

"What about me?" I whispered, slightly alarmed to be left out.

"You can come too," the midwife whispered.

In the laundry room adjacent to the delivery ward, I kitted myself out in disposable surgical gear and washed my hands. Checked the film in the camera. Checked the tape of Madame Butterfly in the cassette machine. Washed my hands again. I joined the wife and midwife and together we moved through to Room 101.

Pat made the immediate mistake of laying on the slab. She had no chance after that. Vanessa and her team of anaesthetists moved in for the spinal injection, needles raised and cackling like witches.

"Curl your knees up dear."

I felt horribly in the way, what with my camera and cassette player. Trying to make myself useful and not being any good at anything else, I pressed play on the tape recorder. Puccini's overture soared. Another needle went in above the collarbone. Pat was hooked up to a drip. The machine that goes ping was moved in nearer and a trolley-load of torture instruments nosed forward, a green-gowned waiter on the end of it.

Dinner was about to be served.

Vanessa began to drizzle water, starting at the toes. "Can you feel that Patricia? No? Good."

As Madame Butterfly trilled at Lieutenant Pinkerton, the anaesthetist headed north, anointing as she went. Before long, the first drip of water Pat could feel was on her neck. This was the signal for the door to fly open. Mr Hare, hero of the hour, strode dramatically into the theatre – his theatre – hands aloft, surrounded by his adoring minions. THWACK! went the left rubber glove. THWACK! went the right rubber glove.

"I'm only here for the opera!" he proclaimed. Opening gag!

His team laid a long green sheet along the length of Pat's left-hand side and another was lovingly laid along her right. A third across her thighs, a fourth across her bursting breasts. A letterbox of flesh was framed in the middle. Great God Hare passed his blade across it, causing a vivid red line of fire to appear. Expecting a blood-curdling yelp of pain, I checked north. Pat was deep in conversation with Vanessa.

"You didn't feel that, did you?" I marvelled.

"Feel what?" she said suspiciously.

I turned my attention south again, to the ballet of blood. Placenta Domingo was in performance with Dame Hari Kiri. The surgeon was folding back the flap of flesh from his incision over Pat's groin, taking her pubes with it and holding it in place with clips, the sort you position around terminals when you have a flat battery. A lumpy line of butter-yellow fat was thrust brutally upwards. Hare trimmed it away like an expert pork butcher. He widened the hole, stretching its parameters. Within the letterbox of cool green cloth lay a roiling red world.

Pat clocked my horrified expression. Her voice rose: "Don't!" she cried, "don't look like that!" The orchestra soared and Madame Butterfly's blood curdling soprano rent the air. I groped for the volume button and turned it the wrong way.

"Did I tell you" Vanessa soothed, her eyes boring meaningfully into mine, "that I went gliding a couple of weeks ago?" She stroked Pat's hair. "It was so peaceful up there, calm and serene."

Southside, Hare was manhandling organs to squeeze more room; it was all far more physical than I thought it was going to be. He looked as though he was locked in a fight to the death with a pulsing octopus.

"What's going on down there?" wondered Pat.

"Believe me, you don't want to know."

"Can you push for us?" asked the mighty surgeon, casually. "It won't feel as though it's doing anything, but it will help, I promise you." He was Roger Moore with a charming dolly bird on his arm.

Pat started pushing for England –and Italy, as Madame Butterfly's weeping soliloquy reached its crescendo. The surgeon prised apart roiling tentacles and there I caught the first glimpse of our baby, submerged beneath the surface of the red sea.

"I'll have to stop pushing. I feel queasy."

She felt queasy?

"Take a rest and then try again."

Hostilities were suspended. There followed a brief musical interlude as Pinkerton arrived on the shores of Nagasaki with his new American wife. Just before an anguished Madame Butterfly could take her own life, Hare cried: "Okay, one more big push!"

A new sense of urgency gripped the room as Pat pushed. The tom-tom was beating faster you sensed and sweat pouring from the galley slaves, their oars ripping ferociously at the water. "I can see an arm!" I yelped, "and a bum!"

The baby breached through into our world, a marbly, blue-veined skein of wonder and remoteness. The flat back was coated in lard like a cross channel swimmer. The umbilical cord was severed and our child born aloft.

"I think we'll pass the baby to the parents to sex," Hare declared, and thrust the child towards us. A pinkerton dangled before our eyes….

"It's a boy" said Pat.

This was the cue for the Paediatric Team, like Monty Python's Spanish Inquisition, to burst through the swing doors and snatch the child away from us, whisking him across to the Resuscitator in the corner.

Silence.

More silence.

It seemed to be an eternity before he cried. Then baby noises struck up and he was handed to his father. Rosy and blue and shawled too, I laid him in Pat's arms.

Rory Indiana.

The surgeon was rummaging around in the letterbox of flesh as if it contained the resignation he'd posted, just before the rise in salary. He fished out something round and popped it up upon Pat's beached stomach, to create a bit more room.

"What the hell"s that?"

"Uterus, old boy. Any other organs you'd like to take a look at, while we've got her open?"

"Yeah," I said, after a bit of thought. "Her liver. It's taken quite a hammering over the years. Let's have a look at that."

It was the happiest time of Pat's life, those first few months at home. Seeing an article headlined: 'P.S. Babies' she wrote in to the *Daily Mail* to highlight her joy at breastfeeding and nurturing a new baby at the age of 42, 17 years since the last one. It was letter of the week. *Woman's Own* saw it, dispatched a reporter and snapper and now we were a two-page feature in a magazine. An independent TV company saw that and dispatched a crew to spend a few days filming us at home. They ran the half-hour documentary on Channel 4. The BBC saw that, and come Valentine's Day, we were watching our programme on BBC2, under the title: 'True Romance'.

It was a chain of events not unlike that old Burl Ives chestnut: 'There was an old woman who swallowed a fly'.

Chapter 23
Orchard Road
- 1995 -

One beloved new family member gained – another lost. My most treasured mother. For some months she had fought the good fight against cancer. She would grope for breath as I fiddled with the gas bottle beside her bed. "No, that's not the way Hereward" came her words, distorted slightly but carefully expended from behind her mask, words riding on breath she couldn't afford but had to spend all the same, because I was doing it wrong. I did everything wrong in those final weeks when it was vital I did them right. I remember her howling with pain as I tried to shove her further up the pillows. I held her as she whimpered. I cried inwardly as she stroked my head.

"Cry properly," she cooed. "It's good for a mother and son to cry."

"I can't."

"Why?"

"Because I'm English."

Mum faded fast – even her great beauty. She had always been a rather fabulous creature – though mainly Dutch, she was descended, on her mother's side, from Pakoe Boewono the Second, an Indonesian Prince. My Dad was lucky enough to cross paths with my mother in Java and somehow talk her into marriage. I think it was the fact that she didn't speak a word of English that worked in his favour. From the very beginning she displayed a fabulous talent for not listening to Dad properly and so, believing him to be a rich farmer, set sail for England's green and pleasant land, only to find Middlesbrough's dark, satanic mills. From technicolour to monochrome. There she was, a bird of paradise trapped in a gilded cage. She was far too exotic for Middlesbrough. We didn't even have a Chinese restaurant back then.

Now she was gone. The house I grew up in had been left to my two sisters and myself. Impulsive as ever, I sold the house I had and bought them out. Pat and I knew

The annual Kaye's Tools staff photo (Peter & Tjitske Kaye to the fore), 1974.

it was a perverse idea moving up North when all my work was in the South. But having lost my mother, it was more than I could bear to lose the gilded cage too. So we upped sticks and moved back to Middlesbrough after a gap of some 25 years away. Now my parents house was ours, the house where I was raised, the house in which my father was discovered, slumped stupidly on a feed bin in the shed. Heart failure – a businessman's death.

His company had collapsed a year earlier, the tool business I was born to inherit, the family business I hadn't wanted to run. Noël Coward defined work as being 'more fun than fun' but he meant creative work. My Dad did the other kind; 'work work'. "My father said here's a horse, ride it, and I've ridden it ever since," he once told me.

Four years before he died British Steel cancelled their account. That was huge. Three years before he died, the shadow of a giant Asda store arose like a frowning God and engulfed our shop. Two years before he died, Peter Kaye had to lay off eight loyal workers, asking their forgiveness. Sandy from accounts slapped his face. We were all upset and outraged by it, though he found excuses for her.

A year before Dad died, he handed his big bunch of keys to the Official Receiver and walked away diminished. He couldn't bear to hear the horse being shot. One year later, he was gone.

Together, my mother and I visited him in the Chapel of Rest, Mum weak on my arm. As we walked into the undertakers, a wide-eyed trainee blurted: "Mr Kaye isn't ready yet!" so we went away and had a coffee then came back. There he lay, his fine brain come to rest on a thinly-disguised block of wood. The pallor fought the rouge. He looked like he'd been in battle with a pair of net curtains and settled back, defeated.

How we love them, how suddenly they are gone, winking bubbles on water. Now I owned the house. Wrestled with the same bills. Lay in my parents' bed on my father's side, listening to Leon and his girlfriend making love in my old bedroom above the ceiling, the room where Pat and I lost our virginity (though not at the same time!) and giggled ourselves to sleep in our teens.

I would stand outside in the garden where I used to chase butterflies, watching my infant son Rory Indiana dig up worms, distant relatives of the ones I dug up when I was three. I'd slice 'em in half and watch each end set off in opposite directions. I used to dig holes out there too; sit in them with a grid across the top and charge my family threepence a time to come past. When they paid up I issued a ticket to the forthcoming attraction: a network of underground tunnels beneath the lawn. I could see the whole thing in my mind; flaming torches to light the way, set in gleaming chocolate walls of soil. All I was waiting for was parental planning permission to dig a bigger hole. It never came through. In fact, the next time I went out there, they'd filled it in.

And I could still almost hear the ghostly roar that would float across the ether when I was digging those holes. Back in my childhood days, 'the Boro' still played at Ayresome Park; the ground was a mile up the road. Before I was old enough to know or passionately care, that roar was unsettling, other worldly. It was the voice of multitudes in acclaim, faintly heard, but as it passed overhead it left one in no doubt that something miraculous had happened. And it had – Boro had scored a goal! When I had a few more years on the clock, I was allowed to venture into the lion's den, unaccompanied. Match-day momentum billowed up all around me, often on alcoholic fumes, as from pubs and bars spilled Boro fans, all in red and white scarves, some with rattles. Then you're being sucked through the turnstiles and it hits you, the vista opening out – the vivid green of the pitch, the clamour, the expectation. As my heroes in the flesh poured from the tunnel heading imaginary crosses, powering invisible volleys, there was a great, full-throttled roar – a joyful, deafening tumult and my voice a part of the orchestra. It was the one I grew up with floating across our back garden, and the one that came back to me now, echoing down the years as I stood watching my infant son.

Memories. I was awash with them, living in my old house on Orchard Road.

Geographically, my home was at one end of the country and my job was at the other, which meant I was away a lot. It wasn't just the constant touring any more. Now, it was all the travelling to get to and from the constant touring. Periods of rehearsal and even band meetings were trips away.

It involved farewells and reunions with Pat on an almost weekly basis. It meant endless commuting from Darlington to Kings Cross to Timbuktu and back again. One time, I took five trains: the branch line from Middlesbrough to Darlington, the train to King's Cross, tube to Waterloo, Eurostar to Paris and TGV the length of France to Marseille, where we performed. The following morning I did the same train journey in reverse: TGV from Marseille to Paris, Eurostar to Waterloo, tube to King's Cross, train to Darlington.

Only just made that last one. Knees protesting, suitcase skinning my calf and heart yammering like a stir-crazy inmate rattling the bars of my ribcage, I double-climbed the escalators and roared into Kings Cross station, sighting my train and the guard's whistle upon his lip. Back in the main hall, the clitter-clatter of the Departures board was already wiping the train's existence from history. I squeezed on board by milliseconds and immediately wished I hadn't. It was a late night football special, and I was wedged up against Newcastle United fans.

The trolley girl battled her way through.

"Tell me pet," asked the Geordie paying her for the dozen cans of McEwans, "do you swear when you're making love?"

A fifty-something, silver haired lady squeezed by and the menfolk shamelessly began touching her up.

"Fuck off" she said calmly, adding: "I'm Steve Howie's mum."

They roared with laughter. Judging by their reaction, Steve Howie was clearly a Newcastle player and not exactly at the top of his game. "When are yous bastards gonna get off his back?" she complained. "You're ruining it for him!"

"Now now, bonny lass," soothed one of them, "he's not *that* bad…"

I was well used to sliding up and down the spine of England. Sometimes the train stopped in the middle of nowhere or at a platform long enough to make me lose the will to live. A middle-aged woman shoehorned herself into the seat beside me once, even though the rest of the carriage was empty. I threw her a look: really? – which she ignored. Her friend stationed herself outside my window, to wave her off. As the train wasn't going anywhere, they picked up their conversation.

"This is the same seat ah sat on when ah come!" she shouted.

The woman at the window smiled encouragingly and pointed to her ears, as if to say 'can't hear you'.

"I say, this is the same seat ah sat on when ah come!"

Window woman shrugged. Train woman decided to over-mouth her words with exaggerated precision, so her friend would be able to lip read: "same seat, but they don't have a little cloth on 'em."

"What?" mouthed the woman at the window.

"I'm saying, they don't have a little cloth on 'em!"

The woman at the window shook her head.

"Hold up, I'll come to the door."

She struggled out of her seat and the two rendezvoused in the open doorway.

"I'm saying, it's the same seat I sat in when I come but they don't have the little cloth."

"No."

"Shame."

Now they'd run out of things to say. The woman on the platform racked her brains.

"Do they have a little tray on the back? They do? They don't… oh, shame."

"Anyway, we're going now," said the one in the doorway, "who's kissing?"

On arrival in London, it was a familiar routine. Slide into King's Cross, a few coins for the same old down-and-outs where I left them, still bickering. Cross the road, down the street, check into my hotel. Feeling rather guilty about the amount I was costing the band in expenses, I'd sought out the cheapest B&B I could find. A desperate pit it was; Chateau Despair.

"Any particular room?"

"Ah, yes, the tiny hot one smelling of fags with the prostitute in the room next door please."

At breakfast I'd make my way down, heavy bags cannoning off the narrow corridor walls. The smoky basement was always full of builders and the smell coming off the chip pan was overwhelming.

"Coffee dahlin', tea?"

"Coffee. And I'm vegetarian, remember."

"That's awright dahlin', I'll do you beans and tomato."

"What kind of tomatoes are they today, grilled?"

"Tinned." And she sashayed away, singing to the radio.

If I was coming back the other way and getting in late I would trundle into Middlesbrough station on the branch line train and from the back of a taxi survey my hometown: teeming hordes of hard-faced girls blissfully impervious to the biting wind in their flimsy garments, funnelling through pulsating doorways; earrings, nose-rings and eyebrow-rings momentarily gleaming in the neon and tattoos ghostly upon their skin.

As the taxi pulled into my drive, I was the guy in that Talking Heads song: This is not my house! This is not my car! This is not my wife!

I'd creep upstairs through the stilled house to our bedroom and undress in the dark. In those early days at Orchard Road Rory would stir beside Pat, waking her.

"I didn't know when you were coming back love." The sleep was still thick in her voice and the warmth of the bed upon her. "I'll put him in his own bed."

"No, leave him."

As carefully as possible I'd lift the covers and, settling back, my arm would enfold the two of them. Laying in the dark it was not the words of Talking Heads I heard but George Sand. 'There is only one happiness in this life, to love and be loved'.

In the morning – that wound-licking re-entry period – I took refuge in my headphones. I had a studio to magic up new songs for the next Pickets album or tour, or new demos for Robert's ever-more eccentric versions of Moby Dick, or songs for other projects in which I was involved. For many months we had the builders in, as I poured money and love into my childhood home.

Outside the window just inches from where I work with a live microphone, lies Mitch in a drainage ditch. I abandon my 'take' as he yells to Tony: "Ah've got my fookin' end mate. 'Ave you got your fookin' end…? Can't hear you pal. 'Ang on, the fookin' mobile's ringin'. Is it mine or yours?"

Ah Middlesbrough. The dulcet tones.

"I'm off for some fookin' chips," shouts Tony. "D'you want any, like?"

"Gerrus a fookin' pie. Mek it two."

Silence from outside. Back on with the headphones. Then it's Rory interrupting.

"Daddy, I need to do some horse whispering."

I bend my ear. A whoosh of tickly breath. I lift up again. "No way! No way can I build you a hill!"

"I thought you probably couldn't."

He looks crestfallen yet resigned and I feel instantly guilty.

"But I can dig you a hole to sit in!" I say, snatching away the headphones, bending to pick the boy up.

"Come on Rory Indiana, let's go in the garden. See what I can do."

Chapter 24
Dystonia
- 1996 -

Queasy from breakfast at Chateau Despair, I dropped down to the tube, en route to the latest round of Flying Pickets rehearsals. A busker boarded my carriage and my heart sank.

"Hello Ladies' n' Gennlemen and welcome to the show!"

I kept my eyes glued to the floor in the traditional 'cast-down' position. He was telling us how 'wunnerful' it was to be here and referring to us as the audience, even though we were commuters, trapped and squirming. Three stops and one revolting version of 'Norwegian Wood' later this hell was over and I was bowling along the road to our rehearsal rooms where the band awaited. We'd made an album for release in the Benelux countries (Belgium, Netherlands and Luxembourg) and with tour dates coming up, we had to learn how to sing the bloody thing.

We had a new Flying Picket on board too; Nick had left, replaced by Henrik, a young Sean Connery lookalike. Get him to say 'Mish Moneypenny', and the similarity was uncanny. His James Bond looks were complimented by a body-builder's torso and a mellifluous singing voice. These qualities, coupled with a double first in 'Carry On' films and a pair of zebra skin trousers, attracted many admirers. His girlfriends were international beauties. His male drinking pals were mainly medical professionals, dropping in on Henrik as he toured, enabling him to indulge his unhealthy obsession with human plumbing long into the night.

Before we could get going, Burt Burm, the head of our record label in Belgium, arrived with publicist Marlene in tow. He slapped the artwork for our new album down on the table.

"What do you think?" he beamed. "Don't you think it's great? They've done a good job, I think."

The Ship Hits the Fans

What we were looking at was a photo of ourselves, onstage at the end of a show, basking in the applause, hands aloft. The name of the band rested upon our upraised hands.

"It's shite," said Kis.

Although Burt didn't quite understand the intrinsic Englishness of the word, nevertheless its essential message had somehow conveyed itself and he bristled accordingly.

"What is this 'shite'? Do you mean shit or what?"

"No, it's worse than shit," Kis replied, "it's shite. Shit with an 'e'. S-H-I-T-E. Shite."

Seemed conclusive enough to me, but the two Belgians looked alarmed.

"We thought it was good," said Marlene.

"Yes, that's what worries me," replied Kis calmly.

"What is wrong with it?"

"The letters look like they belong on the side of a bouncy castle. The title ought to be 'The Flying Pickets Pop Party'. It's destined for the bargain bins. I wouldn't show it to any one of my friends, do you understand what I'm saying? It has no integrity. It's deeply uncool. It's… Seventies."

Disgruntled, Burt and Marlene left. As we attempted to knuckle down to rehearsal, the receptionist appeared at the door. "Is there a Herod Kaye?"

It was a fax from my wife. Gary snatched it away from me and tried to crumple it up. Henrik snatched it away from him and stuffed it down his underpants. Just then, Brian came in with our tour schedules. "Chaps, I'm sorry to interrupt," he apologised.

"Not at all!" cried Henrik, full of the joys, "you're doing a great job, Brian. A great job." He eyeballed the rest of us and we moved in singing: "for he's a jolly good fellow, for he's a jolly good fellow." Before he knew it, Brian was being chaired around the room as we boomed, Harvard style: "And so say all of us! And so say all of us!"

"Chaps," cried Brian, "put me down, put me down!" We didn't and each chorus grew louder and lustier than the one before.

This is what we by and large referred to as rehearsing.

After our first day's heavy work we adjourned to The British Queen next door to structure the set. Gary was waving his money around, having just been paid £800 for a solo gig in Stuttgart. He got a round in then waved his money around a little bit more. "I'm rich and you're not!" he sang in sing-song.

24. Dystonia

Kis went home early and Henrik left soon after, to finish with his girlfriend, long distance. "Can't you tell her you don't want to shag her any more but we do?" inquired Gary.

"It's not that I don't want to shag her…" Henrik's handsome brow knitted into a troubled frown.

"No, but we do."

Now I was left with Gary and Mike, Britain's 'Two Man Bob in The Hedonistic Games', both former world champions. "I'm gone," I said, draining my pint. Just then, the Ladies Darts Team walked in, office cleaners in shell-suits.

"Hi boys," they said, "fancy a game?"

"H, get your round in," instructed Gary.

"Same again," added Mike.

Might have guessed when we walked in we'd be the last to leave. I spent what was left of the night on Mike's floor and we hit the café early the following morning to force the blood sugar back up. Gary was there already, obviously with the same game plan. The three of us, bruised, stirred our tea. Then Gary said glumly: "I got mugged last night."

It wasn't the beating he deserved – I'd bagged that – but it was that wallet again, the one he'd been waving round under our noses the previous evening. Two sensible chaps had relieved him of it.

"What about the bike?"

"Stolen."

"Again?" Mike gasped. Gary's previous bike, left chained to the railings of the Houses of Parliament would you believe, had been nicked just 4 weeks earlier, the bike-chain hacksawed straight through.

"Do you know, Gary" I told him, "I describe you to friends as the only man I know with a monthly cycle?"

The tour grew more imminent and rehearsals grew less shambolic and more purposeful. Then we were back in Berlin for the first of our dates. With 900 Germans waiting in the pews, we felt perky. Same old vestry but no need for a bucket outside anymore: they'd installed a toilet, praise the Lord. Talking of which, Christ's withered hand had dropped off completely, since last time. Still the sacrilegious effing and blinding, seeing Gary savouring the reek of his own armpits and hearing Henrik's cries of 'Nurse!' from the toilet. I donned the Kohl eyeliner, crammed into a new pair of leather trousers, hit the apse with the rest of 'em and laid into 'Don't Fear The Reaper' – perhaps not the most devout choice of songs for opening number.

Then it was Stuttgart, to sing to the Teachers Union. Very Sixties, these German teachers, all clean living hippies. There were about 3000 of them out there as we sang, thronging a beer tent longer even than a German teacher's address to his union. Balding men swung their silver ponytails from side to side in time with the music. Women jiggled face-painted kids in their crushed velvet arms.

Next morning in the van, sound man Paul studied me for a moment. "How bad's your hangover mate?"

"So bad that I'm going to have to change my name to Gideon Sick."

"That's not what we were calling you last night."

"What were you calling me last night?"

"Duncan Disorderly."

Paul nudged Henrik playfully in the ribs. Henrik pressed stop on his Walkman and patiently removed the two earpieces from his ears.

"You all right Henrik?"

"Yeah. Just feel quiet, that's all."

"Okay," said Paul. "No need to go on about it."

That evening – a theatre this time – pulling out all the stops in 'Billy Jean', I dropped off the front of the stage to deliver a verse in the audience. "She said I was the one!" I moaned, moving up the centre aisle as the punters in the aisle seats either side preened in pleasure or sunk back aghast, "could've danced, on the floor, in the round!" I turned to face the stage with a swagger. Now I looked at it, it was a bit high, but no matter. "So take my strong advice" I sang, back to the audience, "remember to always think twice!" Still in the aisle, I turned to look over my shoulder into the spotlight. I had a parting shot. "Don't think twice!" I cried.

I took a run at it and landed upon the very lip of the stage. My arms immediately began windmilling as I discovered I had as much backwards momentum as forward momentum. It was the brand new leather trousers, you see; they were a bit tight, without quite the requisite 'give' in the knee. The faces of the group told me all I needed to know. Mike, with whom I was momentarily face to face, seemed to have weighed up my dilemma and his lips were forming a perfect 'O' in wonderment, as he watched me struggle with the laws of gravity. Kis was beside him, and yet beside himself at the same time. As I toppled backwards off the stage like a deep sea diver from the side of a boat, the last thing I saw was Gary's face. Unalloyed joy suffused his features.

So the tour rolled on – and the one after it. Summer became Autumn became Winter – we were still on the road. One icy night at the end of Bob Marley's 'Buffalo Soldier', we marched off stage in our usual fashion, singing "O Yo Yo", leaving the audience bellowing for an encore. We were clearly visible from the wings so we stepped out onto the street through the stage door, which clicked shut behind us. Finding ourselves locked out we, hammered round to the front of the theatre, with the brilliant idea of reappearing through the audience, who we could hear inside, belting out the "O Yo Yo" refrain and clamouring for more. We couldn't wait to get back in – it was freezing out there. Unfortunately, the front doors to the theatre were also locked. We stood outside dripping with sweat in 10 degrees below for a full 10 minutes, hearing the audience response grow more and more ragged, interspersed now with boos and catcalls. Eventually, the doors burst open.

"What the feckin' 'ell you doing out here lads?" shouted Brian.

The road-show rolled on and the months rolled by, measured out in motorways and air miles, from Iceland down to South Africa, from Belgium across to Slovenia, and up and down every European country between. It was never my intention to become a dinosaur of rock, growing old in an industry defined by adolescence. However, as I found myself in my mid-40s churning gigs out on the road, I still had one thing left in the world to rebel against: extinction. So there I was performing festivals to the great unwashed from here to eternity in tight leather, skinny ponytail and eyeliner, hurling myself at a microphone before the latest crop of disaffected youth. With any luck, they'd take one look and go home and study.

"Keep smiling, keep singing son!" Hereward on stage with the Flying Pickets, 1996.

It was when we were in Rome doing a series of shows and I stood waiting on the pavement in a melee of hangers-on, listening to another restaurant being lined up, another club to follow, that I started to feel all these good times were beginning to become bad times. I shared a taxi back to our apartment in the early hours with Gary, who began haranguing me about my singing. He'd taken to these harangues more and more recently, creating an alarming sense of insecurity in my breast, over the one thing I always felt secure about, the fact I could sing. Arguing back and forth we sped across the Bridge of Statues, the Castel Sant Angelo shining like an upended usherette's torch. It was where Tosca threw herself from the ramparts, I knew. Tosca was the Puccini opera above all others in which Pat and I gloried when I was home.

"My voice isn't as clean as yours Gary, it's rock and roll."

"It's horrible."

"It isn't horrible," Kis assured me the next day as I turned to him for support. "What he says about your voice is horrible."

"He hates my singing."

"He hates you, that's the point. He wants you out mate."

I'd never had to think about my singing before, I just opened my mouth and sang baby! But now that bastard had planted a seed of doubt, I felt self-conscious every time I burst into song. The seed he had planted began to germinate into a full-blown, self-fulfilling prophecy. Suddenly I had a problem. Is it psychological, I asked myself, or medical? I needed to know.

The Ear, Nose and Throat Hospital on Middlesbrough's Newport Road was a soot-darkened building with a dowdy interior of cream walls, sickly green paintwork and dreary lighting. The waiting room was populated with pasty and pinched faces. It had a defeated feeling about it. However positively I'd entered, determined to get to the root of this problem, by the time my name was called I looked as defeated as everybody else. And if the exterior of the building was Victorian, it was nothing on the bare room to which I was summoned. An illustration from a dusty tome on medical experiment plucked from the bookcase, everything in there was brown; air, walls, creaky boards underfoot and fixed to them in the centre of the room awaiting my arrival: 'Old Smoky' – the chair into which I was now being beckoned.

I squirmed in my seat as a small tube was introduced to my left nostril. "There's a tiny camera embedded in the end of it," the consultant informed me cheerfully. "Keep sniffing all the way up, that's it." The length of tubing continued to disappear up my nose. "That's it, good chap. When it gets to the top, start swallowing to pull it down the back of your throat." It was a disgusting experience but then, on a TV screen nearby the picture of the inside of my mouth flickered into life.

"Do you see the two flaps of flesh in the shape of a V, like butterfly wings?"

"Yes," I gargled.

"They're your vocal chords. You see how they're constantly quivering? They're supposed to be still."

"Why are they not?"

"They're in shock."

The length of tubing was slid from my nasal cavity. Now came the consultant's verdict. "I'm willing to bet you have Dystonia of the vocal chords. You've maybe sometimes seen people in the street with spasticated movement, unable to control their limbs? That's Dystonia. But with you it's only local; it just seems to be in your vocal chords."

"What's going to happen to me?"

"In 5 years time people will begin to notice a change in your speaking voice. In 10 years time you may be unable to speak – but by that age you'll have plenty of other things to worry about." He actually chuckled.

"I'm a singer," I told him seriously. "It's my job."

"And do you find you sing better when you've had a drink?"

"Of course. Doesn't everybody?"

"They do," he agreed. "But in your case it's relevant. Alcohol anaesthetises the vocal cords, calms them down so you can sing normally."

"Am I to understand you're prescribing alcohol?

"I think I am," he chuckled, "but don't tell anybody."

I sat in my car and brooded for a long time, before I turned the key in the ignition. I'd reached a crossroads in my life. I was a professional pop singer – with Dystonia of the vocal cords. My mind was already turning it into a song: Dystonia Dystonia, vocal ammonia, they'll hurt ya, they'll stone ya for singing all wrong.

It was growing dark when I arrived back in my drive, where Pat and Rory came out to greet me.

"Bring him in with you," she said, "I'm just about to give him his bath."

Pat turned indoors and gifted me my son. I picked him up and tenderly held him in my arms. Above in the night sky, Comet Hale-Bopp nestled in the Northwest, blazing its two trailing tails over the Conservative Club.

"Comet Hale-Bopp," I whispered; "it's only here for the next two days."

I'd be up there too in 48 hours time, flying to Johannesburg.

Chapter 25
Perg
- 1999 -

I carried on touring with the Flying Pickets – and anaesthetising my vocal cords – as another two years slipped by. My ponytail grew skinnier as my hair grew thinner. So I shaved it all off. I took the shaven-headed look a degree further by adopting heavy mascara and a bowler hat. I was striving for the menace of Malcolm McDowell in 'A Clockwork Orange', though Gary said I looked more like a Homepride flour grader. It didn't help when a local promoter provided a backstage ironing lady and she burnt my trousers, melting an imprint of the face of the iron into the fabric, five minutes before we were due to go on.

"Shall I wear them?" I asked the group, in a last minute flap.

"Might as well," Gary said. "You've made the group look ridiculous for years anyway."

He dug about in his bag and pulled out a pair of black jeans. "They should be alright," he reckoned, "I bought them before I lost all this weight. You just might be able to squeeze into them."

At home, missed birthdays and anniversaries rattled through the turnstile. Everyday moments of childhood magic flowed under the bridge. I was reading a book, 'The 60 Minute Father' which painfully reminded me: 'the door of childhood closes so fast and so finally'. Today was Rory's fourth birthday, the second year running I had missed the occasion. My book told me to 'kneel to talk to toddlers. Listen with your eyes'. Under the circumstances, picking up the phone was the best I could do. I tried to give my son some idea as to why Daddy always goes away.

"Did you get a lovely shiny bike?"

"Yes, a lellow one. From Mummy."

"No. From Mummy and Daddy."

"From you?"

"Yes, I bought that bike. That's why I go away all the time, to earn money so that I can buy you a bike."

Silence on the other end, though I could hear his confusion.

"How did you get it here, by magic?"

Towards the end of an Austrian tour, we were playing a private show in a brewery owned by an Austrian Count. Contrary to the popular saying, he certainly knew how to organise a piss-up. Following the show, Brian sensibly opted to go back to the hotel. As for the rest of us, wave after wave of strong beers and fearsome schnapps arrived at our table. "We make this spirit," said the boisterous Austrian next to me, "and then we bury it in the ground for a whole year. We dig it up only for the Flying Pickets!"

Well, it seemed to be working. Looking along the length of the table, our whole happy Pickets posse, the Austrian Count and every one of his cronies were red faced, shit-faced and shouting.

We weren't in great shape the following morning, I have to say. None of us could remember how the evening had ended or how we'd got back to the hotel. Paul awoke to find a trail of clothes leading from his door, with his shirt screwed up in the bin and one of his socks hanging from the chandelier. And Mike hadn't even made it back as far as his room – we found him eventually asleep in the middle of a roundabout.

There were further delays before we could slog to the next gig. We had to drive 20 kilometres back to the last one to retrieve jackets, shoes and suit-carriers. Befuddled, bamboozled by booze, we'd left half our stage gear behind.

"What's next Brian?" Henrik called up front.

"Beer tent."

Groans.

"Where?"

"Middle of nowhere."

When we arrived at the next hotel I didn't bother taking any of my bags out of the van. I was too tired to lift an eyebrow, let alone a briefcase, guitar and heavy suitcase. I could do without it all for one night, it was home first thing in the morning anyway. All I needed was a bed. If I had taken my bags out of the van however, I'd have noticed I didn't actually have my briefcase. I'd left it back at the last hotel.

We came, we saw, we probably didn't conquer but we got away with it, and the following morning we checked out at 8.30 for the three hour drive across the border from

25. Perg

Austria to Germany and on to Munich airport. Tour over! I couldn't have been more relieved. As all the usual banter went on around me, I listened to the singing tyres and thundering road beneath my feet. The tour bus seemed to be devouring the kilometres to speed me home. Pat had told me on the phone the night before she "loved me to bits" and I was in bits at the thought of basking in the warmth of her again.

Henrik was discussing the delights of kissing two bristly-faced female fans who had materialised backstage after the previous evening's gig. "Next time," he declared, "I'm going to say, do you mind if I kiss your armpit? It's pleasanter."

Upfront, Gary was eating crisps. "What's that rustling sound?" someone asked.

"It's Gary scratching his alien pubes," said Kis.

"It's Brian taking down his plastic underpants," mocked Henrik rather unkindly – Brian was several years older than the rest of us.

We crossed the Austrian border into Germany. One hour from Munich airport we paused for a piss-stop in a lay-by, as rock groups do. It was time to pocket my passport, which was in my briefcase.

I rummaged amongst all the bags. Kindling unease combusted into forest-fire panic as I unpacked everything and it wasn't there.

"Brian, I haven't got my briefcase!"

"What was in it?"

"Passport, credit cards, everything!"

"Oh no-o-o!"

"Can I fly without a passport?"

"Don't be stupid," said Gary.

"Let me think, let me think." Brian clutched his head. He grabbed his mobile and jabbed at it, walking away to find somewhere he could hear the person on the other end.

"How long till our flight Brian?" demanded Gary, as Brian moved out of bullying range.

"I seem to recall seeing a bag sitting in reception at the last hotel but one," Paul mentioned helpfully. "I remember thinking someone's left that bag, don't know who it is but someone; could be Brian, could be Henrik, could be Gary, Kis or H, don't know which, but someone's left that bag."

Brian came back. "Yeah. It's in Perg."

"Which one was that?"

"Pizzeria in basement, red carpet," groaned Mike, head beneath a blanket.

"Oh that one," remembered Kis, "that was the one after that fucking night in the Brewery, no wonder you left your briefcase."

They all chortled.

"Brian," I said. "How far away is it?"

"Perg? It's not even in this country. It's back there, in Austria! We're in Germany now. And without a passport, they'd never let you back through the border."

"Look," pleaded Gary, "can't we just go on to the airport? We can talk about all this there. It'll be much better there."

"Not for him it won't," assured Brian, jabbing his thumb my way. "It's a hundred K in the wrong direction."

Kis was amused by Gary's discomfort.

"What do you mean, better? Do you mean there's coffee and croissants and cakes and things?"

"Well… yes!"

"Good idea!" Kis agreed. "Let's all think of ourselves for a change!"

"Lads!" Brian urged. "Will you all simply shut up for a moment while I think."

Gary said: "You haven't got time to think Brian. If we don't go now we'll all miss the flight, never mind him."

We headed for the outskirts of the nearest town that had a railway station. The van hove to and spat me out at the roadside. Brian armed me with his book of European timetables. I felt abandoned, yet humbled. He was entrusting me with his bible.

"Germany should be somewhere between pages 6 and 700," he said, counting out and handing over some money. "See you then," he managed, "good luck."

Then they were gone. The last image to echo across my retina was one of sniggering faces at windows. To a Picket, my bandmates were experiencing deep, squirming schadenfreude – delight in another's misfortune.

My spongebag containing my wedding ring and father's signet ring had been mislaid earlier on the tour, somewhere in Belgium. My briefcase, diary, credit card and passport were marooned in Austria. My wife was stranded at home feeling like a music widow. I was stranded in Germany.

I reckoned this might be the start of my mid-life crisis.

I started running.

I have no doubt I looked a mess as Pat and I surveyed one another across the threshold. She was smiling and shaking her head, this woman who was in charge of everything in our lives and upon whom everyone depended: Dorothy, her mother, nearing 80 and living with us still. Our two elder sons, secure in her constant love and guidance. Our infant boy who relied on her for everything. Six dogs that followed her around the house. Whinnying ponies that cantered across the field towards her at the sound of her call.

"We thought you were never coming back," she said softly.

I moved into the hall and set down my briefcase, guitar, suitcase, suit carrier. I seemed to have been lugging them forever. My arms went around my wife and I hugged her for all she was worth, whispered into her scented neck: "you couldn't be more wrong."

Pat pushed back and beheld me strangely.

"I'm back for good."

For the past 13 years, apart from the one year when Moby Dick dragged me all the way to the West End, I had been performing a hundred shows a year as a Flying Picket. I'd been on one hell of a fairground ride: gigged with Ray Charles and Miles Davis, danced with Joan Baez and swapped songs round the piano with the Dutch Royal Family (and only found out who they were after they'd left). I'd sung to cynical female prisoners in an Adelaide jail. I'd signed bosoms and bottoms, got pissed and stoned and left clothing in dressing rooms around the world.

It was no wonder my vocal cords were in shock.

We shared a heart-to-heart at the kitchen table that night, Pat and I. "The tour's over," I told her. "I knew it the moment Brian dropped me off at the roadside."

Pat said nothing but looked troubled. I tried another tack. A new millennium was looming and I said to my girl: "I refuse to spend another thousand years in that bloody group!"

"What about our income?" she fretted.

"I worry about that too love, of course I do…"

"But something'll come up?" She looked at me through her hair, sceptically, for quite some time. Sitting back, she seemed to have made up her mind and I awaited the verdict.

"It's probably time to give your voice a rest."

"Hell yeah."

Our hearts were full, the light was soft and Tosca sang sweetly in the background. I took her hand across the table. "We'll be fine, baby."

"How can you know that?"

"I'm sure."

And as if to convince the both of us, I went out the following morning and had a key cut. Coming home, for the first time in a long long time, I let myself in at my own front door.

Part Three

The Nearly Man

Chapter 26
Campo Dog
- 2002 -

Welcome to Andalucia, Spain. Summer doesn't come any hotter than high noon out here in the campo, in mid-August. The dust bowl burns under a brutal sun and its horizon resounds with the howls of stray dogs. In front of our finca, the Rio Seco slithers not with water but with snakes. You can just catch a gleam of white, up where our nearest white-walled village lazes on a mountainside. To reach it is an uphill sword fight through invasive bamboo. This is usually followed by another sword fight at the Ayuntamiento (the local Town Hall) with bureaucracy. Afterwards, driving back home, we leave the village's tarmac road at a pretty picture-stone and bump along a descending track, bamboo swishing against the windscreen. Carefully manoeuvring our 4x4 down onto the dry riverbed and negotiating around craters, I come to a halt as a goatherd crosses our path. We can see our finca from here, but we'll just have to wait; there's no way through his dawdling, tinkling flock. Thar she blows in the distance, shimmering in the heat: our half-built house.

I am 'Campo Dog', an incognito diarist in a trade magazine to the ex-pat community. I write at my patio table, bothered by wasps. Not your little English ones either, oh no. These are big bastards with dangly legs. I have a swat, antihistamine cream and repellent spray set out before me, ready to be snatched up in an instant to do battle.

I sit, wrists and ankles afire with bites and body tensed. As I lean forward to snatch up the swat, an army of ants march up my arsehole, because I left my swimming trunks on the floor and forgot to check when I put them back on. Little fuckers are everywhere! Flip open the door to the dishwasher and you find a million of them circulating the plates in a blur of activity. Happiness would be the appearance of 'Europest' – though I don't know how they'll find us, I didn't really have an address to give them. Finca Rosa, Rio Seco, Andalucia was the closest I could get to pinpointing our whereabouts.

I have taken to styling my letterhead 'Finca Rosa, Tether's End'. I feel like the man in the moon or one of the hotter, less-inhabitable planets.

Back in Middlesbrough when the calendar flipped over to January 2000, it seemed to trigger a sequence of endings in our household. Two of our six dogs succumbed to old age. Then a third, Doris, went into kidney failure and our beloved King Charles Cavalier 'The Whuppy' (who's gilt-framed portrait hung above our fireplace) went into heart failure. 'The Rat' – a Chihuahua we thought would go on forever – also lost the good fight and suddenly we were down to one: a sweet little thing called Charity. That was unfortunate, that one. She was dancing about on her hind legs begging for food as I slaved over a hot stove. I lobbed a boiled potato her way, it shot down her gullet and wedged there.

First time I've ever seen a dog turn blue! I have never been forgiven.

Then a big one: Pat's mother died, lovely Dorothy, who had been with us for all of our married life. Though desperately sad, with her passing a huge weight lifted from Pat's shoulders. For the first time since her father left home when she was 12, she didn't need to feel responsible for her mum any more. As the grief began to subside, a strange new lightness of being entered and lifted her spirit.

Middlesbrough is a leaden overcoat in the winter months and even in Summer the sky can often look like the underside of an army tank. My grandfather, who as well as founding Kaye's Tools, was a poet, described it thus:

Twenty blast-furnaces belching a pall

Nine months of winter,

Lord what a hole!

Now, with 9 months of winter under her belt, Pat began to feel her wings; a migrating bird beckoned by warmer climes. She became exhilarated at the idea of emigrating.

"Where would you live if you could live anywhere?" she asked.

I flirted with the conversation, for it seemed no more than a game. Having always been infatuated with Italy, I replied "Tuscany."

Pat clicked away online, though it soon became apparent in this game of ours, that Tuscan property was way beyond my pay grade – not that I had one of course; we'd been trying to find a proper job for me ever since I'd left the band. Then she started looking at Spain online and everything changed; property was so cheap out there.

"We could build our own," she said excitedly, "you could be a property developer; we could sell up here and build a cheaper house in Spain!"

26. Campo Dog

Now I started to get a little sucked in. Ever the idealist, compounded by my grandfather's poetic tendencies, I began to imagine a life spun in sunlight.

Pat was beetle-browed over the computer: "We may even be able to build two properties, if we get enough for this one. There's this thing called a 'Casa di Perro' she told me, "a 60 metre construct that's really cheap to build and easy to get planning permission…"

I had no idea what she was talking about, but now I was the one getting excited. There was a property boom going on over there; why not be a part of it? Trips to Spain followed and before we knew it the deal was done, though I gulped at our naivety and more than once grimly remarked: "better not be another Lincolnshire." But any doubts I had were buried in an avalanche of enthusiasm from the rest of my clan. Leon and wife Issy, Joe who was now 25, sister Cora, Raphael and Ros, best friends Jessalinda and Pete – it seemed the whole lot of us were mad on emigrating.

From simply flirting with an attractive idea, we were now heading towards the point of no return. Our finca was being built and the Middlesbrough house in which I had been raised was on the market. It represented a monumental break with the past, but I convinced myself the longer I stayed in the house at Orchard Road, the more I was turning into my father.

Then a buyer came along. A 'House Sold' sign went up and now it really was too late to look back.

I looked forward. My mind beheld a vision of Spain where, bronzed and beautiful, we played like children in the waves, we stamped our heels and cried 'Ole'!'. In those final days before we packed up the house, we raised our glasses towards the sun, high hopes surging in everyone. We climbed on our chairs and toasted the future not once but three times: "To Spain! To Spain! To Spain!"

Approaching our completed finca that first time in the Summer of 2002, there in the middle of our newly-laid lawn sat a stray dog, creeping towards us at a hundred wags a second. I went to stroke him. His willy came out, a purple lipstick, dribbling with joy. He peed all over my hand.

"You're frightening him!" scolded Pat. Then, on the spur of the moment: "We'll call him Pablo."

"No we won't darling, because he's not bloody coming in!"

I had been over to Andalucia on multiple occasions to oversee the build but this was the first time Pat had ever set eyes on our new dream home. I was excited for her to see it, hugging myself in anticipation the whole way over. Then, at the moment of our joyful arrival and the big 'reveal' what happens? A bloody dog steals the show. What's more, we'd agreed to just the one dog. I must have reminded her hourly back at Orchard Road as we packed up the house. I'd been overrun for years and this was supposed to be a whole new beginning. Immediately things were going wrong.

"We're not just going to take the first stray that comes along," I said crossly.

"You're always jealous of any animal I have with a penis."

"No I'm not!"

"You were always the same with the horses."

"Ridiculous! It's only we agreed on just the one dog and we'd both choose her together. A bitch," I reminded her, wiping the wee from my hand. "I think we've clearly established this dog…"

"Pablo," she interrupted.

"…Is not a bitch."

Pablo looked up hopefully from one of us to the other. His tail beat even faster and his 'lipstick' which had protracted, protruded. Pat crouched and began squeezing out the tics living in his ears. Without looking up she said: "Why does it have to be a bitch?"

"Because the last one that wasn't cocked his leg and pissed all over my Fender Stratocaster, that's why!"

She cracked a tic between her fingernails. "Still worked, didn't it?"

"You do realise you still haven't said a single thing about the house?"

She smiled up at me. "It's lovely darling."

Within a week, she'd had Pablo inoculated and castrated. He was sleeping on the landing and snuffling at our bedroom door.

The phone signal out in the campo was dreadful. Whilst the rest of the world was in love with their mobiles, mine was redundant. I could have killed for a landline, a proper, weighty old-fashioned telephone. A phone with a traditional ring instead of 'Scotland The Brave'. One where the other party sounded as if they were in the next room, instead of 'can't hear you, hang on, I'm moving outside…. no, you're still breaking up, ring me back… you're out of credit…? I'm down to my last three eur…' Phone goes dead.

It was so hot, the aerial on my mobile wilted then fell off altogether. I stuck it back on with parcel tape but it didn't do much to enhance the reception. Then I dropped the bloody thing in the dog's water bowl. The chances of reaching me were now about nil and the sad device fell into what felt like terminal silence. That was it. My life was over. Lincolnshire – we'd done it again.

When the phone chirped to life around midnight one night, it was so unexpected, Pat sat up and looked at me the way Frankenstein's monster looked at Dr F. after that first bolt of electricity.

"Hereward?" came a dry voice. "Cameron."

"Hello!" I crashed outside and hammered up the steps to the swimming pool, the highest available point to maintain reception. I was stalking around ethereally underlit water, insect-bombed, holding my phone at different angles to find two bars, top right.

"What on earth are you doing in Spain?" he said, oozing charm like a fat cheese.

"Waiting for you to call!" I shouted, dodging around the pool, desperate to keep the signal.

My mind was racing. There had been distant developments on the Moby front for some time, though I'd given up all hope of anything actually happening. Music Theatre International – the go-to-site for the hire of musicals – wanted to include Moby Dick in their catalogue. But to be included, the show needed to be in far more presentable form. The project had been handed over to a member of their personnel in New York, one Russell Ochocki, who had put together a cut-and-paste version of the show from all the various scripts with which Robert had been bombarding Cameron since we fell off the radar in '92, a whole decade earlier. For my part, before I left England I had sent Russell every demo I'd created in those intervening years, to accompany Robert's ever-changing scripts.

Whilst I did all I could to help Russell, however pointless it seemed, Robert simply became enraged at the guy's involvement. He had been bombarding CML and me with poisonous letters and emails ever since Russell came on board. He opposed any attempt to take away from him editorial and creative power. Moby was his and that was that.

In reality, total control had begun to slip away from him the moment he had been removed from directing Moby Dick at the Piccadilly in '92. There'd been a whole production in Germany in which he had not been involved, having been unable to bring himself to attend the initial meeting, as it included a director he had never agreed to. This was Steven Dexter, who happened to be a friend of mine. Instead of turning up, Robert had absented himself with a legal note instead. 'I hereby hand over the show to Hereward Kaye' it stated, with two signatures at the bottom. And so that meeting had begun with Cameron asking if I was up to the task of rewriting the show.

"Of course I am!"

"In that case," he'd declared, "we're going to sit down and reshape the show and we don't go home until I am happy."

For several hours we'd thrashed out, chucked out, plotted and planned. I went away to rewrite, then updated the score with Martin Koch. A German production in Hof ensued. I flew over there for the opening night and squirmed my way through a very formal and operatic interpretation of the piece, my hand death-gripping a good luck card from Cameron: 'Moby lives! May your fabulous score send syncopated goose-bumps across Germany'.

It didn't.

There'd followed a further bout of redevelopment and a workshop production at Mountview Theatre School, all without Robert.

"I've had my spies out," Cameron told me back then; "they tell me it's all working very well, the story's working, the singing's lovely, it's just not very funny!" He'd rifled through the pages from the Mountview production then eyeballed me, challengingly: "you know I can never produce this show? It's known as 'Cameron's Flop'. It would be seen as me trying to prove the world was wrong. The public simply wouldn't accept it. Somebody else, completely separate to me, has to put it on and have some success with it. Then, I'd have it back like a shot."

"All I ask is that you read it on the flight to Australia with fresh eyes. Couldn't you interest anyone over there?"

"The trouble is, there aren't any fucking theatres in Australia!"

"Cameron, I haven't got any contacts, whereas you're the most connected man in the world."

"Look. Freddie's interested. Send it to him and he'll find a couple of theatres to put it in, somewhere in America."

"Will he?"

"He has to like it first, but, yes, he will."

"How can you be so sure?"

"His company is Music Theatre International, largest publisher of musical theatre in America. Who owns fifty percent of Music Theatre International?"

"You do?"

"Exactly."

Cameron's private secretary, Tee, entered.

"Cameron, Gillian Lynne's arrived and it's awfully hot in my office. Shall we take her somewhere else, or..?"

"Gillian darling!" He had risen and flung open the doors.

All that seemed a century ago – and it was! A hell of a lot of poisonous missives from my collaborator had flown across the ether or dropped into letterboxes since then; rants from Robert's pen, dipped in green ink. And I'd given up the game, gone to live in Spain. Now however, as I paced the pool in search of a signal, it seemed as if that conversation about Music Theatre International had moved forward. There'd been a read-through presentation in New York of script and songs, attended by a private audience of MTI staff and those in the know, including this man on the phone.

"Hereward?"

"I'm here, I'm here!"

"I thought I'd report to you first hand Hereward. I've just attended the read-through in New York."

"Oh! How did it go?"

"Extremely well. The real winner," came his gravelly voice, "was your music, which everyone agreed was wonderful. But don't get carried away. There are still many moments in the show that need to be improved."

"Is that where I come in?" Now I was Pablo whimpering to be let in.

"Possibly. I feel there may be a chance – no, I'm certain there could be a very strong chance, that this is a show whose time has come. When we did it 10 years ago, the time wasn't right."

"It was politically incorrect," I agreed eagerly. "Now you've got clubs in London where everyone dresses in school uniforms, a restaurant called School Dinners…"

"Shows like Hairspray and The Producers. It was when I saw The Producers in fact, that it struck me Moby was a show whose time had come. Some shows do take a long time. Look at Chicago. It did nothing when it was written 40 years ago. Look at it now."

"So what now?"

"We can't have Robert rewriting the whole thing again, it's just… mad. But you should be grateful for that madness. It was his whole madcap vision that got us all interested in the first place and drove you to write such wonderful songs."

Cameron went on: "I've asked Russell to send you a copy of the script used for the reading – also a live recording of the presentation. They'll be FedExed to you shortly. Where exactly are you?"

"I only wish I knew!"

"Well I'm going to have to fly you over. We need a meeting. As soon as they arrive, go through the materials I send you very carefully. Then we'll get together."

And he was gone.

It was remarkable. My mobile phone had held it together for more than half an hour. To be honest, if I'd had nothing more than a tin and a piece of string, I think he still would have reached me across the Atlantic. I came off the phone with a sense of having been filled to the brim, almost as if I had become the dried-up riverbed I lived beside and was now a roiling Rio, leaping with salmons of hope and rushing forward.

I ran. I weight-trained. I assumed yoga positions. I renounced alcohol for an entire week. Then I flew – first class darling – back to dear old Blighty.

I met up with Martin Koch and Stephen Metcalfe at Waterloo and we trained it down to Cameron's country pile in Somerset. Stephen was CML's current Musical Director in residence. Previously, the job had been Martin's, a golden era when he had conducted all the legendary musicals to emerge from that stable, so familiar to the public that the world knew them all by nicknames now: Les Mis, Saigon, Phantom. Martin had been doing more than well ever since I'd known him, though back in '92 when we were in the West End, he'd been constantly at Cameron's beck and call, which must have been exhausting. I had spent many hours with him back then, pouring over Moby songs. We worked at his flat; rustic inner-walls, brickwork tastefully uplit; a smart apartment overlooking St Katherine's Dock, by London's Tower Bridge. "You should see the penthouse upstairs," said Martin, "that's the one I really want."

As resident Musical Director, his brief was to look after all Cameron's shows. Then came an offer outside of Martin's exclusive, 'golden handcuff' contract with CML. He was approached to musically arrange a show created by Judy Craymer, based upon the songs of Abba, to be called 'Mamma Mia'. He went and begged Cameron for a 6 month sabbatical, which was refused. However, Abba's songwriters Bjorn and Benny launched a charm offensive and Martin went back to his boss cap in hand. "I think I really need to do this." "Look," an exasperated Cameron had told him, "go and do your little musical. Come back in 6 months when it's all over."

Martin had flown out to Sweden where Bjorn and Benny, with grave trust, handed over the master-tapes to all their anthemic hits. What this meant was that, once they got it up on the mixing desk back home, Martin and his tech-savvy friend Nick were able to separate off the various instrumental elements that, woven together, constituted the actual sound of all those great Abba records. The boys painstakingly sampled then uploaded these separate sounds into three different synthesizers, which they gave to the Mamma Mia pit band to play. Result? The band sounded exactly like the original records, because in a way, they were the original records. Bjorn and Benny were so delighted with Martin's work, they cut him in on one percent of their 'little musical'. Needless to say, that sabbatical lasted a little longer than 6 months – he never went back.

I worked with Martin a year or so after Mamma Mia opened. Home was now a lovely house in Islington, albeit with an annoying shoe factory at the end of his garden. And the next time I went round to his house, many more months of that 1% royalty later, I was sent to an address one street behind. It was the shoe factory, now a chilled-out recording studio. The door was answered by a member of staff.

Martin's studio let out onto his back garden, where we stood enjoying a beer in the sunshine and watching koi carp sliding under lily pads.

"I used to prefer your flat at St Katherine's dock mate," I joshed.

"Oh, I've still got that."

"I thought you wanted the penthouse above?"

"Yeah. I've got that too."

Now here we were in the next millennium, rattling along to Somerset. I was both amazed and grateful to see he was still on board. It just showed our little gem of a show continued to fascinate friends in high places. I didn't kid myself, Moby was a flawed gem – but not paste, or this train journey would simply not be happening.

"I read in the paper" – the coffee trolley interrupted and I waited till it had resumed its rattling progress up the aisle – "that Mamma Mia takes £400,000 a week in London. You're on one percent of the box office, so that puts you on four grand a week from that production alone, is that right?"

"I'm not telling you!"

"I know. Nosy. How many productions are there around the world at the moment?"

"Ten."

"Do they all earn as much as London?"

"Some of them earn twice as much."

"Bloody hell, you're earning more than a Premiership striker!"

"I'm doing very nicely, thank you very much," he laughed, embarrassed.

Cameron's estate manager, John, met us off the train. I settled into the soft leather upholstery of his 4x4. How different from the interior of my own 4x4 back on the campo, rubble on the floor, burst feedbags in the back. John's soft west country burr, as he recounted a recent trip he and his wife had enjoyed in New York (a gift from the boss), occupied the journey. Then we turned off the main road and manicured fields to left and right came sliding by, grazed by bison, West Highland cattle, alpacas.

"Whose are these?"

"Cameron's."

"How much land has he got here?"

"A thousand acres. Here we are," he said, as we crunched to a halt in gravel. He leapt out and opened the door for me and watched me gawp. "Used to be a monastery," said John. "Come in, make yourself at home."

Our host appeared in the hallway, fresh from indoor swim and work-out. He'd been at the Grecian 2000 by the look of it, bastard looked younger than me. "I can either give you the grand tour" he joked, "or we can work on Moby Dick today."

Face-to-face across the hand-made Steinway (only two in the world), Martin Koch at the keys and Stephen rifling through reams of piano parts trawled from the archive, we crawled our way through script and CD of the recent New York reading that had been the catalyst for all this renewed endeavour. Cameron's technique is to start off incredibly aggressively and shoot everything down in flames; he nails you to the floor in the first 5 minutes. It's an effective strategy, to which the only counter is to agree with everything he says, then gradually increase the pressure on the pedal of one's own ideas.

Hostilities were broken for lunch. As we entered the room, the refectory table was being laden with tureens of mash, a roast guinea fowl, quiches, fine wines. Beautiful males materialised; Cameron's partner of 20 years Michael, his resident personal trainer Simon, his ever-attentive personal assistant Anthony. Pudding was spotted – Dick of course.

"Come on," cried the knight of the realm at the end of it all, springing from his chair and heading back towards the piano. In we followed and on we battled, working through till late in the evening. Bottles of Bolly marked the end of the session and, having toasted the great white whale, the campaign ahead was discussed. I was tasked with pulling together all the changes we had made that day into a coherent script. This would be the version of the show we would present in workshop performance to a select audience of movers and shakers in New York.

I spent the next 5 days redrafting Moby Dick from a suite in Bloomsbury. The phone glowed hot with long calls from Cameron monitoring my progress and reminding me to make sure Russell received my work as soon as I was finished. There were follow-up calls from affable second-in-command Nick Allott, concerning contracts. No contract existed between ourselves and MTI. A deal would need to be negotiated, one that carried the signatures of both creators of the musical. Likewise, the 10 year contract that tied Robert and I to CML was about to expire and if I wanted the workshop presentation in New York to happen, a new contract would have to be arrived at and – here's the rub – Robert would need to agree to it.

Unfortunately, my collaborator was so overjoyed our contract was running out, he was counting down the days. In the 10 years that had passed since our blaze of glory in the West End, the Cameron Mackintosh organisation had become evil incarnate, in Robert's eyes. Mackintosh was in cahoots with Lloyd Webber. The whole thing was a plot. Moby Dick was being suppressed, as was Robert's entire career.

The situation could hardly have been more thorny. There was nothing else for it though; I would have to go and see Robert myself, and see if I could talk him round.

He looked pretty dishevelled when he came to the door of his council flat. But he asked me in and, assuming his usual master/pupil stance, Robert began updating me on all his latest Moby developments. He was building a website, he'd rewritten the show. Once we were free of our contract, there were any amount of producers itching to get their hands on the work, we only had to name our price.

I gently had to let him know I was in possession of the script MTI had presented recently in New York and that I had been tasked with tidying it up.

"Who by?"

"Well… you know."

"Mackintosh?" he exploded.

"Uh-huh."

"What's in it?" he demanded.

"It's a cut and paste of highlights from your many versions of the show over the years," I replied.

"How come you can see it when I can't?"

"You'll see it in a couple of days when it's ready," I somehow managed to say. I'd struggled to find that gentle word 'ready' but it was another detonator. He angrily accused me of rewriting his work. No I wasn't, I promised him, I was representing both his work and his interests. But he was growing more and more upset.

"Just give me a couple of days Robert, please." I begged him. He subsided into a shape in a chair and ground away at the hole in his thumb.

Easy bit over! Now I had to break it to him, I was here as an emissary of CML with the offer of a new contract.

"Agree to sign up with that lot again?" Robert was incredulous.

"There'll be an advance," I pointed out.

"They couldn't afford me!"

Back in my hotel room and brooding over bitten nails, the phone jolted me from introspection. It was Nick.

"How was Robert?"

"Difficult."

"I'm sure."

"Fucking difficult. Collaboration's hell."

"I know," he agreed with some feeling, "that's why Cameron doesn't bother."

We laughed at that one. Nick said funnily enough, he'd just recently received an email from Robert, the most poisonous email of all time.

"Send it to me. I can take it, I'm a man."

"Not this one you can't!"

Then Cameron called. "Will he agree to a contract?"

"It'll cost you."

"How much?"

"He wants £50,000."

"Between you?"

"For himself."

26. Campo Dog

Cameron practically squealed with pain. "I've just paid £50,000 for the rights to Mary Poppins, Hereward. And with respect, it's a better fucking show than Moby Dick!"

I got my head down and did battle with the written word, this hybrid script that was a distillation of Russell's version which was in itself already a distillation of all Robert's previous versions – not to mention a 10-hour Somerset sword-fight over the Steinway with Cameron. For 5 long days and nights alone, I pored over every line and lyric, trying to make sense of the nonsensical. The mini bar was ravished in true rock 'n roll style, the phone bill hammered, room service run up, 5 days of 'exxes' spent. As a former Flying Picket, one never forgets these skills.

The moment I put in the last full stop, I fired the script off to Russell, as instructed.

Then I rang Robert to tell him it was ready.

"Where shall we go through it" I asked, "your gaffe or here in my hotel?"

"I don't want you standing over me while I read it," he replied testily. As usual with Robert, he didn't exactly ring off, I just realised he wasn't there anymore.

It was time to take my pristine script over the road to Sir Cameron.

"Darling!" Jennifer Till burst into her office, where she found me printing it all up. "Let me get you some wine. Red or white? White would be better. I'll send for some. Darling, how lovely to see you. You look so nice."

Anthony entered with the chilled Sancerre and the fluted glass, looking gorgeous. All the men in this building were exotic. The women, less so – except for Nick Allot's secretarial merry-go-round of ravishing beauties.

Jennifer phoned Tee, Cameron's private secretary.

"Teazy, is it time for us to lurk?"

We crossed the chandeliered splendour of the first floor into Tee's office, with its ceiling to floor windows overlooking Bedford Square.

"Darling!" Tee greeted me as if we once had sex and it was great. Just as suddenly she lost interest, as Anthony ushered in another suitor to the court of King Cameron.

"It's like Heathrow in here," I observed. "I'm going to get you a sign for your desk: Air Traffic Controller."

She roared her approval. I'd won her back.

"I'm afraid Hereward's next," she informed Anthony's visitor. "We don't let anyone gazump our Hereward, do we dear?"

And yet, as the previous appointee was disgorged, this later arrival was beckoned forward and I was left waiting. He was the producer of 'Rent', a show that had taken Broadway by storm. I was the composer of the show that had been labelled 'Cameron's Flop' – what chance did I stand? Just as my name had been stencilled bottom of the register of greats in the EMI building, here was Moby Dick's place in the pecking order at CML – last appointment of the day. Through the great windows I watched London commuters scurrying for home or restaurants and bars. Bored, I listened to Tee go through Cameron's diary for tomorrow with Anthony.

"He's got the Minister of State at 10. He's got his mother at 11. Do you know the vicar? Well he's died. Cameron wants a huge bouquet for the funeral, but not from him, from his mother. And he has to be at the airport at 1.45 at the latest; he flies to Mexico at 2.20. He's got Napier at 12 so we've got to stop them sloping off together or we'll never find him."

The two mahogany doors open grandly, disgorging the Rent producer.

"Hereward."

Tee hands Cameron a print-out of an email. He's frowning as I follow him through. Russell has emailed a list of objections to the script I have just completed, the script I am about to hand over, the script Cameron has yet to see.

I wait.

He looks up from the email, clearly in a foul odour. "You've done a tremendous amount of damage."

"But you said Russell had to see it as soon as possible!"

"Not before I'd seen it!" If he'd had a leather glove he'd have dashed it from one side of my face to the other. Clearly I'd done things very much in the wrong order. I handed him the script.

"Crap. Crap!" he exclaimed. "Why's this here, who's joke is this? Get rid of it." On he went on and on, one page to the next, flipping forward, flipping back, cross-checking every line and lyric as it grew dark outside. Each artistic decision I had made was pulled apart. Not one page was left unscathed and we still had the whole of Act Two to go. Mercifully we were interrupted by a phone call Tee told him he simply had to take. But then he was on the phone to 'Trevor' for half an hour. At one point I wandered over to the grand piano and shaped a restless chord.

"Don't! I'm on the fucking phone!"

26. Campo Dog

I shot down to reception. "My brother-in-law Raphael and sister Ros are meant to be arriving? If they turn up, please please interrupt my meeting."

"They've been and gone," said reception. "They're waiting for you in the restaurant."

I went back upstairs with sinking heart and continued to wait until Cameron came off the phone. Conversation switched to The Deal. I had received a draft offer from solicitors on both sides of the Atlantic setting out terms agreed – that is, terms agreed with me, but not yet with Robert. That joyful experience was still to come.

This was a tough gig that had landed on my doorstep. I'd ended up demanding £25,000 each for Robert and I in advances from CML and the same amount in US dollars from Music Theatre International. Even Nick Allott had been impressed on the phone, saying: 'you should have been an agent.' It was meant to be a compliment but I flinched at the very word. That was something I would never aspire to be, not after my experience with the last one. After all, Moby Dick had only cost Captain Ahab a leg. It cost me an arm too!

"Did you take advice?" Cameron asked. He'd offered me a lawyer but I didn't trust the impartiality of that scenario. I told the impresario I had gone through the document with my mate Sacha Brooks. Sacha was producer of 'The Full Monty', a musical soon to close after a 6 month run at The Prince Of Wales, one of Cameron's theatres.

"I'm about to spend 7 million pounds refurbishing it," he rather proudly informed me.

"Do you know what you're like?" I said, "you're like the guy in Monopoly who's got Mayfair, Park Lane and all the green ones."

"I usually get all the yellow and red ones as well," he laughed.

"Yeah, well," I said with feeling, 'I've just got the brown ones."

"And Water Works."

Water Works was Moby Dick, an addiction this marvellous bully clearly couldn't shake.

Last to leave the building, we locked the place up together, punched the alarm, hugged-out on the doorstep. "Come with me," I said on an impulse. "My sister and brother-in-law are waiting round the corner in a lovely Italian restaurant. It'll be completely cool, I promise."

"I'd love to" he said sadly, "unfortunately I have to pack for Mexico…"

I met his eyes. "I'm not going to do the Cameron thing. I don't have to. You do know that, don't you?"

"Yes," he said. "I do."

Once again, my return flight to Malaga was changed, as I prolonged my visit to crawl through the script and pacify every objection raised by Russell on one side of the Atlantic and Cameron on the other. I photocopied, bound and biked the final result across to Robert, along with the draft of the legal document setting out all the terms I had negotiated on our behalf.

I gave him the evening to read, then rang him next morning.

Silence.

"Robert?"

He let out a sigh, such as I have never heard since my father-in-law died under my nose.

"I've been crying all night."

There then began a deadbeat litany that would have been improper to interrupt. No magic. No romance. And the final condemnation: it's 'Middlesbrough'.

"This isn't Russell what's-his-name's show" he spat, "it's yours."

"Ours."

"It is not mine."

I swear I empathised. Why wouldn't I, after my own bruising career? And why wouldn't I, after my own experience of having lyrics rewritten and music misappropriated? Robert had painted his masterpiece, and I had painted all over it.

To compound the felony, I had been a filter for Russell and a conduit for every idea of Cameron's, without ever consulting my creative partner. I know why I didn't consult him – he was too bloody difficult to work with! But I also knew how this must look; I had imposed my own vision upon the script, and restored and developed many of my original lyrics. But actually, fifty per cent of the work was still Robert's, plus the whole original concept. If we could make it fly, champagne flutes across theatre land would be raised in praise of Robert Longden.

I had been cast in the role of professional mediator and contract negotiator. I was clearly neither of those things. I had been played, there was no doubt about it. On one side of the contract negotiations: Cameron Mackintosh and Nick Allot for CML, Freddie Gershon and Drew Scholfield for MTI. Their two teams of lawyers.

On the other side: er… me. And, I suppose, one non-negotiable writing partner, who was blanking me on the other end of the phone.

"What about the contract?" I ventured, with morbid trepidation. "Are you in or out?"

I held onto the receiver a long time listening to lapping waters of silence from the other end. But I knew he was there all right.

It all hinged on this moment.

"The deal will go through or fall through Robert. Your call."

I tossed it like a pebble into the still lake between us. There was a ripple of breathing in response, but no more.

"I understand how you must feel. It's up to you."

There then came a sigh even greater than the first, if that were humanly possible.

"Okay."

Chapter 27
New York
- 2003 -

It started tentatively, like a celestial drummer riffing round the kit; a few desultory plips as brushes were drizzled lightly across cymbals. Then an insistent rhythm of rain drumming on the roof, increasing in tempo and intensity as we moved through downpour to thrumming deluge. Light-bulbs flickered as the storm gathered into an electrifying crescendo. The waterfalls cascading down the windows were back-lit by flashes of forked lightning, snaking from the heavens above to strike at the earth below.

Blackout.

A juddering WHOOSH went through the whole house, as if it had been shaken by the very devil. We hardly dared breathe as we lay there in the aftermath, in darkness. Presently, a grave voice came from downstairs. It was our Joe, over from England, sleeping on the sofa.

"You better come down Dad."

I wished I hadn't. The whole ground floor was knee-deep in water, dirty brown and swaying slightly in the torch-light after its charge through the house.

Outside, the garden was a roiling river, indistinguishable from the torrential waters beyond, trading under the ironic title of Rio Seco. We were cast adrift.

"That's it," wailed Pat from the stairs, surveying the desecration. "I've had enough!"

The next day Pat and Rory took refuge in a local hotel, as Joe and I sloshed about the ground floor in our wellies bailing out water. I borrowed a pump from a couple of ex-pats further up the valley and by the time my Pat – very nearly my ex-Pat from the look on her face – returned the next day, we were mopping the tiles. Gloria, our motorhome, had survived the onslaught and so there we lived, for the 3 months it took to salvage the house. Gloria was toasty and snug, with curtains to partition us off from our troubled house across the lawn, where the moon shone into deserted rooms.

Winter came on and our abandoned finca grew cold to its bones. Damp drew mottled graffiti across the inside walls. The air turned dank and stale. Dozy from a night's sleep on the bus, floor tiles were icy as one or other of us crossed the kitchen to fill the kettle, and an obstacle course of dog-shit. Our two adopted strays, Pablo and Scruffles, confused at being left home alone in the dark all night, expressed themselves by leaving desultory turds.

It was Pat one morning, crossing the crunchy lawn and entering the Siberian wasteland of downstairs to fill the kettle.

No water.

"That's it, the last straw, the LAST one!"

Now we used giant bottles of water from Lidl and grew smellier. When we finally did manage to get the water back on, my wife celebrated by having a bath. Letting it out, it inexplicably set the downstairs toilet moaning deeply, as if this was a portal to Hell. Monstrous gurgles presaged a spew of sewage all over the tiled floor.

"Right, this is it," exploded Pat, hands in the air and spinning on the spot, her voice ringing from the four bare walls as dogs, children and I all cringed. "This is IT!"

"I know love, I know," I soothed, "I feel the same."

"No you fucking don't!" She rounded on me. "It's alright for you, you're off to New York in the morning!"

* * *

In the Business Class lounge at Malaga airport I poured myself a coffee, picked up a copy of the *Times* and settled back into a sofa. I felt a slow smile spread across my face as the tensions of the last few weeks slid away.

America!

It had been some years since my last time in New York and as I waited to board the plane, my mind went back to a promise I had made to myself the last time I left that city behind. As we were jostled left and right by Chevies, Lincolns, stretch Cadillacs heading away from the Big Apple, I remembered twisting back in my taxi seat to see it all receding, to drink in the glittering skyline of Manhattan gradually diminishing as we churned through Brooklyn towards JFK. Craning my neck for a last look, I took in the Empire State lighting up the sky in red and green neon, the Chrysler building scaled like a fish and diamond-white in the night. Dwarfing all else, the two towering shoots of the World Trade Centre. At Shea Stadium, where the Beatles triumphed, we turned a corner and that last glimpse was gone from view, the whole mad world of delis and noodle bars, of steam rising through pavement grills, of bagels, pretzels and roast chestnuts on every street corner, a film crew just around it, leafleteers and tin-rattlers striding the length of it. I turned to face forward and whispered: "I'll be back".

From Malaga to Manhattan. From a desecrated house on the campo to Cameron's luxury apartment on 7th Avenue. It was to be mine for the next 3 weeks, as we rehearsed then presented Moby Dick to an invited audience, followed by a cast album recording in an uptown studio. For the first 3 days I would have the place to myself. After that I would be joined by Musical Director Martin Koch and Cameron himself.

Limo driver Anuj dropped me off at the front and doorman Benny handed me a key. Lift attendant Frank took me up to the 11th floor.

"End of the corridor, door on the left. Have a nice stay!"

I let myself in on a circular reception area, the walls hand-painted with views of Provence; Cameron's French vineyard of course. At the centre stood a table and on it, a note from Esme the housekeeper. She'd see me on Monday; meanwhile everything I needed was in the fridge. Propped against a vase of flowers was an envelope with my name upon it and, inside, an itinerary plus $900.

I padded into a living room of Persian rugs, tapestry sofas, antique furniture and Old Masters upon the wall. In the still, oak-panelled study stood a Steinway Grand, so highly-polished you could see your face in it. There were three further bedrooms, three bathrooms and a kitchen hung with shiny pots and pans.

It wasn't home, but it would have to do.

With the rest of the day to myself, I baffled up against the elements – it was 10 below that January – and stood beside Benny on the steps outside. Bitterly cold! I wound the scarf over nose and mouth and pulled the NYC woolly hat down over my ears to meet it. Tugged my coat collar up as high as it would go. Only my eyes were exposed. I looked right: Central Park and Museum Mile. I looked left: Times Square and Broadway. Left it was; I set off along the length of Broadway, to see if everything was just where I left it.

At Times Square I gazed up at the Marriott Marquee. A lift was whizzing its way up and down the side of the building. Arnie had ridden that lift, on horseback, in 'True

Lies'. I had ridden it too; this was the hotel where I had stayed on my first time in New York. I'd sat in the revolving restaurant on the 48th floor, straight off the plane and jet lagged, not knowing if it was me going round or the restaurant – I couldn't work out how the piano player kept getting louder, or why he was suddenly beside me, when I came back from the bar. I was working on another musical at the time produced by Sacha Brooks, and I shared a room there with my two musical collaborators, Dexter and Clark. They were both Stevens, so we dispensed with Christian names.

The three of us were resting up mid-afternoon on our beds, when Clark's phone rang. "Tonight?" I heard him say, "great! Yes, me and Steven Dexter." He fired a quick look my way: "can I bring a friend?" He was hand-over-the-mouthpiece saying "do you want to come out with me and Dex to meet Stephen tonight?"

Not another bloody one! "Yeah, why not."

Far from another Steven, this Stephen turned out to be *the* Stephen Sondheim. I found myself sitting next to the man who had penned 'Maria', 'Somewhere', 'Send In The Clowns'. He was a little traumatised, because his house had just burned down. "My fault entirely. Started in the study – papers everywhere. I had a whole pile of 'em under the standard lamp, which turned out to be faulty. I kept sayin' I'd tidy 'em up. I should've had that lamp fixed."

He looked anguished. "Here, have some wine" I said, filling his glass. And after he'd had a couple, the stories began to flow. This Stephen I found out, had for 25 years compiled the New York Times cryptic crossword. He'd been a raw, 23 year old lyricist when he'd accepted the 'West Side Story gig' as he put it. Rather strange to hear a musical of such magnitude reduced to a mere gig. He'd been about to turn it down but his uncle Oscar Hammerstein talked him into it. Richard Rogers the producer hated him apparently. And he said he was ashamed of his lyrics.

"Surely not!" I spluttered.

"There's a place for us, somewhere a place for us. The emphasis is in the wrong place" he growled, like a gridlocked New York cabbie, "it's all on the indefinite article."

Over the course of conversation, he discovered I was the composer of Moby Dick and began to look at me with some appreciation. "I saw it in the West End and adored it," he enthused gruffly.

"Tell that to Cameron!"

"Well" he'd said doubtfully, "I'll try."

Leaving Times Square I resumed my icy odyssey through Manhattan, fingers aching inside thermal gloves. Fifty-seven blocks I walked, down through the theatre district, past the Flatiron Building, across Madison Square. At the Empire State I took the lift to the top. Up there the cold was brutal but worth it for the view. Frozen like Narnia and spread out below, there lay the whole of Manhattan. The surrounding 'U' of the Hudson River was solid ice. Stalagmites of buildings scraped the sky. There was the Rockerfeller, there Grand Union, there was the Chrysler Building. There *weren't* the Twin Towers.

It seemed inconceivable they could simply have vanished. One was the tallest structure in the western hemisphere; the south tower was the second tallest building in the world. Last time I was here I'd shopped in the underground Mall, explored the ground and mezzanine floors – and been unable to ride the elevator 110 floors to the observation deck because of high winds. Now, as I saw from the top of the Empire State, it just wasn't there anymore.

I walked on. A bread van came past: 'We move our Buns for you!' The numbers on the crossing streets were in their teens now and the vibey, multi-ethnic human stream flowing towards me had become a trickle. A black guy called across to a woman waiting outside a shop: "Hey girl, where's yo husband at?" Amazingly, this blatant piece of chat-up worked, for now they were grinning and walking off together.

A fire truck sailed by, 'Tower Ladder 7' emblazoned upon its gleaming side, and the names of two members of their crew who had lost their lives in the furnace of 9/11. On the radiator grill: 'Still the Greatest Job on the Planet'.

I reached Ground Zero. The railings were draped with messages, flags, a battered fireman's helmet, photos of loved-ones lost. Everywhere you looked were the words 'God Bless America'. A giant cross was set in the ground; two pieces of girder forged together by molten flame.

"That cross you're staring at," spoke a guy coming towards me and setting his bag on the ground, "came outta the rubble just like that. What looks like cloth draped on one of the arms is the outside of the building." Now he began to shout: "Know the history! Don't let it be mystery!" Instantly, we gathered a crowd.

Russell Ochocki and I met up for the first time. We had communicated long and hard on this re-launch of the musical, but I still had absolutely no idea what he looked like. Ochocki, to my romantic mind, was a native American with flowing, crow-black hair – someone far younger than myself, as everyone seemed to be these days. What I got was a stocky, balding and combative New Yorker, the shaved beard of a jazz musician framing his garrulous lips. Turned out he would be turning 50 that year of 2003 – and his birthday was only 3 days after mine. We were doing lunch in a Thai restaurant and he beat the table joyfully:

"Yes! I knew I'd be younger than you."

"What? I was still covered in blood when you were born, they'd barely cut the cord."

"I was early."

"So was I. Very. And what about the time difference?"

We shivered down the street to his office at Music Theatre International. Walking in upon all the open-plan activity, there I espied our spanking new logo on a far wall, next to the logo for 'Les Mis'. Oh God, I thought, here we go again. I was presented to all the bigwigs (apart from Freddie Gershon, the mighty boss), who all assured me this time Moby was going to make it. One of the talking heads was Head of International Marketing. There were some big players coming to the reading I was informed, particularly this one theatre – huge – in Chicago, who went for long runs of their productions. "We're talking forty, sixty thousand dollars a week royalty," he told me. After all the pain I had endured at the hands of this musical, I didn't want to build up hopes again. And yet, it was almost impossible not to.

Spotting a vacant desk on the other side of the room, I waited till interest in me had fizzled out and everyone had gone back to their jobs, then sloped over and sneaked a call to Pat. After a while, I became aware of a bloke standing, waiting to speak.

"Hang on babe," I whispered, looking up.

"Hi. Freddie."

Caught red-handed running up the phone bill by the head of the company!

"Walk with me to the elevator," he instructed.

He talked Moby Dick for all of the 30 seconds it took to walk there, and the 30 that followed waiting for the lift. He entered and pressed the down arrow, still talking. I tried to squeeze in a word or two before the doors slid shut, but found myself talking to shiny silver metal and Freddy already two floors below.

From MTI to rehearsal room, where the cast filtered in and the jabber of conversation rose animatedly. I leant against the piano, playing the usual guessing game of who would be playing what. That older guy would be mad Elijah, clearly, the striking black girl Queequeg, the innocent-looking one over there our narrator Ishmael, and so on. There was a particularly charismatic young man doing the rounds, who wasn't a member of the cast at all, but appeared to be the friend of everyone. Bert V. Royal was a writer and artist, and it was his new Moby Dick logo that adorned the wall at MTI. It would adorn the front cover of our new cast album too, when we'd recorded it.

Bert's first words to me, whispered conspiratorially, were: "you know you're the only straight person in the room?"

I looked around. The perceived ratio of gay to straight in society at that time was 1-in-18. Observing the heightened flamboyance and freedom of expression on display, it seemed he was bang on. Looked like the whole room was gay! I felt almost sheepish about my own, boringly predictable sexual orientation.

During the third day of rehearsals, Cameron blew in off the icy street dressed like an Inuit kitted out at Harrods, in a woolly coat that touched the floor. He was cracking Captain Pugwash double entendres as he entered, having programmed his mind towards the nautical. The atmosphere in the room instantly gathered electricity. Words flew off the page and songs flew off the stave. Elvis was in the building.

He was also in the apartment on the edge of Central Park in which I had happily luxuriated alone. So too was Martin Koch, who flew in soon after. The three of us became… domestic. I have to be honest, it was a little unsettling walking into the kitchen at breakfast time and bumping into Sir Cameron in his underpants.

Attempting a little matey banter, I said: "hey, look at you with your muscles!"

"I work out every single day," he snapped and glared. Then (rather ungraciously), "how do you like your eggs?"

At the breakfast table Martin and he discussed the Prince of Wales Theatre in London's West End. Having recently acquired it, Cameron was planning to give the place an overhaul. He was having the auditorium rebuilt and seating capacity increased, adding new bars, re-imagining the exterior.

"When do you think you'll be ready for us?" asked Martin casually.

"This time next year."

"Us" meant Martin's show obviously, the second most successful show on the planet, after Cameron's 'Les Miserables'. Once all the refurbishments had been completed, to a grand fanfare the theatre would reopen with 'Mamma Mia'.

"What are you up to after this?" the producer asked Martin.

"Vegas. We're opening at the Mandalay Bay. I go straight from here actually."

Cameron nodded approvingly.

It was during the course of one of these sociable breakfasts, I was invited to ring the office for tickets to any Broadway show I fancied. And so I attended 'The Producers', 'Oklahoma' and – after Cameron staggered into the kitchen with food poisoning and

The Ship Hits the Fans

Bert V. Royal's logo for the re-imagined 2003 version of Moby Dick, which appeared as a mural inside MTI's New York headquarters.

gave me his ticket – Baz Luhrmann's delicious production of 'La Boheme'. I had the best seat in the house and as if that wasn't enough, beside me sat a beautiful princess. This is not an exaggeration. She was beautiful, and she was an actual princess. We talked all through the interval and continued animatedly at the end of the show. She gave me her card as Americans do, saying: "promise you'll give me a call next week? I'm in the Caribbean for a photoshoot from tomorrow."

So that's what she was doing next. Luckily, she didn't ask me what I was doing next. Mopping up sewage just wouldn't have cut it.

Rehearsals continued. Brian Batt, our leading man, was recovering from laryngitis and informed us he wouldn't be singing until the actual performance. He was holding back on the comedy too, but it would all happen on the day he promised. Last time around he had been wildly funny, everyone assured me – including Cameron, who had found him so hilarious at the original workshop production, it had kick-started all this renewed activity.

Then the first read-through presentation was upon us, with another to follow the next day. Our handpicked audience filed in and took their seats. Once all 50 chairs were occupied, the performance got underway. It seemed a little stiff and inhibited that first half; Captain Ahab was playing it carefully. The magic we had been promised from Brian Batt failed to materialise. Cameron was so incensed by the time we hit the interval, he tried to stop the rest of the show. I was used to this kind of tension by now, but Russell, experiencing it for the first time, was profoundly shocked. He told the producer it was simply impossible to cancel Act Two. Out of respect for all the actors taking part, it was our responsibility to continue.

A grim-faced Cameron was forced to agree. Against his will he sat through the second act. Looking across, I knew a murderous biopsy was on its way.

The moment the last member of the audience had filed out, he rounded on us with the butcher's knife. Everything had to be put back to how it was the last time he saw it. "The show's got better," he said, turning to glower at me in particular, "but it's got worse!" He even turned on Martin, saying his arrangements were too slick. "The show's just not funny anymore," he concluded. He gave us tonight to fix it, tomorrow morning to implement changes and tomorrow's performance to come up with the goods or else.

I was bleary-eyed as we bumped into each other in the kitchen early the next day. Cameron immediately became scathing about Brian Batt's performance, this leading man he had previously adored. "The problem was drugs."

"Yes," I conceded, "he was perhaps on medication."

"That's not what I mean at all Hereward. I mean he should *be* on drugs. Before he plays Ahab."

"What sort of drugs?"

"Terminal ones!"

Be that as it may, I told him, Russell and I worked long into the night making all sorts of cuts and changes that should result in a tighter, funnier show. "I'm sure you'll approve," I said.

"I won't be able to make today unfortunately" said Cameron, "I have meetings."

This upset me. "So your last memory of Moby in New York will be something you hated?"

He attempted to be conciliatory: "I saw Steve last night."

"Steve?"

He looked at me as if I was mad. Martin was hovering and muttered sotto voce: "Sondheim."

"He's doing The Frogs" Cameron said, assuming I would be as familiar as he with the Aristophanes oeuvre. "Steve said he wished it could be as vulgar as Moby Dick, which he always loved."

That made me smile. It had taken 7 years, but looked like Sondheim had made good on his promise to put in a good word with Cameron.

We went on to discuss the upcoming recording session. The cast album was my responsibility, I was told. For the umpteenth time I was warned it had better be funny.

"Have you done your sleeve notes?"

"I have, yes." I proclaimed to the kitchen ceiling: "no more maybe, Moby!" – then stood there in my towelled bathrobe as if awaiting a round of applause.

After an appalled pause: "Did you thank Russell?"

"I did, I said we were two nations divided by a common language and thanked him for translating it into American. Also grateful thanks to Freddie and yourself."

At this, he became flustered. He knew his name had to be on it somewhere, but he needed to control exactly how his involvement was presented. His signature was all over the thing of course, as was Russell's, but the writing team was Robert and myself; that was sacrosanct. He also didn't want any more shit to stick on him. He was as bruised as Robert and I were by last time around – and a million and a half quid down.

"I came up with a credit that wrapped it up nicely... what was it?" Cameron stood racking his brains then jabbed at his phone to call England. "Put me through to Nick." We waited... "Nick? Hello dear. What was the credit we came up with for the CD? You were with me. it'll be on a piece of paper somewhere..." He listened for a moment then snapped: "well find it!"

Three minutes later his phone rang. After listening for a moment or two he cried "that's it, that's it!" Turning triumphantly to Martin and me: "The authors would like to reluctantly acknowledge interference by Russell Ochocki and Cameron Mackintosh."

So he missed the show that afternoon, but Freddie turned up with Mrs Gershon swathed in furs and a moody John Kander, composer of 'Cabaret' and 'Chicago', in tow. The performance was altogether better, driven by Brian Batt, who was very much restored to former glories. Russell and I had wasted no time imploring him to go utterly bonkers.

I stole a glance or two across at the Gershon party, hoping for encouraging signs. Though Freddie seemed amused enough, his wife looked on with an unchanging, unblinking, uncomprehending stare. John Kander stayed slouched in his seat, 'unimpressed' tattooed to his bored forehead. My heart sank, looking at them. Somehow I didn't think we'd be seeing weekly royalty cheques for $60,000 anytime soon.

The following day in the studio was a long one. The cast were lined up behind microphones, on the other side of the glass from where Cameron, a sound engineer and I moved about the control room. In a separate booth sat Martin, at a baby grand. His fingers stabbed out the chords on the piano and mine jabbed at the talkback button on the mixing desk, whipping the cast onwards, through all 27 songs. It was a happy and spontaneous day and by the end of it, several moments of 'funny' were down on tape.

Waking up in the apartment the following morning, clothes were being folded into Louis Vuitton baggage and farewells called. Martin and Cameron were leaving for different parts of the world, to continue mining their seams of theatrical gold. As a parting shot, the producer informed me Moby's beginning needed looking at again.

27. New York

Knowing I had time to kill before my flight back to Spain, he tasked me with writing an attention-grabbing opener to the Show. In his study he flipped through a library of LPs and CDs, spinning out musical after musical with classic opening numbers.

Then this benevolent tyrant was gone, leaving almost as big a hole in the atmosphere as the absent Twin Towers outside the window.

I had the apartment to myself and the luxury of time rolled out at my feet like a red carpet. Three whole days, before I swapped skyscrapers for hillsides that collapsed in winter and combusted into flame in summer. Three more days before I swapped cosmopolitan comfort for a septic tank that spewed sewage all over the floor. Three days more before I changed this prime Central Park address for: 'The House That Jack Built, Back of Beyond, Tethers End, Spain'.

I kicked off my shoes and moved from room to room, savouring the splendour at my disposal. I took a bath. Prepared some food. Curled up on the sofa with a book of Norman Rockwell illustrations, so absorbed, the backbeat of the street and symphony of car horns outside receded to nothing.

Eventually I peeled myself away and returned to the oak-panelled study. There stood the Steinway, gleaming blackly at its centre, expectantly awaiting.

I spent a peaceful afternoon shuffling through the pile of CDs, listening carefully and making notes. Then, when I was ready, I set a few pages of pristine paper against the music rack, picked up a decent pen, pulled up the dimpled piano stool – and began for the thousandth time to rewrite Moby Dick.

Chapter 28
The fridge

When I got back to my finca, a delightful surprise was in store: Leon, my responsible eldest – 26 by now, married and resident in a village 10 kilometres away – had toiled all 3 weeks of my absence to transform the place. I'm not saying it looked like a classy condo on Sixth Avenue, but our mouldy wardrobes were mouldy no longer, the plumbing worked and the floor tiles had been stripped back to terracotta. He'd patched up the old pantile roof, sealed up leaky cracks in the walls, tiled the bathroom and repainted inside and out.

'Gloria' returned to being a motorhome and we moved back into our finca. Best of all, I got my little studio working and son Joe gave it a name: Costa del Soul.

Getting online and picking up a mobile signal was still but a dream in this bowl of hills, so a morning trip to internet café Cyber Lucia was my only hope of connection to the wider world. The café was my postal address too; I had a mailbox. It was there I went on a morning after dropping Rory at his International School, where the kids all had blond streaks, the mums had Range Rovers, jangly jewellery and Essex accents, and the teachers looked like the cast of 'Neighbours'.

You'll know by now that the middle of nowhere has never been my preferred address. Therefore, I was constantly on red alert for a message from Cameron. He was my best – possibly only – chance of rescue. On an early Spring day of 2003, he duly obliged, though the message in my inbox wasn't exactly what I wanted to read. The subject was my new opening number.

> Dear Hereward, I hope you had a safe journey home. I have now had a good look at the new pages you sent me. I think the ideas are very good but the lyrics are not up to it yet. I suspect this opening number could be a very important song but I think you need to write it with Robert. It is his ingredient that is missing. I'm sure it will be a nightmare, but just maybe, him being asked to contribute something towards a show he feels has left him might get a positive response.

So I wrote to Robert, struggling to find the right words. By this stage in our relationship, finding the right words took half the day. After reading and re-reading my message, I finally pressed 'Enviar' and logged off with relief. I then drove back down the mountain to England-on-sea (or Fuengirola as the Spanish called it) to collect Rory. Here he came, swinging his schoolbag and looking embarrassed at the prospect of climbing into the one scruffy vehicle in a long rank of shining chrome. He paused a little way off, before reluctantly coming forward. I leaned across to open the passenger-side door.

"Hi Dad."

"Hi darling! What did you learn today?"

His face brightened: "Jesus Christ Superstar, walks like a woman and wears a bra. Bra's too big, wears a wig, that's why they call him sexy pig."

"Goodness, that must have been exhausting. Jump in."

"Can you buy me an ice-cream?"

"Yep, you're in luck, I need to check my messages." Long as it had taken me to write to him, somehow I knew Robert would already have fired off a reply.

"Three scoops?"

"Two."

Negotiations concluded, he climbed in the car.

Logging on back at Cyber Lucia, there awaited Robert's positive response:

> Moby Dick is MY creation. Every stupid interference goes to damage and dull the magic. All you have both done is open the curtain and shoot the wizard and the whole of New York knows it. Cutting and pasting Cameron's personal taste and humour is a 100% stupid and meaningless. Cameron's frankly childish behaviour is a symptom of somebody stealing somebody else's show to play with. It better work because in forty-eight months if it doesn't then I will come down on you all like the Red Queen.

There was another salvo from him immediately beneath the first one, sent a few moments later. I had produced a hybrid of his work apparently and he demanded I explain myself.

So that went well.

There had been another try-out of the script I had so recently helped develop and present in America. No workshop performance this one, it was a full-scale production playing to paying audiences in Dayton, Ohio. I needed building up after Robert's pa-

28. The fridge

rade ground dressing-down, so I dropped a little line to the musical director, who I had met in New York. He'd attended the second read-through presentation and loved it.

"Hereward" he replied, "it's a huge hit, literally. Completely sold out on the first night. Standing ovation as soon as the finale was finished. It was crazy. The feedback was extremely positive and honestly, a tad overwhelming. People truly loved the show. You're a hit!"

I suppose I should have forwarded this eulogy on to Robert, but why bother? It would only invite another torrent of abuse. I'd had enough of playing subordinate to his sergeant major.

Whilst I still had three bars on my phone, I plied my child with two more scoops and rang Martin Koch about the progress of the cast album. He'd taken the master recordings from our New York session back to his state-of-the-art shoe factory at the end of his garden, to polish it up. Now I had him on the phone though, he honestly didn't know when that might be. He'd just started arrangements for 'Jerry Springer the Opera', due to open at the National in April. As ever he was up to his ears in more important things and it was clear we were just going to have to wait. He could sense my frustration.

"You should do it" he said, "I'll see if I can have a word."

It was as if he'd summoned the genie of the lamp. Cameron called almost immediately. He was encouraged the show was being enjoyed so much in Dayton, Ohio and everyone was now panting for the "oral instruction manual" – as he put it.

"We need you here in London, Hereward."

"When?"

"Now!"

Martin had described me to him as 'king of the home demo' and it seemed that was the very quality Cameron was looking for. He didn't want slick, he wanted rough and ready. He was giving me 5 days flat and not a day more in the studio at CML to overdub all instruments, sound effects and mix the album. Though I begged him for more time he wouldn't give me a minute longer; he wanted it amateur and unglossy. Nice of him to think of 'amateur' and 'Hereward' in the same breath – he'd almost managed a compliment. Cameron was far more generous with my accommodation however: I could have his house in Regent's Park. It was a magnanimous gesture; I'd been there just before Christmas and the place was a palace.

"That's most kind."

"Anything else?"

"I'll need an engineer, Protools, per diems…"

"Look. Sort it out with Chris Grady; I'll get Tee to transfer you."

Click.

Teleported from Andalucia to One Bedford Square, I stood before Tee's desk and nodded towards the large mahogany doors.

"Is he in?"

"No dear, he's in Oxford at Sir Tim's inauguration." She handed me the key to Cameron's London residence. "We're all rather worried you might have forgotten the details for the alarm system."

"I managed it last time without setting off the alarm, didn't I?"

"You did dear, but it was 3 months ago."

It had been in the run-up to Christmas, when I was in London preparing the script for New York and tiptoeing through the minefield of contract negotiations with Robert. CML had teamed up with their partners-in-creation DeWynters, as they did every year for their festive bash. This year it was at Cameron's property. A pillared, cream-coloured Nash house on Regent's Park, it had 21 rooms and on this occasion, a striped marquee attached to the side, industrial heaters blasting through as though it were a hot air balloon. Buses had arrived, disgorging staff from both companies wafting in on clouds of scent and excitement, one hand closing around the proffered Bellini, the other plucking a nibble from the outstretched tray, as Bing crooned 'White Christmas'. There were some great frocks, and the women had dressed up nicely too.

Cameron stood at the entrance to the marquee in full Santa regalia, flanked by Santa's little helpers, Anthony and Adrian, in kinky boots and ermine trim, Esteé Lauder make-up and flowing blond tresses. He embraced me as I went through and then as an afterthought, squeezed one of my buttocks. Sticking firmly to my policy of refusing to 'do the Cameron thing' I gave the fruity old knight of the realm an arse-squeeze of my own. The eyes above the white beard widened in disbelief.

There were name cards at each table setting. Locating mine next to Tee, I'd taken my place and pulled crackers with her as party poppers streamed all around us. On the top table Santa Cameron delved into his sack, roared out a name and flung the gift at the recipient with all the venom he could muster, more often than not sending wine glasses smashing as the package spun in.

28. The fridge

It was all very Christmassy. At midnight we'd crammed into the drawing room for carols round the piano. Then Cameron was shoving me in the back to play some numbers from Moby Dick. "I can't!" I protested, "there's no mic." Against the cacophony I was yelling in his ear: "and I've got a REALLY QUIET VOICE!"

"*We'll* sing 'em!" he roared, giving me another shove.

My vocal cords, thoroughly anaesthetised, found themselves taking a familiar battering as I hammered out the songs from Moby. And it was gratifying how many partygoers knew all the words. Then I was banging out Billy Joel, as the piano man from wine bar days took over my soul.

That was the last time I had been a houseguest at Cameron's and entrusted with the details to the alarm. Now I was in a taxi from Tee's office, winding round Regent's Park's inner ring road, repeating to myself the digits I needed to input. I wasn't quite so sure of them now, going over them in my mind. I hoped to hell I had them in the right order.

I struggled through a wrought-iron gate with guitar, suitcase, laptop, shoulderbag. Turning the key in one lock then the double lock beneath, I pushed open the front door.

BeeBeeBeeBeeBee!

Thirty seconds to disarm the alarm. Carefully I typed in the numbers and waited a heart-in-mouth moment or two, until the VU display informed me the thing was disarmed. Date and time began to scroll across. Phew! I'd remembered correctly, I was in.

Opting for an early sober night and no food, I ignored the ensuite and took instead a long soak in the bigger bathroom downstairs. The tub was a classic Victorian clawfoot, the clotted cream towels were warm and the Martin Guerre bathrobe made me feel like Marilyn Monroe. I took whiffs and dabs from the little row of Liberty's bottles on display. The skin balm calmed and the eye gel soothed. Then I padded upstairs to my bedroom like Pooh Bear after a jar of honey. Turning back the bedclothes on my baronial bed, I remembered I'd forgotten something: the burglar alarm needed resetting for the night.

Padding back downstairs I inputted the numbers, plus the extra digit needed to prime it. The VU display didn't confirm my action this time but all was well, nothing to worry about here. I turned and plodded up the wooden stairs to Bedfordshire. Extinguishing the bedside lamp and snuggling down, I experienced a zen-like calm, as my embalmed and pampered skin luxuriated in the soft sheets.

But somewhere at the very back of my subconscious I felt I'd forgotten something.

I was awoken by booming male voices from downstairs that morning, interspersed with heavily-accented and highly-agitated protestations from a female. Suddenly I felt sick with apprehension. I dressed quickly, but came down a lot more slowly. The house was crawling with coppers, big burly men in uniform filling the hall. Anna, the Portuguese housekeeper, turned on me wide-eyed: "You set off alarm and police come! Cameron will be very unhappy. Doesn't like police in house."

"I didn't set off the alarm!"

"You set it wrong!"

"I absolutely did not!" I repeated the sequence to her, under my breath.

"Then ON? You didn't press ON before black button?" She was hyperventilating. I grew lightheaded and feather-legged in a way I hadn't felt since school. The constabulary stared on sarcastically. No doubt they had cast a raping eye over Cameron's portraits and pictures of him with the Queen. I'd tainted the place.

"Oh for fuck sake!" I snatched up my guitar case from where it leant by the door and barged outside.

Apprehension was my companion that whole day in the CML studio. I found it hard to concentrate on the New York cast's recordings. Then, at around 6pm, Adrian buzzed me to take me through the alarm system for the premises. As I would be last to leave, it fell to me to prime the bloody thing. Another one! The responsibility was almost overwhelming in my fragile emotional state. I was in a daze as he took me through it all: ensure every door's shut or you'll trigger the alarm, make sure every light's off, check the alarm's fully set. I now had a second sequence of numbers to remember, on top of the first lot I hadn't remembered correctly. My mind found it impossible to visualise the digits.

"Write it down Adrian, please."

Where I lived in Spain I had no need of alarms; my tumbledown finca was so far from civilization a burglar would never find it, let alone break in. No lucrative works of art suspended upon my walls – unless I could find an image of the Virgin Mary somewhere in a patch of mottled damp. And yet, I'd ended up with responsibility for two substantial Central London properties, both hot-wired to the police.

Adrian left, everyone left. Goodbyes were called, lights extinguished, doors slammed. Then I was quite alone in the building, slaving over a hot stave. When I was done for the night, I passed like a ghost through the silent headquarters checking from top to bottom, every door and light. Finally I primed the alarm and let myself out. I stood outside for a long time staring up at the place, before I felt reassured enough to leave.

28. The fridge

At Regent's Park I wrestled with the double locks and let myself in on a deathly dark townhouse.

BeeBeeBeeBeeBee!

With shaking finger and, I prayed to God, the right sequence of numbers, I disarmed my second alarm of the night. Bomb disposal would have been less nerve-racking. The scrolling VU assured me it was access all areas, but it took me a full 3 minutes to believe. I went straight for his wine cellar and uncorked a bottle of red, a good dusty one. I took a hefty gulp. I needed it for the phone call I was about to make.

"Cameron?" I said, "it's Hereward."

A Robert-like silence floated from the other end of the phone as he heard out my earnest explanation of the morning's incident. Finally I ground to a halt.

"I'll give you this one," he said evenly, "but if anything else happens, you're out."

"Absolutely. It won't happen again. I promise."

In more conciliatory fashion he asked: "have you discovered the wine cellar yet?"

I had to confess, indeed I had.

"Help yourself" he said, "but don't drink anything with dust on it."

There were further nightly calls as my work progressed. Towards the end of my stingily-allotted time, tracks that were finished were biked over to him in Somerset. He came back at me with a long list of tweaks. At this stage, I had but one day left of the five I had been granted.

"I can't possibly implement these changes, as well as do final mixes on 27 tracks, all in one day."

"You have to."

"It's impossible."

"It's showbiz."

I did manage to get a few more days out of him in the end, though he was grumbling it would mean me staying on in his house, when he was due back in a couple of days.

"I'll find somewhere else if you like?"

"No," he said. "Just as long as you don't set off the fucking alarm again."

* * *

I came in with a couple of bags of shopping and endeavoured to find room for it all in the fridge, which I saw, as I opened the door, was already heaving. Anna must have filled it. Then I remembered: Cameron and Michael were due to arrive. Fitting all my stuff in called for a careful rearrangement of the contents. So I cleared the bottom shelf then populated it with all the bottles, theirs and mine. Vintage champagnes and Grand Cru St Emilions reluctantly shoved up to accommodate bargain bin Sauv. I could shove things up no further and I still had two fat bottles of Bolly in my hands. I gave up trying to find room in the body of the fridge and turned my gaze to the door. There, on the bottom door shelf, it might just be possible. The squashed-up organic milk and hand-squeezed orange juice cartons all but burst their seams but I managed to cram the bottles in. I filled little gaps in the upper door shelves with all the remaining food product I had removed from the bottom shelf.

Gently, I pressed on the door to see if it would close. It would, but only with a final determined push and a few clanks of complaint from within.

Unbeknownst to me, that last little nudge I gave to force the fridge shut, tipped the horizontal bottles of champagne on the bottom shelf slightly upwards, so that the wire encasing their corks became entangled with the wire of the magnums of champagne standing in the door. It was effectively a bomb primed to explode, unless the fridge door was opened very very gently.

That evening, after a session in the private gym followed by a luxurious soak in the clawfoot bathtub, I bounded down to the kitchen to pour myself a drink. Still pumped from the workout, I wrenched open the fridge door.

They must have heard the eruption in Camden Town.

Out exploded the contents, bottles detonating like bombs, corks flying like live bullets. The whole lot – shelves, food, booze – cascaded down with a sound that still reverberates in my memory, a crash akin to the top floor of a house collapsing through the conservatory roof below.

It was a Michael Crawford moment. I trembled at the settling epicentre in a state of shock. Then dread eyes lifted to survey the carnage. Glass was scattered far and wide, cartons of orange and milk were still gurgling into rivulets of red wine. Every food-spattered surface looked like a Jackson Pollock painting. Fridge door shelves were skidded across the floor and the metal rails that belonged to those shelves lay far flung, twisted all out of shape.

The door of the fridge swung upon its hinges, laughing at me. With horror I noticed its inside surface was devoid of shelves, wiped completely smooth, where once it was groaning with Anna's goodies.

28. The fridge

I was thunderstruck by a new thought: Cameron and Michael! They were due back, perhaps any minute, maybe their car was nosing its way round Regent's Park inner ring road at this very moment! Frantically I searched for a utility cupboard with dustpan, brooms, cleaning products, mops. I was wrenching open doors with more venom than the force that destroyed the fridge.

Now I was filling bins and buckets, mopping at the floor and viciously swiping it dry with bathroom towels. Spattered food art I smeared about, rinsed and attacked again till all the cupboard surfaces were wiped clean. But the fridge door shelves refused to slot back into their grooves and the metal frames that held them refused to go back in, they were so bent out of shape. The more I panicked, the less they fitted. I gave up in the end, leaving them in neat little rows along the sideboard.

With no time for a note of explanation – not that I could have come up with one – I bolted upstairs to my bedroom, slammed the door and locked it. The time was just seven in the evening but the day – my life! – was over. I climbed into bed, unplugged the bedside phone from the wall and pulled the pillow tight around my ears. First the alarm, now this! Any moment now they'd be in the house hungry and thirsty and make straight for the fridge. I'd hear a shout, I'd be found out and the rap of Headmaster's knuckles would fall upon my door.

I tried to get to sleep and blot out the world, and after an hour or two of silence from below, I believe I did get close. But as my consciousness began to drift, so too did a memory come bubbling up to the surface, a memory of the last time I had felt exactly the same way as this: in trouble. Some traumas never quite leave you, however many steps away you take from childhood…

I was 12 years old and under the spell of Sarah Lodge, my first girlfriend. At the bus stop after school we allowed every bus to sail by while we passed chewing gum from her mouth to mine and back again. Occasionally, when absolutely no one was around, she let me feel under her blouse. This was quite often, for the rest of the school were in 'prep', an outrageous measure recently introduced by Kenyon, the new headmaster. You had to spend a deathly hour and a half in the school hall under the gaze of an invigilator. I hadn't quite got into the swing. I'd spent every night this week in the bus shelter and now it was Friday.

I was in Latin when light knuckles fell upon the door. Kenyon! I knew it before his smug moustache appeared beneath the glittering eyes. "Sorry to interrupt, Mrs Beeston, but…"

"Not at all Headmaster!"

"May I just have a private word with Kaye?" He met my apprehensive eye: "if you wouldn't mind? In my study?"

His hush puppies conveyed him ethereally along the corridor. I followed in a dream, knowing from his back that my hour was at hand. He disappeared into his study and closed the door. I realised I was expected to knock.

"Come in," he called.

Asked to explain my absences, I began making up lies about my whereabouts from Monday to Thursday. Visit to my Nan, family outing to the cinema, that sort of thing. I swore I was telling the truth but he looked doubtful; clearly more was needed.

"Scouts Honour!" I blurted, "Scouts Honour Sir!" – and I stood there giving the awkward hand sign. I might as well have given the V sign. After all, it was easier to do and as it turned out, it would have got me into a lot less trouble.

"It's alright Kaye," he murmured. "I know you wouldn't betray your Scouts Honour."

But I still had one day unaccounted for, and I made up one untruth too many. Thursday found me out. After a quick call to cross-check with my distracted mother who didn't have a clue what he was talking about, Kenyon came off the phone and stared at me with silent loathing.

"A pack of lies," came the grim verdict. "Worst of all, you betrayed your very highest pledge: Scouts Honour." As he looked down upon my bowed head, my eyes scuttled across the floor to the cane in the corner. "Quite what your Scoutmaster will have to say about that is a matter for this evening, I don't expect he'll be too impressed, do you?"

"No Sir."

"I don't suppose your fellow Scouts will be too impressed either."

"No Sir."

I was getting vertigo.

"Well. It falls to me as your Headmaster to administer the maximum punishment. Bend over the back of the sofa there. Remove your jacket first."

I waited an age, tipped over like Pinochio on his night off, till the air whiffled and the pain spat. Hard tears flecked the rims of my eyes. I presumed I was in for five more and tried to pace myself. By the fourth I was writhing to avoid the next one. Five and six killed me.

"Go now to your classroom."

28. The fridge

In the school hall that evening, we scouts stood to attention in a semi circle as the lanyard was ceremonially raised. After the Scouts Prayer, our Scoutmaster Mr Moody said "at ease" in a distracted, troubled manner, before snapping: "not you Kaye!"

Without a further glance in my direction and taking a good 30 seconds before he spoke, Moody told the troop: "A Boy Scout's word is his bond, an unbreakable oath represented by a sign, the sign we give to the outside world. Our Scouts Honour. This day," he continued darkly, "one of those in our midst has betrayed that trust. In doing so he has weakened us all." His eye passed from face to face before finally settling upon mine. He was a big man – 6 foot 6 inches – who looked fucking ridiculous in shorts. He stared me out for a full minute. Then he stepped forward and his long right arm swung to grasp the badge on my left shoulder. 'Camping'.

Rip!!

He passed the badge into his meaty left hand and the long arm swung again, to the badge up on my right shoulder. 'Knots'.

Rip!!!

'Firelighting' followed, 'Cycling Proficiency', 'First Aid'. When all were gone and my proud green jersey was threadbare, he pointed to the door.

"Go!"

It was a quite dreadful feeling walking the walk of shame out of that School Hall. The experience changed me. Perhaps the experience even redirected my feet into this version of the future, where I lay in bed in 2003 in my benefactor's mansion, with that self-same feeling of dread.

"Hello?" came a voice from the landing the next morning, "it's Cameron." I carefully assembled an expression of delighted, innocent surprise, before unlocking and opening the door.

We stood face to face. He seemed a little flustered and embarrassed.

"I'm afraid I have to serve an eviction order. It's just to do with the insurance; Anna can't be here for the next couple of days and the insurance people won't cover it, so we have to shut down."

Embarrassing as it was to be evicted, his story mercifully allowed us both to sidestep the issue. I was off the hook, though I suspected I'd driven away his housekeeper. I imagined Anna running down the road, hands fluttering in the air, not stopping till she reached Portugal.

"Look, I'm running late. I'll see you at the office. Who are you dealing with there?"

"Maria."

"Get Maria to find you a hotel. I'll try and find the time to join you in the studio."

I didn't see him for another 13 years.

* * *

Back once more in Spain, I wrapped myself in the loving arms of my family. Stayed at home licking my wounds. Opened the fridge door very very carefully.

Four stray dogs were following Pat around the house now, and a cat. But I forgave everything; I was back in the bosom. I wasn't the only one: Pat had come across a day-old chick the size of a stamp, blown from the nest. She had it popped down her cleavage to incubate. Before long she was popping dog food down there on the end of tweezers, into the creature's beak.

"It seems to have taken to its environment" I remarked, "maybe it's a tit?"

A full 2 weeks went by before I emerged from the finca, to bump along the dusty riverbed in our rickety rackety Terrano and wind my way up the hillside, where the white-walled village lay and the church reached up to God. At the internet café I opened the first email with some trepidation.

> Dear Herry, I have just listened to Moby Dick. You have done a stupendous job. All in all it has come out better than I could ever have expected. A score for you to be proud of. Love Cameron.

I pushed back on chair wheels, rolled my eyes heavenwards and let out an exhalation.

An email from Nick Allott informed me Moby Dick was now fixed and would henceforth be licenced via MTI in its current form, with a full page in the catalogue.

"The show is set," wrote Nick, "and hopefully can now set sail for a long and prosperous voyage."

Finally there was this one, and I knew now I truly was forgiven:

> Dear Hereward, we are developing a new musical based on the television series Sex, Chips and Rock 'n Roll by Debbie Horsfield, to be produced here, hopefully prior to a commercial run. Your name comes recommended to us by Cameron Mackintosh as a composer. Would you be interested?
>
> *Braham Murray, Artistic Director, Royal Exchange Theatre, Manchester.*

Chapter 29
Fin
- 2006 to 2020 -

We rode into Manchester, burnished and weary after the long drive from Andalucia to the north of England. I'd been 2 years removed from English life, holed up in my little studio, writing music and lyrics for 'Sex, Chips & Rock 'n Roll', and waiting for the production date at Manchester's Royal Exchange Theatre to roll around. Now that time had arrived and here we were, parking up at our rented terraced house in Bury, feeling like aliens in a world we once knew – particularly Pat, who hadn't been back in the country for 4 long years. We had dogs with us of course: Pablo of the pink lipstick, and one you haven't met yet, Toffee, a chihuahua with indescribably bad breath.

"Can you just turn her face towards you and her arse towards me?" I plaintively asked. "It might smell better."

12a Clegg Street, Bury! Imagine those words sung by angels and spelt out in the sky by stars – well that's how it sounded to me. The place was ours for the next 6 weeks and I was humble with gratitude. My contract ran until opening night – 5 weeks of rehearsal and 1 week of previews. Then we would have to drive back home to Spain, whilst the show was scheduled to run for the whole of the summer. Now I was back in Blighty, I wished my contract could run the whole course.

How we craved to get back to old ways! For it wasn't just me, Pat felt the same. Our hearts sang at the sight of people collapsing umbrellas and entering familiar shops from the rain: Littlewoods, Mothercare, Clarks, Everything For A Pound. We grinned in the Post Office, hearing again the recorded voice rising to a peak and cascading down the other side: "Cashier number ten please… Cashier number two please…"

Most thrilling of all was the red carpet Manchester city centre had rolled out for me. Within a half-mile radius of the Royal Exchange, every other lamp post was draped with a long flag, bearing the name of our show and beneath it a quote: 'The hardest quality to find in musical theatre is a composer with a unique style and sound. Hereward Kaye has it and he certainly knows about Sex, Chips & Rock 'n Roll! Cameron Mackintosh'.

There I stood outside the Arndale Centre, nut-brown and covered in mosquito bites, sandals in the rain, wally chain, hippy bracelet – the full nine-yards – and my eyes travelled from first flag to last, a whole city street of them. I couldn't stop smiling, I felt as if I had been handed a new life.

I settled into the routine of going out to work in the morning and coming home every evening to wife, child and supper. At first it was as if I was playing a role, but the sense of somehow being an imposter gradually wore off. I began to feel I could happily live the rest of my life going to and fro from Bury to work and back again.

At the theatre, I found great reward in being a cog in a project of mutual endeavour. I joined in with the morning's vocal exercises, I sat in concentration through rehearsals with co-author Debbie Horsfield, the two of us watching director Jonathan Moore and the cast go through Debbie's scenes, or my staged songs. I sat beside the MD or rehearsal pianist with my guitar, there to help if needed but not intrude as the Principals went through their big numbers. Lunch was shared with fellow creatives, cast or crew. Or skipped altogether as Debbie and I poured over lyrics and made changes as necessary for the afternoon. We were collaborating and agreeing, or respecting one another's point of view when we didn't – it was a whole new sensation.

Manchester Royal Exchange's poster for Debbie Horsfield and Hereward's 2005 stage musical, based upon Debbie's hit TV series of the same name.

Before I knew it we were 4 weeks into rehearsals and the first preview was almost upon us. Opening night and departure from Manchester for Spain were not far behind. Soon all of this would be over. It was an alarming prospect. I couldn't admit it to myself or others, but I knew in my heart with gathering certainty as each day passed that I couldn't go back. The Wild West was the last thing I needed.

Then the band arrived. Smiles were wide and all was excitement and expectation. The lead guitarist however, rocked up with quite a different attitude.

29. Fin

"I'll be available for a few of the performances" he informed us dismissively, "but most of the dates will be filled by my dep."

He was sacked on the spot. A hasty meeting was convened between the production team in which I was not involved, and as they emerged, all eyes turned towards me.

"You will do it, won't you?"

It wasn't so much a question as an assumption. Here surely, was a ready-made replacement; I'd written all the songs after all. But the score was unrecognisable from the one I had created. An arranger had gone to work on my tunes. Principals had arrived and told the MD "I can't sing it in that key". Some songs were duets between male and female and the key switched back and forth. Furthermore, we were only days away from first preview, no time at all to get my head and fingers round a whole new score. Nor was I the accomplished guitarist they all assumed; I'd never used any of the effects pedals that transform a jangle to a lion's roar at the press of a toe. And the last time I'd been a pit musician was 20 years ago. And I didn't even have my guitar here, let alone a pedal board. This was a terrible idea on so many levels.

"I'll do it," I agreed immediately.

I had a hell of a lot to learn and no time at all in which to learn it. But it was a job, a proper, normal job back in England – and jobs don't get better than playing your own songs night after night. I wasn't the MD – I was under the musical leadership of another. I was simply a pit-band guitarist playing himself back into form and right then, that was all I aspired to be.

So Pat, Rory and pooches all flew home after opening night and I moved into the Royal Exchange's 'director's flat' in the centre of Manchester. There I lived, until the summer-long run of Sex, Chips & Rock 'n Roll came to an end in September. By that time I had spent five long months in England and the Spanish spell was well and truly broken. The flamenco dancer had double-stamped the floor for the final time and cried "Ole!"

Pat was back in Spain now, but it felt like home to her no longer. "Just find us somewhere to live in England," she begged on one of our nightly calls. "I don't care where – anywhere."

Anywhere? There was a brief! But I leapt on it. "Pack up the house," I told her decisively. "I'll come back and move us out when I've found somewhere."

I remember coming off the phone and just standing there, thinking what happens next? I might also have asked myself how it had come to this at the age of 50, but I already knew the answer. Where others built nest eggs and paid off mortgages, we burnt bridges, always moving, always slicing our life into dislocated chapters. Where others would stick, we twisted. We were high rollers, we were serial offenders.

Once, as a young man, a girlfriend reading my palm pointed out a break in the lifeline. I'd always wondered what it might represent: Divorce? Revelation? Death? Standing there in a hallway in Manchester, stateless, jobless, homeless, clueless, I reckoned this might be that break in the line on my hand. The future was out there waiting on the other side of the divide… but where? I spun on the spot to take in the four walls to north, east, west and south, mired in indecision.

"Anywhere, she says."

It was like opening a menu with every dish under the sun. I'd still be making up my mind long after chef's gone home. It needed narrowing down.

So… I wanted to be within one hour's striking distance of London, as I used to be (cos you never know, I thought). And after four years on the Costa Del Sol, I was reluctant to relinquish sunshine and sea. City life was out of the question unfortunately; Pat's nature-lovin' soul demanded rural. These then were the coordinates. I felt like a German Major General on the eve of the 'Battle of 2005', sticking a pin in the map:

"Here" I informed the four walls, "between London and Brighton: ve vill attack!"

* * *

The Mid Sussex village of Lindfield unfolded her historic charms as we drove at a fascinated crawl, wriggling around Pretty Corner, with All Saints Church on the left, The Stand Up Inn on the right. A pond almost the size of a lake swam alongside, parented children chucking bread to serenely sailing ducks. Then Lindfield Common hove into view with a cricket match in progress, as the pavilion scoreboard turned over. I heard Rupert Brooke, on some God-forsaken battlefield afar, pining for all he was missing:

Stands the Church clock at ten to three?

And is there honey still for tea?

We'd virtually wept for joy in the aisle of Sainsbury's that first day back in Manchester, so you can imagine what the sound of leather on willow was doing to us! Pat and I promptly moved into the village and vowed never to move out, come hell or high water, neither of which would ever visit Lindfield, we were sure.

That was *where* settled. What about *what*?

29. Fin

For once in my life I needed to lower my sights. Mr Ambition is a constant companion, a ventriloquist's dummy, wooden mouth clacking up and down. I needed to shove him back in his box. Waiting for the next big musical to appear was no kind of plan, it might be years before the next one came along. I could write one of my own I supposed, but how long would that take and what would we live on in the meanwhile? Then I would need to pitch the thing: industry professionals would need to be convinced, investors brought to understand why they should invest in my dream. Scrutiny would be applied with a narrowing of eyes from people who knew a thing or two about risk and success. I'd be hanging on the approval of others, just so I could take the next step forward.

When it came down to it, I'd had enough of being weighed and judged. I'd had enough of being so fucking cavalier! Maybe it was an age thing, but I pined for the road ahead to be as predictable as the one that wove around Pretty Corner, not a heart-stopping joyride, all blind corners and crumbling mountain road.

We enrolled Rory in our local Primary and Pat and I began to make friends. Realising I was 'in the Leisure Business', a school mum asked me if I taught guitar at all? She was looking for private lessons for her child. Teaching was something I had never considered before. I could, I thought, yeah I could teach guitar… I heard a muffled voice from my wooden companion in the box: "If you're going to do that, open a music school, you dummy!"

It could be like that Jack Black movie I'd just seen, 'School of Rock', I thought excitedly, I could do it for real….

"Let me OUT! NOW!"

I found premises, shamelessly traded on my Flying Picket past and threw a jolly at our new site. BBC South East came and filmed us, the local papers ran with it, the phone rang off the hook and 'Rok Skool' was born. Over in Spain, Leon took an immediate interest in what was alarmingly beginning to look like a business and came back to join me. He recognised there were just too many elements to this I would never get together: tax, insurance, all the boring shit.

Now I had a son for a business partner, though I never wanted my kids to follow in my footsteps – I never knew where they were leading at the best of times. And Leon was fabulously unsuited to the job! We were a music school for children and it involved a lot of work. There were only three things Leon hated: music, children and work. But hey, you can't have everything, and he did have my back.

One year became two and two turned into twelve as the business became an established part of the community. Once parents saw what we were up to musically with their kids, they wanted a bit of it for themselves. It seemed everyone had a guitar gathering dust in the attic and every midlife crisis craved a headband and distortion pedal. Before long we had almost as many adults as children and I was running a studio, directing bands and vocal groups, teaching songwriting, conducting a choir. When Pat came on board as vocal coach and Joe came back from Spain too, to join us, the business was providing employment for four members of my family and though the fifth, Rory, was too young, we built a fabulous band around him. At the tender age of 12, he was now lead singer in a rock group and his life was effectively ruined.

Rok Skool didn't set the world on fire, but it gave us stability. After a lifetime of touring and upping sticks, Pat and I had a real sense of putting down roots that would not be uprooted this time. The seasons rolled on and our years became a succession of Rok Skool terms. We lived orderly lives and if we fancied a bit of anarchy, the counter-culture of Brighton was just down the road.

There I could have ended my story. But there was a whale in the room. Not an elephant – it was far bigger than that.

Moby wasn't finished with me yet.

In 2013 Michael 'Chase' Gosselin, a young US director/producer type, became hugely excited when he discovered Moby Dick the Musical online. Robert gave him short shrift but I supported him – even going as far as flying out to New York and helping him stage another workshop presentation. A few weeks later he arrived on my doorstep with his own rewritten version of our show, something he had no right to do at all. The story was as much about the lives of the girls of St Godley's as Moby Dick now. I was hugely dismayed.

I dragged him down the coast to Hastings, where my dramaturgical mentor Steven Dexter now lived, to subject his vision to Steven's expert scrutiny. "You can't tell two equal stories," Dexter told him. "One of them has to become a shell for the other."

"By the end of the High School musical," I informed Nick Allott of CML, "each of the girls needs to have gained something precious from their performance: salvation, forgiveness, closure…"

"A heart, a brain, courage..."

"Exactly! He seems determined to invent a whole new show and reckons he has big bucks backing him."

"You've got to stop the guy," said Nick, flatly.

It was difficult, particularly given that he'd come all the way over from the States just to talk me round to his unilateral rewrite of the show, but we had that awkward conversation and an unhappy Chase went home. After he'd gone – and I really don't know why it took so long – it struck me it was about time I wrote my version. I'd spent half my life trying to please other people, marrying Robert's work with input from Cameron, Russell, and now Chase. How respectful can one man be? Surely I knew by now how the piece should work, better than anyone? Seemed like everyone else in the world had had a go, why the hell – no, why the *fuck* – shouldn't I?

So I wiped the slate clean of everything written before and started again from scratch. This would be the very last time – I swore! – I sat down to rewrite Moby Dick. I had all of Robert's previous scripts, the MTI hire version and every one of our demos and cast album songs at my elbow. And I had my 'phone-a-friend' Steven Dexter, without who's skill and knowledge I'm not sure I would have had the confidence to pull it off.

I built the show up brick by brick in my own image. I wrote new songs. Others I dismantled and reconstructed, or interrupted with dialogue and re-imagined. And when I was done, I sent the script off to Sir you-know-who.

I didn't have to wait too long for a reply. His new PA, Jane Austin – I kid you not – rang and put me on standby to receive a call.

"I'm sorry to keep this short" Cameron opened, "but I have to go to Manila."

"Of course."

"I've read your script," he said dryly.

"And?"

"I have three changes in Act One and two changes in Act Two." There he paused, waiting for a reaction. After all, so few changes were practically unheard of, where Cameron was concerned, his interference was never reluctant! But I stayed quiet.

"What I'm trying to say is well done Hereward."

"Thank you."

"What I need now" he informed me, "is a recording of the music so we know it works as well as the script. It's exactly what we have just done with Barnum and Saigon."

Despite the little fluttery feeling in my chest as I came off the phone, I was determined, absolutely determined this time I would not allow my dreams to run riot. "That was good!" came a muffled voice. "Back in yer box," snarled I.

In common with greater musicians than myself (such as Jamie Cullum and Paul McCartney), I have never been a 'reader'. Therefore I was unable to set down my own music on the stave. So I went to see Martin Koch, who declared himself emphatically in. This being Martin however, his contribution took a hell of a long while coming! His star was in the highest ascendancy these days. The previous year in 2012, he'd been Musical Supervisor of the London Olympic Games no less, overseeing Danny Boyle's epic opening ceremony. Nowadays every time I turned on the telly, there was Martin waving his arms around, in charge of a band or orchestra. His every gig was always going to pull rank: Eurovision, Sports Personality of the Year – brutal competition. But we got there in the end, though it took two years, and Cameron received his materials. After which, Jane Austin – taking a break from her latest novel 'Persuasion' – put me back on standby.

"There's been a change. Someone wants to do Moby Dick."

"Great!"

"Andrew Wright has agreed to direct and in fact, he's investing some of his own money in the production. You're very lucky to have him."

"I'm sure."

"They're expanding the theatre – The Union in Waterloo, do you know it? It'll be in there. And it'll be your new version."

My new version!

After the call, I Googled 'Andrew Wright'. Top West End choreographer and director. His claim to fame as a performer, apparently, was as Candlestick in Beauty & The Beast. Only in musical theatre, eh?

Just a little fringe venue, I muttered to myself. "In London," came a muffled voice, "doing your script mate."

Not only was Mr Ambition out of his box, he was purring in the crook of my arm.

After a 12-year absence, I found myself back at Bedford Square. Andrew was already in the room when I arrived, so I had not been privy to whatever he and Cameron had already discussed; my contribution was clearly being managed with care.

"Herry!" cried Cameron rising to meet me arms outstretched, using a nick-name he'd never even used, as if the 13 years since I trashed his fridge had never happened.

We three spent as many hours crawling our way through my script, with me explaining or having to justify every twist and turn. Finally we fell to discussing the rehearsal schedule. Andrew wanted complete freedom to do his own thing and asked both Cameron and myself very nicely not to attend, if we didn't mind? I did – but

I said I didn't. The big worry – and this came from both of them – was that Robert would rock the boat. I knew the words that were coming next…

"You need to go and see him," said Cameron.

This meeting called for the most genteel of environments possible (in case he wanted to murder me), so I booked an afternoon tea for two at the Grand Hotel in Brighton. Perhaps I could have thought it through a little more. This was where the IRA detonated a bomb in 1986.

It had been such a long time since Robert and I had seen one another. And how far did we go back? We could be mature about this, surely, two guys in their sixties?

I needn't have worried. There he was on the steps as I exited the cab, looking fit and strong, all smiles.

"Robert!"

Together we went through to afternoon tea. Over bone china and scones we caught up a little on intervening years. "Are you still acting?" I asked. His face darkened.

"I can't, no one will have me. He's got at everybody. He's poisoned them."

"Who?"

"The Dark Lord."

"Who's that?"

"You know. Him." The loathing was palpable. "Lloyd Webber," he spat.

"Oh come on, please…"

"I assure you. It's a fact." And he stared me down.

To change the subject and steer it towards the business in hand, I reminded him of the time in '94 when, instead of attending a meeting, he'd sent along a legal note instead, countersigned by a solicitor: 'I hereby hand over the show to Hereward Kaye'. I thought it was an important reminder, before I began my own résumé of intervening years: the production in Germany, the MTI workshops in 2003, the recent workshop with Chase and now this version, my version, one that showcased the best of both our work.

"I've agreed to take a backseat and I won't be attending rehearsals," I told him, as Robert sat stony-faced. "Andrew wants his artistic freedom and Cameron's granted it. Leave 'em to it man," I implored. "Who knows what might come from this?" I begged Robert not to rock the boat, for both our sakes.

"I'll let you get on with it then" he said quietly, rising to leave.

Guess what happened? This was Robert, after all. He set down his napkin, ignored my every word, went home and fired off his own script to everyone in the loop – except me of course. A few days after that, he followed up to Cameron, Nick and Andrew, with: 'You are doing my script, aren't you?'

Andrew Wright responded: 'I do not want to get in the middle of any past issues. I will simply pull out, as well as my investment.'

I only found out because Nick Allott copied me in. Oh God. Here we go again.

With apprehension, I sent Robert the lot: my new home demos, Martin's manu-scripted arrangements that had taken him two years to complete, my script that had already been worked through and agreed upon for this production. I had to show him just how much work had already gone into this.

After that, there was only one further communication: 'It wasn't written by me. Remove my name from the script. I shall send MY script to the critics and explain why I am satisfied that this is yet another gambit to sabotage this show on behalf of the Dark Lord.' He signed off: 'This letter marks the end of my association with Hereward Kaye and Cameron Mackintosh.'

* * *

I arrived at the venue for auditions. The building was humming with performers in a state of heightened anticipation. Three contenders for each of the principal roles had been invited along – apart from Captain Ahab and his wife Esta; those parts had already been promised or just about, to two X-Factor finalists. Star of the latest season, Anton Stephans, had been awarded the role of demented headmistress playing an obsessive sea Captain (is it any wonder this show was so impossible?) and now, into the audition room, tottered Brenda Edwards, a tour de force from X-Factor's second series, back when the whole country watched. Brenda was recovering from breast cancer and 'only at 25%' she said, having only just been operated upon. So she hadn't been absolutely given the role yet, we needed to see if she would be well enough to handle a month of performance.

"Do you mind if I do this one sitting down?" She looked exhausted. "I took the drain out yesterday for this audition," she explained, "I didn't want to put you all off!"

She looked so frail sitting there as the pianist struck up Tina Turner's 'Simply The

Best' – which made it all the more amazing when she blew the roof off the place. The gig was hers from the moment she opened her mouth.

Then Andrew talked her through the part of Esta. "Who's playing my husband?" she demanded.

"I'm not at liberty to divulge, but someone from X-Factor – you know him I think."

"Oh my God it's not Chico is it? Tell me it's not him!" She's shrieking with laughter then holding her chest, groaning: "me stitches, me stitches!"

Slowly, I led her out on my arm to a waiting taxi. Meanwhile back inside, everyone else had moved into a dance studio to work with a choreographer. He demonstrated a four-bar sequence of moves – this was 'One' apparently. Two and Three followed, to be instantly remembered and replicated. 'Four' they were informed, was freestyle.

The beatbox boomed and the choreographer barked out the numbers in rapid succession: "And One! And Two! And Three!" When it came to 'Four', the company combusted into breakdance, back flips, swallow dives. These days it seemed, as well as acting and singing and dancing brilliantly, you needed circus skills too.

Andrew addressed them all at the end: "Cameron Mackintosh is the original producer of Moby Dick and he loves loves LOVES this show. He says he'll leave it to me but he's ringing every two minutes saying have you done this, do that. I say I thought you were leaving it to me? He's going to be there on Press Night, when he turns 70. He says: 'get this right Andrew and it'll be the best birthday present anyone could give me'."

Graham Norton had inquired of Cameron on his BBC radio show earlier in the year: "When is Moby Dick the Musical coming back? So many people are asking about this, to the point where you think you might as well, because if all the people asking questions about it go to see it, it'll be a hit".

Well folks, this was it, Moby's return, presented on the London stage for the first time in a quarter of a century. The musical went into rehearsal, and like a very good boy I kept my promise and stayed away.

Press Night was upon us, and the '25th Anniversary Production' of Moby Dick, as it was being billed. The poster showed two schoolboys in their late teens wearing a skirt, one smoking a fag, the other holding a can of lager. Between them a girl firing a splash of grinning sperm whale from a water pistol. In the hoop of school tie that provided the 'O' of Moby and the 'I' of Dick, a new strapline: 'You'll Be Blown Away!' – tasteful, as ever.

Pat and I took our seats with that old familiar feeling: excitement mixed with the kind of dread prisoners must feel when brought before the firing squad. The Moby Band were in place, shoe-horned under a set of stairs with perspex screens around the drummer and music stands glowing like runway lights to bring my music home. The bass player was rifling through pages of his score. Sound and lighting engineers were behind their mixing desks, dressed in dishevelled schoolgirl uniform. Actors were briefly glimpsed, assembling behind a paint-spattered curtain daubed with 'MOBY DUCK', the second word crossed-out and replaced with 'DICK'. In front of my wife and I, two elderly hacks' backs gingerly rose in objection, before the cast had even had a chance to make hackles rise. Pencils were licked, grumbles exchanged. We tuned into their conversation.

"*Telegraph*," Pat whispered.

"*Guardian*," I grimaced at her. They would hate it.

Cameron took his seat, flanked by Nick Allott and Drew Cohen, the new President of MTI who had flown over. At the last moment Robert inserted himself into the only available space – a school bench smack in front of the stage. He looked flustered and uncomfortable.

The house lights dimmed, Anton Stephans emerged, all dragged-up as the Headmistress of St Godleys.

"Parents, old girls, students we have actually managed to trace..."

He paused for a laugh. It was unforthcoming. But we were underway. For the first time since the last time Moby Dick fell under critical gaze in London back in '92, here came Hermann Melville's classic novel, filleted, fucked-over and fantastically regurgitated by the anarchic girls and boys-dressed-as-girls of St Godleys. What would the public make of it? Perfect for our gender-fluid times surely? But it was hard to tell – they had grown strangely quiet.

This was an untypical, ticketed audience, made up entirely of those who sit in judgement: print journalists of the old and new school, radio reviewers, online bloggers, theatre websites. London's New Union Theatre was a fringe venue with only 80 seats and, apart from we few insiders, every single one of them was taken up by a critic. At applause points at the end of big numbers, there was no applause, which was disconcerting for the cast who had only experienced wild woo-hoos from friends, family and well-wishers in the previews. It was inhibiting for those of us in the crowd who wanted to clap. Were these bastards enjoying it? I certainly wasn't! But it was touching to observe Cameron mouthing all the words to the songs, like a fan.

He came up to me at the end of the show. "Are you happy with what they've done?"

I tried not to look too pained. Happy? I was anything but. Now I knew why I had been asked to stay away from rehearsals. I had been assured by Cameron at the start of all this that "someone wants to do Moby Dick and it'll be your new version". If this was my version, it was unrecognisable.

"It's a very edited version of my script," I said, being as kind to it as possible. "All the exposition's been removed, there's no explanation, no story as we go along." His face darkened as I stumbled on. "The whole thing passed like a bullet. I know jukebox musicals are all the rage but the scenes were cut down to almost nothing, it was song after song. This is Andrew's vision, not mine," I had to tell him. "I still haven't seen my Show. But… Andrew has a lot of talent and the cast are marvellous," I managed. At this he nodded furiously.

Trying to frame appropriate words of his own, Cameron said if anything, there was too much School now and not enough Melville. Now I was nodding furiously.

I watched him turn his back, more kindly than back at the Piccadilly 25 years earlier. Moby still wasn't right: I knew it, he knew it. There he went, this massive enthusiast, always interfering, always seeking to improve, always thinking big. Not only had he taken the musical theatre world by storm, he had taken me by storm. Cameron walked out of my life, and I'm tempted to add 'for the last time' – but I'm sure he'll have something to say when he reads this book!

The reviews came in and Moby Dick was declared the 'marmite musical' you either loved or hated. As for the script I had written but never seen, it was adopted as the MTI hire version and began to be picked up by community theatre groups in the States. This was gratifying, but it seemed it was never going to set the world on fire; that dream was over. As ever in my life with everything I had ever done, I was the nearly man – again.

* * *

I write this memoir four years later. Across the room Pat is on a Zoom call with her team. She runs Small Dog Rescue Sussex, pulling strays from kill shelters in Romania, or the roadsides of Spain, Portugal, Bosnia. Sometimes she brings them over, 30 at a time, placing puppies with a network of foster carers all over this country, then finding permanent adopters. An immediate crisis is always unfolding. She was over in Romania twice last year, while I held the fort at home. There was a moment where the kids and I were discussing some family matter in which she had not been involved.

"When did that happen?" she asked sharply, looking up from her phone.

"Oh…" I said casually, voice trailing away, "you weren't there."

I write this in 2020, in lockdown. All the London theatres are dark, Rok Skool is shut down, Coronavirus ravages the planet. Confined to their homes, Italians appear on their balconies and sing lustily. Ghostly operatic arias float into deserted piazzas below. In the UK we emerge from our houses to stand on our doorsteps and applaud the NHS.

There's a jogger running along the middle of our road instead of the pavement. And where are the aeroplanes criss-crossing the sky above our garden? Parked up at Gatwick 20 miles away that's where, just so much metal; flightless birds. The real ones flute and pipe, filling the air with song that has never sounded sweeter or rang with greater clarity. Is it the song of the mockingbird?

The natural world is re-emerging. In a city in India, an apparition of the distant Himalayas mystically arose one morning, as smog lifted for the first time in decades.

The world has grown quiet. The world has ground to a halt.

Not America though! The imposter in the White House, P.T. Barnum masquerading as President of the United States, declares, pinky in the air: "It's just a little problem. The Show goes on."

And so, as your Nearly Man sets down his pen, a boy dressed as a girl in a community theatre somewhere in America, picks up a placard at the end of a performance of Moby Dick and crosses the stage.

The sign reads:

'FIN'

Acknowledgements

I lovingly thank those select few readers of my early manuscript whose involvement, ideas and encouragement inspired me onwards. You were: Larry Viner, Peter Guttridge, Henrik Wager, Nancy Doyle, Neil Thackray, Russell Meagher, Tom Robinson, Leon and Pat Kaye.

A special heartfelt thanks to all those who contributed and gave their support, to ensure I could publish. You were:

Amy Anzel	Aston Goodey	Roy Rad
Ana Badescu	Adam Guratsky	Perry Rigler
Juliet Bailey	Nancy Doyle Hall	Matt Roberts
Stephen Barrett	Claire Hamill	Tom Robinson
K A Beaven	Jane Haughton	John Sabin
Simon Bowman	Gill Haw	Robert Sanders
Sacha Brooks	Hugo Heathcote	Tammie Scott
Steven Brooks	Stephen Henshaw	Maria Fernanda Sepulveda
Ralph Brown	David Hentschel	Alison Shore
Deborah Byland	Lynn Horsman	Paul Sloman
Phil & Pam Clark	Geoff Howard	Norman Macgregor Skeoch
Brian Cook	Julie Jeary	Chris Strong
Mike Curnock	Adam Jolly	Andrew Sweetman
Stewart Dinsdale	Leon Kaye	Lucy Swinerd
Jane Divall	Mark Langham	Wendy Swinton-Eagle
Sammi Doherty	Frank Lipman	Jeth Taylor
Rebecca Dowden	Tim Lynn	Neil Thackray
Jesse Doyle	Isabel Manweiler	Paul Thornton
Rosamund Doyle	Gemma Martin	Daniel Valenzuela
Jo Elliott	Estelle Maxwell	Henrik Wager
Michi Ellicott-Taylor	Russell Meagher	P. J. Warren
Michael Fergon	Alexandra Mele	Sue White
David Ffitch	Katie Mora	Claire Wickes
Cylvian Flynn	Kate Morrell	Emma Newton Williams
Nicole Furre	Mike Oliver	Brenda Williams
Sally Gardner	Jane Plumb	Ken Wilson
Pete & Jesse Gilgan	Natalie Porter	
Karen Glasby	Alastair Powell	

About the Author

Songwriter Hereward Kaye has, over the last five decades, worked with a number of major names in the UK record industry and West End musical theatre. As well as co-creating the musical Moby Dick with Robert Longden, he was lead singer for Rick Wakeman and toured the world for a decade as a member of the Flying Pickets. More recently Hereward founded Rok Skool in Haywards Heath, where he now coaches and mentors emerging talent. His own back catalogue can be discovered via Bandcamp.

Hereward lives in West Sussex with his wife Pat, and they have three sons.